.37.04/PRE

PREVAS, John :- Hannibal Crosses the Alps.

This book should be returned to any branch of the
Lancashire County Library on or before the date shown

Lancashire County Library
Bowran Street
Preston PR1 2UX

Lancashire
County Council

www.lancashire.gov.uk/libraries

HANNIBAL CROSSES THE ALPS

HANNIBAL
CROSSES THE
ALPS

THE ENIGMA RE-EXAMINED

By
JOHN PREVAS

SPELLMOUNT
Staplehurst, Kent

Published in the United Kingdom by
SPELLMOUNT
The Old Rectory
Staplehurst, Kent TN12 0AZ

ISBN 1-873376-93-6

Published in the United States in 1998 by
Sarpedon Publishers, Rockville Centre, New York.

A catalogue record of this book is available from the
British Library.

10 9 8 7 6 5 4 3 2 1

MANUFACTURED IN THE UNITED STATES OF AMERICA

CONTENTS

LIST OF MAPS

ACKNOWLEDGMENTS

A serious book is not an easy thing to write. It takes a great deal of preparation, energy and determination to accomplish. The author must develop a focus which is concentrated enough to allow him to stay on task and resist the enticing alternatives which life continually throws in his path to tempt him away. It is not easy as well for an author's spouse since there are long periods of solitude to be endured by both partners for the sake of the project. I would like to dedicate this book to my wife, Mavis Gibson. When I first began to think about writing on Hannibal and the Alps she gave me encouragement. When it came time to accompany me to the Alps and venture into those often foreboding heights, she put aside her personal fears and climbed with me. Each year we have returned to those same mountains to climb again. She bears the scars, both physical and psychological, from falls and she has endured endless hours of physical toil to reach yet another ridge which I was sure held some clue to Hannibal's crossing. On one occasion she nursed me for several days after I suffered sun-stroke during one particularly difficult climb. She documented our journeys through the mountains of southern France with her camera and many of her pictures grace the pages of this book. We have enjoyed many good times together following in Hannibal's footsteps, and as we look to the future we are always mindful of the ancient Roman dictum, "carpamus dulcia, post enim mortem, einis, et fabula fiemus."

I would also like to mention in these pages the man who taught me Latin many years ago, Robert Rowland. Currently Dean of the College of Arts and Sciences at Loyola University in New Orleans, this scholar took time from his busy schedule to teach a less than gifted student

Latin. I studied with him for a long time, often in tutorial sessions for which he received not a penny of compensation and during which his patience was sorely tried on many an occasion. In my mind he represents everything that a true teacher should be. He is knowledgeable about his subject, firm when he needs to be with his students, yet ever mindful that teaching is an art which also demands equal parts of patience and understanding. When Robert Rowland taught me Latin he opened new possibilities for me. This ancient language became the key which opened the door to French and then the doors to archeology and the joys of historical research. He selflessly gave me a lifelong gift for which I will always be grateful.

Finally, I would like to acknowledge the support of two very old and dear friends, Clement and Ellen Mitchell. They have encouraged me over the years to write this book and have taken pride in its accomplishment. Ellen took time from her editorial duties at a local Virginia newspaper to read my early drafts and offer many valuable stylistic suggestions. I spent many pleasant hours on their terrace. Clement kept my champagne glass full while Ellen read and corrected my early drafts.

Writing this book has been a wonderful experience for me. I enjoyed the research in the ancient manuscripts contained in the libraries of the left bank of Paris and I enjoyed the climbs high into the Alps. I hope that the reader will enjoy this book as much as I enjoyed writing it.

Washington, DC
February 1998

WHO'S WHO IN THE PUNIC WARS

ANTIOCHUS III. King of Syria, welcomed Hannibal to his court at Ephesus in 195 B.C. when Hannibal was forced to flee from Carthage.

ARCHIMEDES. A native of the Greek city of Syracuse, and a famous mathematician, he designed elaborate war machines that devastated the Roman fleet when they attacked the city during the Second Punic War. When the city fell in 212 B.C. Archimedes was killed by a Roman soldier looking for plunder.

C. TERENTIUS VARRO. Roman Consul defeated by Hannibal in 216 B.C. at Cannae.

FABIUS MAXIMUS QUINTUS (Cunctator). Roman consul who devised the strategy of shadowing Hannibal in Italy and never engaging him in any decisive battles. Fabius was called the delayer (*cunctator*) and his strategy was based on his belief that time would work in favor of the Romans because of their greater numbers and superior resources.

GAIUS FLAMINIUS. Roman consul killed at the battle of Lake Trasimene in 217 B.C. He was outsmarted by Hannibal.

HAMILCAR BARCA. Father of Hannibal and commander of the Carthaginian forces in the First Punic War. Hamilcar established the Spanish empire for Carthage and is regarded as largely responsible for the Second Punic War because of the hatred of Rome that he developed and nourished in his son Hannibal.

HANNIBAL BARCA. Son of Hamilcar and the commander of the Carthaginian forces against Rome in the Second Punic War. Considered to be one of the history's greatest military geniuses.

HANNO. Carthaginian general in the First Punic War. Defeated at the naval Battle of Ecnomus in 256 B.C.

HANNO BARCA. Brother of Hannibal, left to guard the passes between Spain and Gaul during the Second Punic War.

HANNO THE GREAT. Carthaginian politician from 240 to 200 B.C. and chief opponent of, first, Hamilcar and then Hannibal. Favored the development of the African empire and sought an accommodation with Rome.

HASDRUBAL BARCA. Brother of Hannibal, left in command of Spain and North Africa during Second Punic War. Late in the war he led a relief army over the Alps (207 B.C.) in an attempt to come to the aid of Hannibal. Hasdrubal was killed at the Battle of the Metaurus and his severed head sent to Hannibal by the Romans.

HASDRUBAL THE HANDSOME. Brother-in-law of Hannibal, successor to Hamilcar in Spain, assassinated by a slave in 221 B.C.

LIVY. Roman historian who wrote a history of the Punic Wars. His account is considered to be less objective than that of Polybius.

M. PORCIUS CATO. Roman senator who fought against Carthage in the Second Punic War. His hatred of Carthage was a major cause of the Third Punic War and the destruction of the city. Famous for his quote "Carthago delenda est" ("Carthage must be destroyed") with which he ended every speech he gave in the Roman Senate.

MAGO BARCA. Brother of Hannibal, defeated by Scipio in Spain. Invaded northern Italy in 206 B.C. where he was wounded; later died on his way back to Carthage.

MAHARBAL. Numidian cavalry general who crossed the Alps with Hannibal. Fought at the battles of the Trebbia River, Lake Trasimene and Cannae.

MARCELLUS, CLAUDIUS. Roman commander in Sicily and then Italy. Killed in battle in 208 B.C.

MASINISSA. Numidian prince who fought first with Hannibal in Spain but then changed his allegiance to Rome. Fought with Scipio Africanus in North Africa and was recognized as king by the Romans for his service.

PAULLUS, LUCIUS AEMILIUS. Roman commander killed at the Battle of Cannae, 216 B.C.

POLYBIUS. Greek historian who wrote the definitive history of the wars between Carthage and Rome. Polybius was present at the destruction of Carthage. His works are the principal sources for the study of the Punic Wars.

REGULUS. Roman commander who was defeated by the Carthaginians in North Africa during the First Punic War. He was captured and sent to Rome to negotiate a peace treaty. Regulus could not betray his country and returned to Carthage, where he died a terrible death by torture.

SCIPIO, GNAEUS CORNELIUS. Uncle of Scipio Africanus. Roman commander killed in Spain, 211 B.C.

SCIPIO, PUBLIUS CORNELIUS. Roman consul and father of Scipio Africanus. Killed in Spain fighting the Romans in 211 B.C.

SCIPIO AFRICANUS (Major). Roman commander who after the deaths of his father and uncle in 211 was given command of the Roman army in Spain. Captured New Carthage (Cartagena), landed in Africa and defeated Hannibal in 202 B.C.

SCIPIO, AEMILIANUS PUBLIUS CORNELIUS (Minor). Adopted by Publius Scipio, the son of Africanus, he captured and destroyed Carthage in the Third Punic War.

SEMPRONIUS LONGUS. Roman consul defeated by Hannibal at the Battle of the Trebbia River, 218 B.C.

XANTHIPPUS. Spartan mercenary who led a Carthaginian army in the First Punic War and defeated the Romans under Regulus in North Africa.

CHRONOLOGY

1200 B.C.　Trojan War, legendary time period for the founding of Carthage by Queen Elissa (Dido).

1000 B.C.　Archaeological evidence of first Phoenician landings in Sicily.
Phoenician expansion into the western Mediterranean.

900 B.C.　Archaeological evidence of first Phoenician landings in Sardinia.

814 B.C.　Founding of Carthage.

800 B.C.　First archaeological evidence at Carthage.
Greek colonization in southern Italy and Sicily.

753 B.C.　Legendary date for the founding of Rome.

600 B.C.　Founding of Massilia (Marseilles) by the Greeks.
Carthaginian colonization of Sardinia and western Sicily.

509 B.C.　First Treaty between Rome and Carthage.

480 B.C.　Wars in Sicily between Carthage and the Greeks.

348 B.C.　Second Treaty between Rome and Carthage.

306 B.C.　Third Treaty between Rome and Carthage.

275 B.C.   Carthage controls and colonizes vast areas of Sicily.

264 B.C.   Rome intervenes in Sicily and challenges Carthaginian hegemony.
            First Punic War begins.

247 B.C.   Hannibal born at Carthage.

241 B.C.   First Punic War ends.
            Mercenary War at Carthage begins.
            Rome takes Sardinia and Corsica from Carthage.

238 B.C.   Hamilcar Barca takes command in North Africa and defeats the mercenaries.

237 B.C.   Hamilcar Barca establishes the Carthaginian empire in Spain; establishment of the Barca Dynasty.

229 B.C.   Hamilcar killed in battle; succeeded by his son-in-law, Hasdrubal the Handsome.

221 B.C.   Hasdrubal assassinated; Hamilcar's son Hannibal proclaimed new commander of the army in Spain.

219 B.C.   Siege of Saguntum (Sagunto), the ostensible cause of the Second Punic War.

218 B.C.   Roman declaration of war on Carthage.
            Hannibal leaves Spain for Italy; Hannibal crosses the Alps and enters Italy.
            Battle of the Trebbia, in which Hannibal defeats a Roman army.

217 B.C.   Battle of Lake Trasimene, Hannibal again defeats a Roman army.

216 B.C.   Roman Senate votes to seek a decisive battle with Hannibal.
Battle of Cannae, Hannibal destroys a Roman army.
Romans adopt a defensive strategy against Hannibal; no
further major battles between Hannibal and the Romans
in Italy.

211 B.C.   Hannibal marches against Rome.

207 B.C.   The tide of the war turns in favor of Rome; Hannibal has
no reinforcements, Roman allies do not defect to Hannibal
in the numbers he had planned for.
Hasdrubal, brother of Hannibal, leaves Spain with an
army and crosses the Alps. Hasdrubal is killed and his
army destroyed at the Battle of the Metaurus.
Center of the war shifts to Spain; Hannibal becomes a
sideline in Italy.
Scipio the Younger defeats the Carthaginians in Spain.

206 B.C.   Scipio achieves complete victory in Spain.

205 B.C.   Mago, Hannibal's youngest brother, invades northern
Italy; later dies of wounds.

204 B.C.   The Romans land in North Africa.

203 B.C.   The Carthaginian Senate recalls Hannibal and his army
from Italy to defend the city against the Romans.

202 B.C.   Scipio defeats Hannibal at the Battle of Zama in North
Africa. Carthage accepts Roman terms for peace, and after
sixteen years the Second Punic War ends in a Roman victory.

201 B.C.   Carthage is confined to its African territory by treaty with
Rome, loss of its fleet; city under Roman political supervi-
sion and imposition of a heavy war indemnity.

200 B.C.   Hannibal becomes chief magistrate of Carthage, reorganizes the city's finances and holds supreme power for five years.
Polybius, the historian of the Punic Wars, is born in Arcadia, Greece.

195 B.C.   Hannibal flees Carthage and goes into exile in the eastern Mediterranean; continues to fight against Rome.

183 B.C.   Hannibal commits suicide at Bithynia rather than be taken prisoner by the Romans.

150 B.C.   Third Punic War begins.

146 B.C.   Carthage is destroyed by the Romans after a three-year siege. Polybius is present at the fall of the city.

118 B.C.   Polybius dies after falling from a horse.

59 B.C.   Roman historian Livy born at Patavium (Padua) in northern Italy.

A.D. 12   Livy dies at Patavium.

INTRODUCTION

The city burned for seventeen days, and even after it no longer contained life the Romans weren't finished. Once the fires had cooled, soldiers worked amidst the rubble and the thousands of incinerated human remains to obliterate any physical trace of what had once been known as "the jewel of the Mediterranean." First the city was set afire and then it was taken apart, stone by stone. Its inhabitants were killed or enslaved, though some managed to escape into the vastness of North Africa, their subsequent fates among the indigenous tribes unknown. The Romans even leveled the hill in the center of the city upon which the citadel had stood, to make nature's one-time gift to their enemy a less formidable height. Salt was sown in the ground and all traces of the city's civilization, including records, destroyed. Then the Romans' task was finally finished.

The phrase "Carthaginian solution" has endured into the 20th century, meaning not only the total annihilation of one's enemy but the sources of his strength as well. Dwight D. Eisenhower pondered the phrase in 1945 as Allied armies advanced on Nazi Germany, however in that case the post-war arrangement became far less drastic. In 146 B.C. the "solution" was implemented. The Roman Republic not only defeated its greatest enemy but wiped all traces of its civilization off the face of the earth. It was as though the Romans needed to erase a trauma from their own collective consciousness: a time when Carthage lay not at their feet but at their throats.

A Carthaginian had once descended from the Alps into Italy, and for fifteen years his army remained, undefeated. He massacred thousands of soldiers of the Republic, seemingly at will in some of history's great battles, and laid waste to the peninsula. At one point the citizens of Rome cowered behind their gates, humiliated, while the invader stood outside the city's walls, challenging them to give battle. There were three separate wars between Carthage and Rome that spanned more than a century; however, as the Greek-born historian Polybius wrote, "All that happened to the Romans and the Carthaginians was brought about by one man: Hannibal." [1]

The destruction of Carthage was the culmination of the Third Punic War, an uneven struggle consisting primarily of a three-year siege of the North African city. The First Punic War was fought mainly in Sicily and its surrounding waters. The Second Punic War, however, was the largest of the three conflicts and the most costly in lives and treasure. It is sometimes referred to as "Hannibal's War."

The story of how Hannibal crossed the French Alps to invade Italy in 218 B.C. has fascinated generations of readers ever since the feat was first described by historians more than two thousand years ago. Few images in history have managed to capture and hold the imagination over the centuries quite like that of this bold North African. Perched upon a monstrous elephant, Hannibal Barca led his army of mercenaries over the highest and most dangerous passes of the Alps to challenge the Roman Republic for mastery of the ancient world.

Though the crossing of the Alps was only a brief episode in a larger conflict between the cities of Carthage and Rome, it has become one of the great adventure stories of history—and one of its most intriguing mysteries. While successful in achieving its strategic objectives, Hannibal's march extracted a heavy toll in human life and suffering. Nearly half of his army perished before it even reached Italy.[2] Many of the soldiers died at the hands of the fierce Celtic tribes that lay in ambush along the route, while others starved to death on the barren mountain slopes. Hundreds fell to their deaths from the high precipices as the long Carthaginian column slowly struggled its way over the snow- and ice-covered pass. Those who survived the ordeal in the Alps were described as little more than "ghosts and shadows." They were men half-dead from hunger and cold, their strength and spirit drained from them by the Alps. The miracle of this story is that any of them survived to reach Italy at all.

Why Hannibal ever undertook to cross the Alps can only be explained within the context of the power struggle which was then unfolding around the Mediterranean. During this period Rome had not yet become the glorious city of the Caesars and the ruler of a vast empire. It was a struggling young republic seeking to establish a prominent place for itself in the hierarchy of the ancient world.

Carthage, on the other hand, was already a powerful force in the Mediterranean and had been so for several centuries before Rome. The Carthaginians had become prosperous through commerce, primarily seaborne trade, and had built for themselves a city of unrivaled splendor on the shores of North Africa near the site of modern day Tunis. The city was a marvel of architecture and engineering and it afforded its people a state of luxury unimaginable to most others in the ancient world. By the third century B.C. Carthage had reached the height of its power as the largest and wealthiest city in the western Mediterranean.[3] Yet there was a dark side to this commercial empire, which manifested itself in incomprehensible acts of cruelty. They crucified lions for their amusement and their generals for failure; and modern archaeologists have verified the assertions made by ancient historians: the Carthaginians threw infant children into a massive furnace.[4]

The historical destinies of Rome and Carthage became linked just as their myths were intertwined. The legendary founder of the Roman people, the Trojan prince Aeneas, once loved the Carthaginian queen, Elissa (called Dido by the Romans). After he deserted her she commited suicide, but not before making a curse to her gods that there would always be hatred and war between their peoples.[5]

Notwithstanding the curse, the established empire in North Africa and the rising one in Italy were bound to come into conflict. Trading posts and colonies in Sicily, Sardinia and Corsica formed an important part of the Carthaginian commercial network in the western Mediterranean. As the Romans consolidated their power in southern Italy and crossed over into Sicily, they began to encroach on these colonies and threaten valuable trade routes. It was not long before Rome and Carthage were involved in a conflict that would span a hundred years. There were three Punic Wars that lasted intermittently from 264 until 146 B.C. While the first was limited to a struggle over control of Sicily, their scope eventually widened and, in the end, the Punic Wars determined who would rule the ancient world and ultimately influence the very course of Western civilization.

During the first war (264–241 B.C.), Hamilcar Barca, the father of Hannibal, commanded the forces of Carthage on Sicily. While the war was eventually fought to a stalemate, the Carthaginians lost their hold on the island and were forced to retreat to North Africa. Following another, domestic, war, the leaders of Carthage began to look for new territories to rebuild their lost empire. They turned farther west, to Spain, a land rich in natural resources and still undeveloped. There, under the leadership of Hamilcar they established a larger and richer colony than they had previously controlled in Sicily. As Carthage prospered by exploiting the mineral wealth and manpower of Spain, Rome too became more interested in the potential of the western Mediterranean. The rivalry between the two expanding empires increased and, coupled with intense resentment that still lingered from the first war, set the stage for a second and even greater conflict.

By 221 B.C. Hannibal had taken political and military command in Spain, and had inherited not only his father's dynasty but his hatred of all things Roman. While still a boy, Hannibal had vowed upon the sacred altars of the gods at Carthage to wage eternal war with the Romans. History would record that no oath made by a son to his father was ever more faithfully kept, nor proved to be more costly in human life and suffering, than this one.

A key result of the First Punic War was that Carthage had lost its Mediterranean naval supremacy to Rome, which, prior to that conflict, had hardly possessed a navy at all. As Hannibal undertook preparations for the next war he formulated a strategy to protect Carthage from invasion and curtail Roman expansion in the western Mediterranean. The central element of his strategy was a surprise overland invasion of Italy, by way of the French Alps. The entire plan was based upon Hannibal's assessment of the Roman hold over Italy. At the time of the Second Punic War, Italy was not a unified country but rather a land of semi-autonomous city-states and tribes loosely held together in a confederation dominated by the city of Rome. It was this confederation which gave Rome its strength by providing a virtually limitless supply of manpower and resources. Hannibal believed the Italian confederation would dissolve if Roman authority were challenged and that many of its members might even turn against their masters. If member states could be induced to revolt, the legions would be tied to the Italian mainland suppressing insurrections while Carthage, for the short run at least, would be safe. Hannibal's mercenary army would be the catalyst in a reaction that would destroy Rome from within.

The Second Punic War began in the spring of 218 B.C. when Hannibal departed Spain to begin his invasion of Italy. The Carthaginians were merchants and it was their custom to hire others to do their fighting for them. Thus mercenaries had been recruited from all parts of the ancient world to join Hannibal's army and to fight for a cause that must not have concerned them much beyond their next pay date. One aspect of Hannibal's brilliance as a commander lay in his ability to take this disparate mass of hired killers and mold them into a disciplined, cohesive fighting force. The devastation that they wrought on Italy, both physical and psychological, proved to be far greater than could have been imagined from their small numbers. Hannibal and his mercenaries left scars on the Italian countryside and on the Roman psyche that remained for decades and affected the course of Roman political and military development for centuries.

When Hannibal invaded Italy, events unfolded at first precisely as he must have intended. The crossing of the Alps surprised and frightened the Romans, who had anticipated a war that would be fought in Spain and Sicily. When the Romans became aware of Hannibal's presence they dispatched large armies to northern Italy in a desperate attempt to stem the invasion. In the early battles between the Romans and Carthaginians, Hannibal showed that he was one of the greatest tactical commanders in history. He won a series of victories over larger Roman forces by exploiting every advantage he could extract from the terrain, weather and the flaws of his adversaries. Through his effective coordination of the elements of surprise and maneuver, as well as his insights into human fallibility, he enjoyed a distinct advantage over the Roman legions, even though he was always outnumbered.

The Roman legions in the early years of the war were no match for Hannibal's polyglot mercenary army which here, as in previous histories, we somewhat inaccurately refer to as the Carthaginians. History records numerous instances—as when Lee, Jackson and Stuart led the Army of Northern Virginia—when the collective command of an army makes it superior to an opponent. Hannibal's daring Numidian cavalry leader Maharbal, his younger brother Mago and the rest of the battle-hardened Carthaginian officer corps might have formed at this time a confluence of military talent that could achieve success beyond what troop strengths alone would seem to justify.

The success of Hannibal was so rapid and decisive in the early years of the war that it seemed Rome itself would fall before the onslaught of his troops. Even the rumor of his approach was alleged to be enough to send thousands fleeing the city in panic, and years after his death the Romans still used the warning cry "Hannibal ad portas" ("Hannibal is at the gates") to frighten errant children.

As the years passed the course of the war gradually began to turn in favor of Rome as the Romans learned from their mistakes on the battlefield. One lesson they learned, after Cannae, was to avoid major pitched battles with Hannibal entirely. Still, Rome had a vast supply of manpower and resources and was able to replenish her losses, while Hannibal had limited numbers of men and little material support from Carthage to sustain him. In the end only a few of the Italian city-states joined Hannibal. Most remained loyal to Rome, and by the final years of the war the Carthaginian army was no longer the formidable force it had been when it first came down from the Alps.

While the Romans had only to let time and attrition work in their favor to eventually win the war, the psychological pressure of Hannibal in Italy for so many years was almost more than they could bear. Like an arrow shot into a lion, which cripples but does not kill,

Hannibal tortured the Roman beast for year after year. For fifteen years they endured his presence in Italy and watched, often powerlessly, as he devastated their lands and cities at will.

Finally, after successes against Carthaginian forces in Spain and against Carthage's allies, the Romans were able to send an expeditionary force to North Africa to threaten Carthage itself. The Romans risked everything on the ploy, but it worked. The citizens of Carthage, protected from the ravages of war for many years because of Hannibal's presence in Italy, were terrified at the sight of Roman legions landing on their shores. They called their greatest commander home to defend the capital, and even though Hannibal saw the Roman gambit for what it was, he reluctantly returned to North Africa in 202 B.C.

Not far from Carthage, in the deserts to the south at a place called Zama, Hannibal engaged the Roman army and was finally defeated. The victorious Roman commander, Scipio Africanus, moved by the splendor of Carthage and favorably disposed toward Hannibal, spared the city from destruction. Under the terms of the peace settlement the Carthaginians had to pay a huge indemnity to Rome through fifty annual installments. After a few years, however, Carthage recovered from its defeat and began to prosper. So rapid was the Carthaginian recovery from the war that they were able to pay off the indemnity to Rome ahead of schedule.

Carthaginian prosperity only gave rise to Roman anxiety. Influential forces in Rome urged pre-emptive action against North Africa, and the powerful orator M. Porcius Cato ended all of his speeches in the senate with the concluding phrase: "Carthago delenda est."[6] ("Carthage must be destroyed.")

The final Punic War began in 149 B.C. when Carthage was put under siege. The city held out for three years before it was sacked and burned. Legend has it that the Roman fear and hatred of Carthage had become so great by then that a curse was placed over the ruins and salt plowed into the ground so nothing could ever live there again. So complete was the Roman destruction that little trace of the Carthaginian culture remains today. Modern scholars have correctly concluded that "Rome murdered Carthage with very little regret."[7]

The story of how Hannibal crossed the Alps is a small but integral part of the history of the Punic Wars. It is important not only for the achievement itself, made under the most adverse conditions imaginable, but because of what it has spurred in the public imagination over the centuries. The story is controversial because it has still never been determined with certainty where in the Alps the Carthaginians crossed. The location of Hannibal's pass has generated intense speculation, causing generations of scholars to search and re-search the ancient manuscripts for clues. Hundreds of adventurers, soldiers and even emperors have traversed the Alps in search of the exact pass. Hannibal's crossing is a story of adventure and intrigue, triumph and tragedy. It is a tale worth re-telling to each new generation and it is a path into the highest passes of the Alps worth following again.

NOTES

[1] Polybius, *History of the Roman Republic*, Bk. IX, Sec. 22.
[2] Polybius, Bk. III, Sec. 60; and Livy, *The War with Hannibal*, Bk. XXI, Sec. 38.
[3] Carry and Scullard, *A History of Rome*, p. 115.
[4] Serge Lancel, *Carthage: A History*, pp. 233 and 367.
[5] Virgil, *The Aeneid.*
[6] Michael Grant, Michael. *Greek and Latin Authors*, p. 84.
[7] *Cambridge Ancient History*, Vol. VIII, p. 162.

CHAPTER 1

❧ · ❧

CARTHAGE AND ROME

According to legend, a Phoenician noblewoman named Elissa, who possessed exceptional beauty and intelligence, founded Carthage. Forced to flee her native city of Tyre after her ambitious brother murdered her husband, this woman sailed west to North Africa with a band of loyal followers and chests filled with gold. Elissa landed her ships on the shores of what is today Tunisia and was so captivated by the natural beauty of the land that she decided to settle there and build a city. She found a site that was well protected by high hills and that had a narrow entrance to the sea. On this site she envisioned building a great city situated between Egypt and Spain and directly across from Sicily and Italy—at the virtual crossroads of the Mediterranean sea trade.

A local African chief, amused at seeing a woman leading this band of refugees, mockingly challenged her to take all of his land that she could fit within the hide of a bull. To the laughter of the natives and the astonishment of her people the queen accepted his challenge and ordered the sacrifice of a prize bull. When the ritual of the sacrifice had been completed, she had the hide carefully removed from the slaughtered animal, and while the Africans watched in amazement she set about cutting it into thin strips. From these strips she laboriously wove a long and delicate thread with which she delineated the land she had chosen. She named the site Carthage, from the Phoenician word that means "the new city."

Her task completed, Elissa demanded her due and the chief, outwitted by a woman, had no choice but to grant her title to the land. To salvage his injured pride the African proposed marriage, but Elissa rejected him with the reply that she had a city to build and no time for a man. The chief withdrew with his tribe into the deserts south of Carthage, where he became an enemy of the new queen and her city. What the queen could have easily bought with gold she chose instead to win in a contest of wits. With a quickness of mind and a spirit for bargaining she outsmarted the African chief and displayed the traits that would come to characterize her people, first as they ruled North Africa and eventually as they came to control most of the western Mediterranean.

According to the same legend—the *Aeneid*, by the Roman poet Virgil—the founder of Rome was a Trojan prince named Aeneas. Fleeing the destruction of his city by vengeful Greeks, he found his way to Elissa's new city, where the destinies of Rome and Carthage became entwined. In a passionate but ill-fated union the two lovers lived together in the queen's palace for a year. Elissa gave everything to the Trojan prince she called her husband, yet the time came when Aeneas was summoned by his gods to leave Carthage and fulfill his destiny. He left the bed of the queen while she slept and in the darkness before dawn sailed his ship from the harbor of Carthage and across the sea to Italy. There he would found the people who would one day destroy Carthage.

A medieval Latin epigram laments the fate of the unlucky queen.

> Unhappy, Elissa, was thy fate,
> in first and second married state,
> One husband caused thy flight by dying,
> The other caused thy death by flying.[1]

When the queen discovered that Aeneas had left, she ordered that a great funeral pyre be prepared on the roof of the palace. Before the Trojan ship had sailed from view beyond the horizon, Elissa renounced her lover and prayed to the gods that there would always be war between their peoples. Then the she took her own life and her spirit descended into the underworld as the flames of the pyre consumed her body. As Virgil had it, in the realm of the dead her spirit waited in anger for centuries until her champion finally appeared to take revenge upon the Romans.

When Hannibal came over the Alps and descended into Italy he was the embodiment of her curse. From the depths of hell the frightened and besieged Romans must have heard the scornful queen urge on her champion as he devastated Italy with his mercenaries and elephants. Even hell could not contain the fury of the queen as all Italy trembled before her avenger, and the citizens of Rome fled their city in panic at the cry "*Hannibal ad portas.*"

Legends aside, archaeological evidence indicates that the people who founded Carthage did so around 800 B.C. and probably came to North Africa from the ancient Phoenician city of Tyre, situated on the coast of modern Lebanon.[2] The early founders of Carthage were a people whose origins modern linguists believe can be traced to a time in early history when languages with common elements had just started to appear in the Near East and Europe. They were a seafaring and commercial people who established trading stations, or "*emporia,*" throughout the Mediterranean. These were small settlements strategically located along the coastlines, where there was commercial activity. They functioned as places where bargains could be struck with the local natives and goods stored until they could be loaded on ships and taken to Tyre. The city of Carthage no doubt developed from one of these early "emporia."

In the centuries that followed the founding of the city, Carthage became a marvel of architecture and engineering. It was described by ancient commentators as the "richest city in the world" and the "jewel of the Mediterranean." Protected by a combination of natural and man-made fortifications, the city was sheltered against the frequent storms and marauding pirates who swept in from the sea to the north, as well as against the hostile natives who inhabited the deserts to the south.

Within the center of the city archaeological evidence indicates that the Carthaginians had constructed two harbors.[3] The first was to accommodate their warships and the second was for merchant shipping. This system of double harbors, unique to Carthage, allowed ships to be safely moored in large numbers and dry-dock operations to be undertaken throughout the year. Inland, the Carthaginians built a citadel upon the highest point of a series of hills that they called the Byrsa, from the ancient Greek word meaning hide. This citadel was fortified by thick walls and became the most secure place in Carthage. It was here, on the Byrsa, that the Carthaginians erected magnificent temples to their gods, splendid palaces for their nobles and established the seat of their government.

In the lower city that surrounded the harbors there were large numbers of buildings to house the thousands of artisans, laborers and shopkeepers who made the city thrive. The Carthaginians built massive warehouses to store the vast quantities of treasure that flowed daily into the city. Gold and ivory, as well as the hides of a variety of animals, were shipped to Carthage from along the African coast. From central Africa came elephants that would be trained and utilized as the tactical machinery of the Carthaginian forces in war. Metals such as silver, iron, lead, zinc, mercury and copper came from mines in Spain, and tin was brought from as far north as Britain. The city quickly became a center for the metal trade of the western Mediterranean. Pottery and marble were imported from Greece and used to decorate the homes of the wealthy and for building temples and palaces.

Throughout the Mediterranean world the Carthaginians peddled a wide array of goods—from weapons, linen, wool, vases and glassware, to ornaments made of ivory and precious stones. At their height, they managed to control in some way or another, at a profit, almost everything of value that was carried on a ship in the western Mediterranean. They manipulated foreign competition in such a way that their merchants were able to buy cheaply and sell at inflated prices. By the third century B.C., trade in the western Mediterranean had practically become a Carthaginian monopoly, while other states and cities were excluded from competition by commercial treaty or by the menacing presence of the Carthaginian navy.

The descendants of Elissa built a vast commercial empire in the period from 800 to 300 B.C. that brought them enormous wealth and influence in the ancient world. Seaborne commerce caused the Carthaginians to establish trading posts along the coasts of Spain,

France, Sicily, Sardinia and North Africa. There is evidence that their network even extended into the Atlantic, eventually stretching as far south as the west coast of Africa and as far north as Britain.[4] Rarely would Mediterranean navigators venture so far and so frequently beyond the Pillars of Hercules (Gibraltar) until the age of exploration at the end of the medieval period.

In order to protect the sources of their wealth from competitors, the Carthaginians built a military and naval establishment that was too strong to be seriously challenged until the appearance of the Roman war machine at the end of the third century B.C. The Carthaginian navy utilized the most advanced designs and techniques of shipbuilding available at the time and produced large fleets of ships for both war and commerce. These ships were well constructed and expertly sailed by the citizens of Carthage, who gave personal service on the war fleet as a matter of pride and civic duty. The navy was always ready to enforce the commercial interests of the empire.

When the Carthaginians encountered conflicts on land, they hired others to do the fighting for them. Carthage did not maintain a standing army but recruited mercenaries from around the Mediterranean, as well as conscripts and large numbers of auxiliary contingents from the native states of North Africa. Among the groups often hired to fight for Carthage were the skilled Numidian horsemen living in the deserts of Tunisia and Algeria, the primitive and fierce Celtic tribesmen of Spain and France, and professional hoplite infantry from Greece.

Although Carthaginian citizens did not predominate in the ranks, the city nevertheless became state-of-the-art in the science of war. Since mercenaries are, by definition, of suspect political loyalty, command of them was given to a highly trained and dedicated corps of officers, drawn from the sons of influential and wealthy families of Carthage. These young men were aristocrats who had chosen to make a special profession of military service. They gained a wide degree of experience by serving in posts all around the Mediterranean and developed effective techniques to control the mercenaries under their command. The sternness of these officers toward their men, however, paled in comparison to the cruelty that the Carthaginian people could show toward their own leaders who failed in battle. Carthaginian officers who failed in the line of duty faced the prospect of crucifixion outside the city walls.

The land around Carthage was rich in cultivable land and thick forests. Eventually many Carthaginians left their maritime pursuits to develop large estates and plantations in the countryside or to develop industries to harvest and mill the timber of the forests for use in shipbuilding. The Carthaginians used slave labor on their plantations and became efficient at producing not only crops but also great herds of cattle, horses and sheep. Therefore, Carthaginian wealth came not only from commerce on the sea but also from the backs of their slaves on land. The Carthaginians ruled their colonies and estates with a tyrannical hand, and those under the yoke had little chance to win their freedom or share in the wealth of the empire.

Farming became a major industry and the Carthaginians exploited the land as profitably as they had the sea. Eventually a belt of prosperous estates with vast fields of grain, pasture lands, vineyards and olive groves surrounded the city. The Carthaginians worked to its limit nearly all the land that could be cultivated. Estates could be found throughout North Africa, as far east as Libya and as far west as Morocco.

As the centuries passed, the Carthaginians developed a society that blended elements of their Phoenician heritage with institutions and practices unique to their own situation in North Africa. Perhaps more than any other classical people, with the exception of the Egyptians, the Carthaginians were bound to their city by devotion to a peculiar religious practice. The Carthaginians sacrificed infant children to a massive bronze image of their god that stood high upon the Byrsa in an area called the "*tophet*."[5] This practice of infanticide was found nowhere else in the ancient world on such a scale of intensity and frequency.

With ominous outstretched palms this bronze image of the god Baal, "lord of the furnaces," accepted the bodies of condemned infants and then dropped them into a raging inferno while the citizens of the city watched in rapture. There is evidence in the recently excavated ruins of Carthage that this sacrificial area on the Byrsa was in continuous use for centuries.[6] Remains found at the site have been positively identified by forensic specialists as the bones of infant children and are testimony to the long existence of this repulsive practice.[7]

What purpose infanticide might have played in the communal life of Carthage is still subject to considerable speculation, as befits perhaps the most horrific ritual known to have been practiced by a major Western civilization. The practice might have been a form of birth control, euthanasia, a supreme test of loyalty to the city, or as a superstitious way of appeasing the anger of the gods in times of crisis. Perhaps all babies born in a particular month, for obscure reasons of numerology, or during certain festivals, were made victim.

It is also possible that the citizens of Carthage were no more inclined to throw their healthy babies into a burning pit than any other people before or since; the sacrificial site may have been a communal graveyard reflecting a high rate of infant mortality. Or, if healthy infants were indeed sacrificed, these may have been babies born to slaves or seized from enemy tribes in the desert. In any event, while histories written by ancient Carthaginians themselves are virtually nonexistent, the reports of their enemies—whether based on fact or rumor—comprise the bulk of the record of daily life in Carthage that has survived. And in these histories, the theme of Carthaginians as baby-killers recurs time and again.

While the precise reason for the incinerator on the Byrsa remains unknown, it is commonly recognized nevertheless that the Carthaginians were among the most religious and superstitious people of the ancient world.

Worship in Carthage was heavily promoted and actively regulated by public authorities. The priests wielded considerable influence in the city. So widespread and deep was the religious fervor of the Carthaginians that the common names of people often took on a religious significance. Hannibal for example—a name that appears frequently in the history of the city—is interpreted to mean "he who enjoys Baal's favor." Other common names, such as Hasdrubal, "he who has Baal's help," or Hamilcar, "pledged to the service of the god

Melqart," show the extent to which religion played a dominant role in the life of the city.

In spite of their immense wealth the Carthaginians never became one of the truly great civilizations of the Mediterranean. While their accomplishments are impressive in many areas, they never seemed to be able to rise to the artistic, cultural and intellectual level of their Greek neighbors. Whereas the upper classes of Carthage adopted Greek styles of dress, manner and language, they never managed as a society to apply more than a thin veneer of Hellenism to their own materialistic culture.

Most of what is known about the government of Carthage comes from the descriptions of the Greek philosopher Aristotle.[8] In his famous comparative study of ancient constitutions he described Carthage as a government composed of an executive, a senate, a popular assembly and a judiciary. From what can be determined, Carthage appears to have been ruled by an oligarchy of rich merchants and landowners, much like governments have been throughout history. Ruling magistrates for the city and the countryside were elected annually, usually on the basis of their birth and wealth, as were generals and admirals.

Before the Romans appeared to challenge them, the Greeks were the Carthaginians' primary competition for commercial trade in the western Mediterranean. The Greek Empire had reached its peak under the Athenians of the fifth century B.C. and then under Alexander the Great in the fourth. Both of these centuries, however, saw the Greeks looking east toward Persia and less interested in the western Mediterranean. By the beginning of the third century B.C., Greece was no longer a great military power and the Greek city-states posed no serious threat to Carthage or her commercial interests. While the Greeks had founded important cities in eastern Sicily and southern Italy, Carthage controlled the western part of Sicily and the important trade routes to Sardinia, the Balearic Islands and the western coast of Italy.

Greek and Carthaginian interests finally clashed on Sicily, but Carthage never had to contend there with much more than a small number of independent city-states ruled by petty tyrants. The Carthaginians were able to reach an accommodation with the Greeks and there was never a unified or serious threat to their interests until the appearance of the Romans on the island in 264 B.C.

The story of how the Romans came to Sicily and eventually displaced and destroyed Carthage is the story of the Punic Wars. As a result of these wars Rome grew to become the greatest empire in the ancient world. To understand how all this came about it is necessary to begin with a brief look at earlier Roman history.

For many years Rome was considered to be little more than a sanctuary for criminals and runaway slaves in the Italian province of Latium. The city had lain dormant, from an international perspective, for centuries. Largely ignored by the major powers of the ancient world, Rome lay on the perimeter of larger events, in between the powerful orbits of the Carthaginians and the Greeks. The Romans, however, by virtue of their position on the Italian mainland and their own ambition, were destined to play a dominant role in the affairs of the western Mediterranean. It was only a matter of time and circumstances before they would make their move onto the stage of international politics.

The earliest Roman society was fashioned out of a number of tribal groups known as *"gens."*[9] These groups existed long before the founding of the city and had developed their own religious practices, formulated their own types of tribal government and established various systems for the control of smaller and weaker clans. This arrangement persisted for several centuries before the formation of Rome, and from what can be determined, it was largely the drawing together of these tribes, or *"gens,"* under new political arrangements that resulted in the unification of the Romans.

From its legendary founding date of 753 B.C. until 509 B.C., the city was ruled by a series of despotic kings. The first king, Romulus, was the grandson of the Trojan prince Aeneas, who had deserted the Queen of Carthage.[10] Romulus was the first of seven kings who reigned in the 244 years until the creation of the Roman Republic. The last king, Tarquinius Superbus, was driven from the city after his son, Sextus, raped the daughter of a noble and respected family.[11]

From the overthrow of the last king in 509 B.C. until the death of Julius Caesar in 44 B.C., Rome was a republic. During the period of the republic the city was ruled by a senate and two annually elected consuls. The senatorial system provided a means by which the heads of the ruling families controlled the city, and this arrangement worked until other classes—businessmen and workers—grew strong enough to challenge the aristocrats. These groups began to demand more representation in the government and the society eventually developed into two distinct classes: the patricians and the plebeians. The patricians were the privileged, landholding nobility, who wielded an almost complete political, social and financial control over the city, while the plebeians were the lower class of farmers, artisans, laborers and tradesmen. This lower class became increasingly important as Rome expanded, for it provided the labor for the fields that supplied the city with food, a tax base and military manpower in times of war.

The patrician nobility ruled exclusively until the 4th century, when a wave of reforms resulted in the creation of a plebeian governmental assembly and the issuance of a written law code, the Twelve Tables. This code gave the lower classes more civil rights, and by the early 3rd century B.C. the plebeian class had obtained a significant level of representation in the affairs of the city. All these political and social reforms were occurring just as Rome was about to embark on a series of domestic and foreign wars. The plebeian class was crucial to Roman success, as it would supply the resources that Rome would need to conduct its wars. Further, the countryside around Rome supported an agrarian population that could supply the soldiers for the Roman legions and food for the city.

The first step Rome took in building an empire was to consolidate her power over the other states in Italy. At the beginning of the 3rd century B.C. Italy was not a unified country but a land of diverse, independent city-states, tribes and clans. As Rome moved against her neighbors in an attempt to consolidate her hold over the mainland, military superiority alone was not enough to ensure success. The

Romans were not powerful enough at that period in their history to rely solely on military force to bring their neighbors under their control. Diplomacy and a willingness to promote and extend the benefits of Roman citizenship to other Italian cities and tribes played as important a part in the process as military might.

Formal alliances thus became an important component of policy as the Romans set about to unify Italy. The system of alliances developed by the Romans offered weaker cities and tribes protection and a chance to participate in the growth of the empire. With each Italian alliance Rome increased her pool of manpower and resources. Over time, this development generated its own momentum and built for Rome a strong political and economic base. The Romans were generous with the franchise of citizenship and they gave many of the tribes and cities they defeated in war a stake in the future. Time and again the Romans demonstrated, especially in these formative years, a particular skill in dealing with their neighbors during periods of conflict that allowed them to expand their political and economic base in Italy.

As the Romans refined their techniques of diplomacy they were often able to get their way by treating both conquered and ally alike with consideration, generosity and honesty. Allies were granted rights and privileges that often approximated those of Roman citizens, including protection under Roman law. The conferment of these "Latin rights" or partial franchise became a privilege eagerly sought by communities that came under Roman sway, either through treaty or conquest. Often the Romans would leave the local government of a conquered people intact while conferring upon all the members of the society the privileges of full Roman citizenship, including the right to stand for public office. This gave many cities and communities throughout Italy an incentive to support Rome and enjoy the benefits and prestige of Roman citizenship. Some conquered cities and tribes became "*civitas sine suffragio*," meaning they had access to all the private and civil rights of Roman citizens, though not the all-important right to participate in the political process by voting or standing for election.

As Rome became the unquestioned center of a new Italian coalition she behaved with exceptional fairness toward most of her former enemies and her allies. The Romans built a confederation of neighbors who with few exceptions remained loyal in times of crisis and gave them a broad base of support upon which to undertake their conquest of the ancient world. This support from the members of the Italian confederation proved helpful in the First Punic War, crucial in the Second, and decisive in the Third.

By the middle of the third century B.C., Rome had become the dominant force on the Italian peninsula. Within the Roman alliance system was a first circle that encompassed the provinces closest geographically to the capital. These were Latium, Campania and the Sabine territory. They were tied to Rome by strong treaties and grants of civic franchise. Beyond this was a second circle of less favored client states, such as the Etruscans and the Samnites. These groups enjoyed limited benefits of Roman franchise but were bound to Rome by levies of tribute in the form of food and conscripts. By 240 B.C. nearly all of central Italy had been incorporated into this Roman confederation.

Only in the north of Italy and in the extreme south were the Romans uneasy with the inhabitants. In the north was the territory of the Gauls or Celts, who inhabited the Po Valley and the Alps. These were the least civilized of the tribes in Italy and always gave the Romans reason for concern. They had sacked Rome in 390 B.C. The Gauls would be a source of trouble for Rome in the Second Punic War and it would be several centuries before they, too, would be brought under Roman domination.

In the south, the Romans were concerned about the independent Greek city-states. In the decade between 280 and 270 B.C. Rome entered into a series of wars with these city-states that proved to be the first test of the strength of the Roman confederation. During these Pyrrhic wars, named after the king of a Greek city, Epirus, the Romans were exposed to the military tactics of the more sophisticated Hellenistic world. In the early stages of the wars the Romans lost numerous battles, but they were quick to learn from the Greeks and eventually won the conflict. By the end of these wars the Romans had extended their alliance system to the southern tip of Italy and close to the shipping lanes of the Carthaginians.

As the Roman alliance system grew in central and southern Italy, and the Romans moved closer to Sicily, they became a concern to Carthage. From what historians have determined, the relations between Rome and Carthage before the Punic Wars appeared amicable.[12] Even though Carthage had a strong navy and could mobilize effective mercenary forces, the Carthaginians were businessmen first, and they preferred to rely upon diplomacy to remove possible clashes that might disrupt their commercial ventures and thus cost them money. In their early relations with the Italian states, of which Rome was only one, they offered mutually profitable treaties of trade and commerce. During the early part of the 3rd century B.C., the Carthaginians were inclined to avoid conflict where less costly methods could prevail as effectively. They tended to avoid resorting to hostilities unless they had some definite financial gain in view.

Carthage had concluded two treaties with Rome some years before the outbreak of war in Sicily. Both of these treaties had been written to assure the Romans that the Carthaginians had no intention of intervening on the Italian mainland or of challenging Roman hegemony there. In turn, the Romans agreed to accept Carthaginian control of much of Sicily and to refrain from maritime competition with Carthage in the western Mediterranean.[13]

Ancient as well as contemporary historians have blamed Rome for starting the Punic Wars.[14] The motives for the Roman involvement in Sicily are questionable and theories abound as to why they intervened at all in what started as a localized conflict between two relatively minor forces on the island. In later years the Romans justified their expansion beyond Italy and the building of their empire as motivated by an altruistic desire to protect the weak, humble the wicked and bring Roman law and civilization to less progressive societies.[15] Modern apologists maintain that Rome invaded Sicily to assist her Greek allies on the island and that imperialism played little if any part in the decision to go to war. These historians argue that Rome never intended to embark on an imperialistic course but found herself controlling an empire by default at the end of the Punic Wars.

Other historians maintain that the Romans began the wars because they feared Carthage would eventually seek to control the Italian coasts in much the same way that they controlled Sicily and Spain.[16] Even if there was no Carthaginian military presence in southern Italy, the influence of that empire through its traders and other emissaries would undermine the Roman concept of an Italian confederation under Rome's exclusive control. From this perspective the Roman actions were defensive and justified as a pre-emptive strike to protect their security. The last and most likely argument is that Rome had been on the path to imperial conquest all along, whether consciously or unconsciously, and that intervention in Sicily was simply the first step that would bring Rome to the forefront of power in the ancient world.[17] Rome had been moving for some time before the Punic Wars to consolidate her hold over central and southern Italy and must have had a view of her future that included visions of an empire in the Mediterranean.

Rome was certainly on the path of imperial conquest by the time of the First Punic War, and the Carthaginians feared correctly that the path would only end on the ruins of their city. Roman expansion into southern Italy threatened Carthaginian interests in Sicily as well as in Sardinia and Corsica. Carthage, then a richer and more established power, had no choice but to protect her interests and enter into a war with Rome.

The Romans invaded the island of Sicily in 264 B.C. on behalf of a group called the Mamertines. The Mamertines were mercenaries who had originally come from the Italian mainland and taken the name "men of Mars." They had roamed throughout Sicily for years, entering the service of first one local despot and then another until in 289 B.C. they seized the city of Messana (Messina), a coastal fortress on the northern shores of Sicily. They decided to make their home there after they murdered the local men and took their wives and daughters. From this base the Mamertines collected tribute from throughout the island and launched sporadic attacks on shipping in the straits between Italy and Sicily. Eventually they came into conflict with the ruler of a powerful Greek city, Syracuse, on the eastern coast of Sicily. In 270 B.C. the tyrant of Syracuse, Hiero, decided to rid the island of the "men of Mars" once and for all, and he marched on

Messana.

The Mamertines worried they could not hold out for long against Hiero, so they turned to Carthage for help and at the same time sent a delegation to Rome. The Carthaginians agreed to aid the Mamertines, and they sent an army to Messana to assist in defending the city against the Greeks. For reasons that are not entirely apparent, the "men of Mars" convinced the Carthaginian commander, Hanno, who had come to help them against the Greeks, to leave their city. Hanno left Messana and positioned his men in the countryside. The Carthaginians were furious at his stupidity and quickly crucified him for lack of proper judgment. The new Carthaginian commander then joined forces with the Greek tyrant Hiero and both armies set about to besiege the city.

The Roman decision to send troops to Sicily in 264 B.C. on behalf of the Mamertines was not made lightly. The move to invade Sicily was the beginning of Roman overseas expansion and the Senate debated the matter at length. There were senators who believed it was beneath the dignity of their city to ally itself with a lawless gang of mercenaries and pirates, even if they had originally come from Italy. These senators argued that the Mamertines were not worth the price of a war with Carthage, the strongest naval and commercial power in the Mediterranean.

Opposing forces in the Senate, led by Appius Claudius, argued for war with Carthage, claiming that sooner or later Rome would have to deal with this dangerous presence in the Mediterranean. If the Carthaginians held Messana, he argued, they would have an important base from which they could launch future incursions into Italy. Now was the time, Appius Claudius argued, to confront Carthage, not later.

The Senate was unable to come to a decision and so the matter was given to the Roman people to decide through their popular assemblies, the Comitia. There the people voted to intervene in Sicily, and Appius Claudius was elected commander of the Roman expeditionary force. When he arrived in Sicily he tried to negotiate an accommodation with the Greeks and the Carthaginians who had control of the countryside around Messana. Unable to come to terms with either force, Appius attacked the Greeks first. They retreated to Syracuse and the safety of their walls. Then he attacked the Carthaginians, who retreated as quickly as had the Greeks. The dramatic and relatively easy victories of the legions at Messana increased popular support for the war in Rome. The Senate voted to dispatch additional forces to Sicily under the consuls Otacilius and Valerius the next year.

This, then, was the cause of the first of a series of wars that would prove to be the most destructive and costly the ancient world had ever seen. The movement of Roman legions into Sicily on behalf of the Mamertines brought Rome into direct conflict with Carthage and commenced a cycle of particularly vicious wars that would last over a hundred years, from 264 to 146 B.C. While the first of the wars was limited to a struggle over control of southern Italy, their scope eventually widened, and in the end the Punic Wars determined not only who would rule the ancient world but also whether Carthage or Rome would influence the very course of Western civilization.

The first conflict between the two cities lasted more than two decades, generated intense hatred between them and set the stage for the larger and more destructive Second Punic War. During the war the Romans portrayed the Carthaginians as a faithless and cruel people and they coined the word "punica" to refer to this mendacious race which sacrificed its young to a god of fire. The Carthaginians in turn hated the Romans with equal passion and both sides inflicted as much pain on each other as they could through defeat in combat, torture, crucifixion and all manner of other atrocities.

After their defeat at Messana, the Carthaginians convinced the Greeks at Syracuse to join them in another alliance and take back the city from the Romans. Their joint forces confronted the Romans outside Messana and were defeated by the legions a second time. The First Punic War had begun in earnest. The Carthaginians now retreated to their fortress city at Agrigentum on the southern coast of the island, where they assembled a sizable force of Ligurian, Celtic and Iberian mercenaries. Additional ground forces were brought in from North Africa to reinforce the garrison at Agrigentum. The Romans attacked the city in 262 B.C. and the citizens and soldiers of

Agrigentum who survived were enslaved. The Carthaginian mercenary armies had lost a second battle against the legions, and as a result many Sicilian towns declared openly for Rome. In general, however, the coastal cities of Sicily stayed loyal to Carthage throughout the war. This probably happened because of their fear of Carthaginian naval superiority over the Romans. On the other hand, many of the cities in the interior of Sicily went over to the Romans because of the strength and presence of Roman ground forces.

The Senate at Rome was overjoyed when it received the news of the victory at Agrigentum. The Romans were now resolved to drive the Carthaginians completely out of Sicily and increase their own power on the island. A number of minor battles followed in the countryside around Agrigentum in the years 262 and 261 B.C. During these battles the Carthaginians used war elephants against the legions. While the Romans had initially panicked at the sight of the charging beasts, and even avoided fixed battles for fear of them, they eventually developed defensive tactics that proved effective. The Romans stationed spear-throwers in their front ranks to torment the beasts at the onset of the battle and then positioned their infantry in a formation that was so thick with men it could not be breached even by the charging elephants. On many occasions the Romans were even able to drive the elephants back into the ranks of the Carthaginian troops.

Not long after the defeat at Agrigentum the Carthaginians came to the realization that they could not win against the Roman legions in pitched battles. The Romans seemed willing to sacrifice however many men it might take to win a battle and they always seemed to have unlimited numbers of men to refill their ranks. To compensate for Roman superiority in manpower the Carthaginians modified their tactics and placed their mercenaries in several well-fortified coastal cities. The Carthaginian navy could keep them supplied by sea and at the same time these forces could be deployed into the countryside to harass Roman supply lines throughout Sicily. The Carthaginian navy would land small groups of these soldiers over much of the Sicilian coastline and they would engage the Romans when conditions were favorable, then quickly withdraw if conditions changed. These tactics

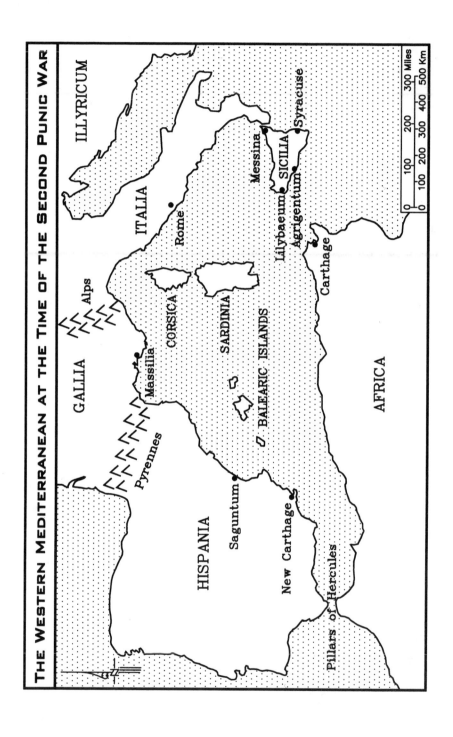

THE WESTERN MEDITERRANEAN AT THE TIME OF THE SECOND PUNIC WAR

ILLYRICUM

ITALIA

Rome

Messina

SICILIA

Lilybaeum

Agrigentum

Syracuse

GALLIA

Alps

Massilia

Pyrennes

CORSICA

SARDINIA

BALEARIC ISLANDS

Carthage

HISPANIA

Saguntum

New Carthage

Pillars of Hercules

AFRICA

0   100   200   300 Miles
0 100 200 300 400 500 Km

succeeded for several years as the Carthaginian politicians waited patiently for the Romans to tire of the war and reach an accommodation. During this period Carthaginian fleets were active along the Sicilian coastline, cutting Roman communication and supply lines and even attacking the southern Italian coastal cities. These attacks on the Italian coastal cities had more of a psychological effect than any strategic value.

The Romans now realized that they would have no chance for a decisive victory over Carthage by continuing to follow their present course. It was not in their interest, nor was it in their nature, to fight a long, drawn-out war. The Romans wanted a quick resolution to the conflict, so in 260 B.C. they made a major change in their military thinking. They decided to take the war to Carthage while defending the Italian coastal cities against the Carthaginian navy. Both of these strategies required a strong navy and at that time the Romans had little experience of the sea. They had virtually no ships of their own and had been ferrying their legions across the Straits of Messana with ships they had leased from the seafaring Greek cities of the southern Italian coast.

The Senate voted funds to build a large fleet of ships. This was a significant decision for the Romans since they had always been land-based fighters and knew very little about naval warfare. They were embarking on a venture that was new to them and they were engaging an enemy which, in the words of one ancient historian, "had enjoyed unchallenged supremacy of the sea for generations."[18] The Romans however, were undaunted, and determined to commit whatever amounts of money and manpower it would take to accomplish the task.

The pride of the Carthaginian navy was the quinquereme, a one-deck ship of fifty to sixty oars with five men to an oar. These ships were slow and heavy but very seaworthy and were used principally to ram enemy vessels. The Romans had no ships like these in their navy; however, by chance, not far from the Straits of Messana on a shore in northern Sicily, they happened upon a Carthaginian quinquereme that had run aground and been abandoned. Capitalizing on this opportunity, they dismantled the ship, board by board, and transported it back to Italy. There they used it as a model for the construction of their new fleet.

The Roman fleet of quinqueremes was built in less than two months. Contingents of sailors from the Greek coastal cities of southern Italy were recruited to man the first ships while the Romans trained their own soldiers in the skills of seamanship. The Romans went so far as to establish schools on land to train their men in the arts of rowing and sailing.

The Romans were already skilled fighters on land and they developed a unique device that allowed them to bring their successful style of fighting to the enemy at sea. The Romans outfitted their ships with a device called the "*corvus*," or crow's beak. This was a platform approximately four feet wide and some thirty to forty feet long made of planks nailed across each other and containing a large iron spike in one end. The device was attached by hinges to the front deck of a Roman ship and then fastened to the mast in an upright position by a rope running to the spike end through a pulley. The *corvus* could then be dropped into the deck of an enemy ship where it would embed itself and hold the enemy vessel fast in a death lock. Roman soldiers, using the *corvus*, would then swarm aboard the enemy vessel in large numbers.

The first contingent of the Roman fleet put to sea, and its first naval encounter was a disaster. The consul Gnaeus Cornelius Scipio was heading for Messana when he stopped at the small coastal island of Lipara (Lipari) to attack the Carthaginian garrison there. The attack turned into a fiasco when the fleet was unexpectedly trapped in the narrow harbor by a larger squadron of Carthaginian war vessels, and the Romans abandoned their ships.

A second contingent of the new Roman fleet encountered the Carthaginian navy not far from the Straits of Messana in 260 B.C. The Carthaginian admiral, anticipating an easy victory and having nothing but contempt for the inexperienced Roman seamen, launched an impulsive frontal attack. Relying on the traditional Carthaginian method of ramming, he was not prepared for the effect of the Roman *corvus*. As the fleets engaged, the crow's beaks of a hundred Roman ships slammed into the decks of the Carthaginian quinqueremes. The ships were held fast and the Roman legions swarmed aboard, winning their first naval victory. The Roman admiral was honored at Rome for his triumph while the Carthaginian admiral was immediately crucified on the island of Sardinia.

Bolstered by this unexpected victory at sea, the Roman Senate voted to strike directly at Carthage. In 257 B.C. the consuls M. Atilius Regulus and L. Manlius Vulso set sail from Italy with a large fleet of warships and a sizable army of legionaries for the coast of North Africa. They encountered a Carthaginian fleet off the eastern coast of Sicily. The Carthaginians drew the Romans into their center with the intent to ram their ships, but the Romans, utilizing their technique of grappling and boarding, defeated the Carthaginian naval forces and enjoyed their second major victory. Carthage no longer had any sizable naval force in the waters between Sicily and North Africa, and the city was open to invasion.

When the Roman forces landed in North Africa at Cape Bon near Carthage, they encountered little resistance and proceeded to ravage the rich countryside. The Carthaginians sent out two small armies to engage the Romans but both were defeated. Regulus offered terms, but the Carthaginians refused. Their purses and lives in peril, the Carthaginians hired a Spartan, Xanthippus, a specialist in the use of elephants, to come to their aid with a sizable force of mercenaries. In the spring of 255 B.C., with an army of Carthaginian citizens and Greek mercenaries, the Spartan commander met the Romans outside Carthage in the valley of the Bagradas (Medjerda). His elephants broke through the Roman lines and trampled to death many of the massed legionaries while skillful Numidian cavalry, hired by the Carthaginians, outflanked the survivors. Nearly the entire Roman army was destroyed in what was Rome's greatest land defeat of the war.

The consul Regulus was captured and the story of his captivity in Carthage developed into an important part of Roman historical lore. Latin writers in later years, such as Cicero, Livy and Valerius Maximus, recounted with pride the story of how Regulus conducted himself while a prisoner of Carthage. The consul was sent to Rome in 251 B.C. as an emissary with instructions to obtain an exchange of prisoners and negotiate an end to hostilities. Regulus was compelled to swear upon his honor as a Roman that if he failed in his mission he would return to Carthage.

Regulus appeared before the Senate at Rome and, placing his own welfare aside, he advised the assembled leaders of his country not to release the enemy prisoners because they were experienced soldiers who would only return to Carthage to fight another day against Rome. Nor, he advised, should Rome negotiate with Carthage for an end to hostilities. Rome had the upper hand in spite of the defeat in North Africa and would eventually prevail. Regulus urged the Senate to continue the war. The senators approved and the noble Roman, despite the protestations and pleadings of his family, friends and countrymen, returned to Carthage, where he died a terrible death by torture. Regulus came to epitomize those virtues of patriotism, duty, honor and self-sacrifice that would become the foundations of Roman civic pride in the centuries to come.

As the war continued the Romans suffered enormous losses at sea. Some of the sailors died in battle fighting the Carthaginian navy, but most died as a result of bad seamanship and the elements. A Roman fleet en route to Africa with reinforcements for the remnants of the Roman army there was lost off the coast of Sicily in 255 B.C. The admirals of the Roman fleet had ignored the warnings of their experienced pilots to avoid the southeastern coast in making the passage from Italy to North Africa. The fleet was caught by one of the sudden storms that characterize this area of Sicily and dashed upon the rocks of the shoreline.

The Romans, however, were stubborn and once they had committed themselves to a course of action they would continue no matter how high the cost. While utter determination had its advantages in conflicts with human opponents on land, it did not work against nature. In 253 B.C. another Roman fleet ran aground because of bad seamanship at the legendary island of the Lotus-Eaters, Meninx.

The Roman ground forces, bolstered by reinforcements from their Italian allies, pressed the war in Sicily. By this stage of the war only two Carthaginian strongholds remained and they were located at the western tip of the island. The first was the fortified city of Lilybaeum

(Marsala) and the second was a naval base nearby at Drepana (Trapani).

There were political developments in Carthage at the same time that would affect the outcome of the war more than Roman troop movements in Sicily. The Carthaginians were losing their interest in the war with Rome. Influential factions at Carthage had become interested in expanding the empire in Africa and were considering a vast expenditure of money and effort in that direction. This change in policy indicated a shift of power in Carthage in favor of those who wanted to abandon Sicily to the Romans and concentrate on building a greater African empire. Such a move, they argued, would be cheaper and more profitable than continuing a war that had no favorable outcome in sight. It appeared the war might thus have ended in Rome's favor had it not been for the result of a naval battle fought off the coastal city of Lilybaeum in 248 B.C.

A fleet of Roman warships under the command of the admiral Claudius Pulcher (the Beautiful) was moving to engage a Carthaginian naval force near Drepana. On board his flagship Claudius prepared for battle, but like any pious Roman he was obligated first to consult his high priests for omens. The priests reported that the omens were, for the moment, inauspicious as the sacred chickens aboard ship were refusing to eat. The priests advised postponing the battle until another, more favorable day. Claudius, anxious to win a victory, impetuously ordered the sacred chickens thrown overboard and the attack begun. The Romans suffered a costly naval defeat. Claudius was put on trial in Rome, where, while condemned for the disaster and heavily fined, he just barely managed to escape the death penalty.

Apart from a few naval victories, the Romans had not been able to acquire the experience of the sea that could only come with decades of sailing the Mediterranean. Heavy weight, as well as inexperienced rowers, hampered the Roman ships. Their naval victories had been won largely because of their use of the "*corvus,*" yet this device also made the Roman ships unwieldy in bad weather and vulnerable to capsizing. The Carthaginian ships were faster and better handled, and after they adjusted to the novelty of the "crow's beak" they were able to gain back their advantage on the sea. Furthermore, Carthaginian ships were able to ram and sink many Roman vessels because the Romans were simply bad seamen. A combination of naval disasters resulting from some sudden squalls off the shores of Sicily, compounded with poor seamanship and incidents of running aground, ended for a period the advantage the Roman naval forces had enjoyed when they first engaged the Carthaginians.

The Carthaginian victory off the coast of Lilybaeum renewed their enthusiasm for continuing the war. Their senate appointed a young but experienced general to conduct operations in Sicily, Hamilcar Barca. A man of exceptional ability, both as a strategist and a tactician, Hamilcar took command of the mercenaries and improvised upon the earlier strategy of guerrilla warfare against the Romans. That strategy had worked well in the war's early years and Hamilcar revived it through a combination of quick moves behind the Roman lines combined with daring raids upon the Italian coastline.

While Hamilcar managed to alter the course of the war in Sicily in a relatively short time, divisions in the Carthaginian government still hampered his chances for winning. There had developed two factions. The first were the commercial investors who had considerable ties to international trade and sizable investments in Sicily. The second group was composed of wealthy landowners who wanted the resources of Carthage directed toward the development of an African empire. This faction was convinced that the potential for great agricultural productivity—agribusiness—in North Africa was far more lucrative and much safer than the continuation of a war in Sicily that had dragged on inconclusively for years. This faction, led by a politician called Hanno "the Great," had little interest in providing the resources necessary to allow Hamilcar to win the war against Rome. These landowners eventually gained the upper hand in the government and ended support for him in Sicily.

The Romans, undaunted by their defeats and losses on the seas, voted in the Senate to rebuild their lost navy. The Senate persuaded the wealthiest citizens of Rome, individually and in consortia, to donate funds for the building of a new navy. By 242 B.C. a Roman fleet of some 200 warships had been launched from Italy and appeared in the waters off Sicily. The new Roman navy caught a Carthaginian supply fleet headed to Lilybaeum by surprise. The supply ships could not out-run or defend themselves against the Romans and they were easily sunk or captured. This was a naval disaster that Carthage could ill afford. The garrison at Lilybaeum could no longer be supplied and it would be only a matter of a few weeks until it would be starved into surrender and Carthage would lose its last large base in Sicily. Hamilcar had no choice but to enter into negotiations with the Roman commanders to end the war.

For Carthage the continuation of this war showed no further prospects for success in spite of the presence in Sicily of an exceptional leader. The Carthaginian land forces could no longer be adequately supplied by their navy, and they were too weak to capture the fortified cities of Sicily that had been lost to the Romans in prior battles. While the Carthaginians were never decisively defeated in Sicily, their leaders realized that no definitive victory against Rome was possible, so they submitted to a peace under less than ideal conditions rather than continue a war they could not win.

The Roman consul Lutatius Catulus, victor of the recent naval battle, made the terms of the surrender relatively light by Roman standards. He agreed to allow Hamilcar to evacuate all his forces from Sicily intact. Carthage was to pay an indemnity to Rome over a twenty-year period and abandon all claims to Sicily. The Roman Senate, however, found the terms too lenient and increased the indemnity, shortened the repayment period and required Carthage to keep its merchant ships out of all "Italian" waters.

As a result of the First Punic War, one of the longest and most costly wars in ancient history, the fortunes and futures of both sides had been dramatically altered. Carthage retreated to Africa and emerged from these decades of war in a weakened state. The loss of Sicily was the first major tear in the fabric of her empire and it would soon be followed by the loss of Sardinia and Corsica. With Carthage no longer a presence in Sicily, Rome seized the latter two islands despite the recent treaty—but without opposition. With these first overseas possessions, Rome was on her way to building the empire that would enable her to dominate the ancient world for the next six centuries.

Unfortunately for Carthage, the end of the First Punic War did not end the bloodshed of its citizens. It marked the beginning of a period of domestic warfare more savage than had been the fight in Sicily against the Romans. Carthage was left with a force of 20,000 mercenaries in Sicily who demanded to be brought back to North Africa and paid for their services. That force, under the command of Hamilcar Barca, was repatriated in small groups so as to minimize its potential for disrupting the city. The plan was to pay the mercenaries off quickly as they arrived and then send them back to their countries of origin. The Carthaginian government, however, unhappy over the enormous indemnities to be paid Rome, balked at paying the mercenaries their full due, especially since they had lost the war. The Carthaginian senate preferred crucifixion of the mercenaries rather than payment.

A volatile mix of Iberians, Gauls, Ligurians, Balearic islanders, Greeks and Africans began to mass outside the high walls of Carthage, impatient for their pay. There were negotiations between the Carthaginian senate and the mercenary leaders followed by delays. The Carthaginians, from the heights of their city walls, threw worthless promises down to the agitated mercenaries. Finally they rebelled and started a war in which, paraphrased in the words of a Greek historian, the armies of both sides were not content with mere "human wickedness" but ended by assuming "the ferocity of wild beasts and the vindictiveness of insanity." The mercenaries invited the African states to join them in their attack against Carthage, and according to the ancient sources nearly all did. The solidarity between the mercenaries and their African allies can only be understood within the context of their mutual hatred of the Carthaginians. Revolt against Carthage flared up everywhere in North Africa. The citizens of Carthage would have to fight for themselves, as there were no mercenaries to be hired, and no Greek specialist in elephants to come to their rescue. Hanno "the Great," the Carthaginian politician who had favored withdrawing from Sicily, took command of the citizen army but his greatness failed to achieve military success. The situation became increasingly alarming. The senate then entrusted command of a new army to Hamilcar Barca.

Hamilcar recruited a few mercenaries from Italy, employed some renegades from his old army in Sicily, and conscripted more citizens from Carthage. When he was ready, the Carthaginian commander led his army out from the walls of the city to fight against men he had commanded for years in Sicily. The fighting was fierce and the atrocities terrible. Feelings ran high on both sides and there seemed no way to end the war except through the annihilation of one side by the other. After three years, during which all manner of torture, crucifixions and cold-blooded brutality were committed by both sides, Hamilcar in 238 B.C. brought matters to an end when he lured the greater part of the mercenary force into a cirque, or gorge, outside Carthage known as the "saw." There the mercenaries, already exhausted at the time by hunger and fatigue, were trapped and massacred by Hamilcar's army using elephants. Those who survived the carnage, including the leaders of the mercenaries, were taken back and crucified before the walls of the city.

Rome remained largely neutral, at least by ancient standards, throughout the mercenary war in North Africa. The Romans made profits selling supplies to both sides and even allowed Carthage to recruit small numbers of troops in Italy. Roman traders provided the mercenaries with supplies and made handsome profits just as the Carthaginians had done in other regional conflicts years before. It was in 237 B.C., as the mercenary war ended, that Rome seized Sardinia in a blatant violation of her recent peace treaty with Carthage.

Carthage, worn out by years of struggle, and with no fleet left with which to fight, was in no position to challenge Rome's actions. Even though voices in the Carthaginian senate called out for another war, Carthage was forced by a new treaty to renounce her claim to Sardinia and to pay even higher indemnities to Rome. After the treaty was signed, Rome seized the island of Corsica in a second display of her new power. The two islands together thus became the second Roman province, and with Sicily became the foundations of the dawning empire. The Carthaginians, worn out by two wars, their resources depleted, and a large portion of their empire lost, submitted to a Pax Romana, a peace under humiliating conditions. They remained in North Africa to tend their wounds and await a new champion and another war.

Rome emerged from the First Punic War stronger than she had ever been and ready to expand her control over the Mediterranean. Even though Roman admirals had lost fleets of ships through faulty seamanship, and Roman generals thousands of men through poor tactics, these losses were more than compensated for by Rome's abundant reserves of manpower and her willingness to commit all the resources necessary for a decisive win against Carthage. The Romans had endeavored to force the issue with Carthage at every juncture in the war. They displayed time and again their readiness to learn from their enemy the lessons necessary to beat him and to adapt to changing circumstances. The Romans had been forced to develop in areas that were new to them. They built new fleets time and again after they lost the old ones through poor command, defeat or the sea. Citizens of modest means as well as the wealthy came forth with donations for the war effort and Roman men were willing to leave their homes and fields to take up arms in order to advance the aims of the Republic. As a people the Romans came together in this war as they never had before. The war made Rome the strongest naval power in the ancient world and opened Roman eyes to the profitable potential of governing territory outside the Italian peninsula.

Large cities throughout Sicily and southern Italy now readily asked to become Roman allies. Within a decade of the end of the First Punic War Rome had sent legions of public officials to Sicily and Sardinia and had begun the administration of her new empire.

NOTES
[1] Thomas Bulfinch, *Myths of Greece and Rome,* p. 289.
[2] Serge Lancel, *Carthage: A History,* p. 40.
[3] Lancel, p 172.

[4] *Cambridge Ancient History*, p. 17.

[5] Lancel, p. 227.

[6] Ibid.

[7] Lancel, p. 228.

[8] Aristotle, *Politics.*

[9] Cary and Scullard, *A History of Rome*, p. 49.

[10] Barry Cunliffe, *Rome and Her Empire*, p. 24.

[11] Cunliffe, p. 46.

[12] Carry and Scullard, p. 116.

[13] Carry and Scullard, p. 596.

[14] *Cambridge Ancient History*, p. 44.

[15] Virgil, *The Aeneid.*

[16] Cary and Scullard, p. 116.

[17] R.J. Rowland, *Rome's Earliest Imperialism*, p. 761.

[18] Polybius, Bk. I, Sec. 60.

CHAPTER II

⋘⋙ · ⋘⋙

THE RISE OF HANNIBAL

"Angebant ingentis spiritus virum Sicilia Sardiniaque amissae"[1]

Hamilcar Barca was a proud man, and the loss of Sicily to the Romans at the end of the First Punic War made him determined to gain revenge. He had come close to defeating the Romans in Sicily, and, if not in winning the war, at least in fighting it to an honorable draw. Then the politicians in Carthage withheld the support he desperately needed in the final months of the conflict, leaving him no alternative but to surrender. Hamilcar negotiated the best terms he could and the war concluded. On his return home he was called upon to fight yet another war, caused by the same politicians who had deserted him against the Romans, against the very men he had led for so many years in Sicily. After the mercenary revolt was finally crushed, Carthage was exhausted and weak. It could only look on helplessly as Rome seized Sardinia and then Corsica in blatant violation of the peace treaty. The Carthaginians could do nothing more than accept the loss, endure the humiliation and wait for another time to avenge themselves.

The Barca family was wealthy and influential in Carthage. Hamilcar, as a young man, could have followed a life of leisure or devoted himself to commercial pursuits. Instead, he chose a career of military service to his city, a life that often took him far away from his family for long periods and frequently placed him in harm's way. As with any soldier, he lived with the knowledge that he could fall in battle, but as a Carthaginian officer he lived as well with the fear that he could be crucified by his own people should he fail to achieve victory.

39

Hamilcar had a wife, daughters and sons who waited for him in Carthage. He must have seen his family only rarely during the war in Sicily and then the three more years of fighting that followed in the deserts and mountains outside Carthage.

After the safety of his city had been secured, Hamilcar, as commander of the army, turned to building a new empire for Carthage in Spain. Carthage had lost three of its most valuable possessions as a result of its ill-fated war against Rome and it needed new areas to exploit in order to maintain its wealth and position. One influential faction in the Carthaginian government favored the concentration of all resources toward the development of an African empire while a second, led by Hamilcar, favored the establishment of a new empire in Spain and a continued Carthaginian presence in Europe. If Rome, with its incestuous ties to Greek culture, could be expected to look for opportunities to the east, Carthage would spread west to rebuild its empire.

Driven by his hatred of the Romans, Hamilcar may have had a hidden agenda as he undertook to convince the Carthaginian senate to let him conquer Spain. He was determined to build a base on the Iberian peninsula from which he could launch his next war against Rome. This would be a war to punish Rome for her humiliation of Carthage, to recapture the lands that had been unjustly taken from her and to restore to Hamilcar Barca his honor. The natural wealth of Spain would be used to finance the next Punic War.

Hamilcar was not content to pledge only his own life and fortune to struggle against the Roman republic, but he dedicated the lives of his sons as well. The seeds of his hatred found fertile ground in the hearts of his four sons: Hannibal, the eldest, followed by Hanno, Mago, and Hasdrubal.[2] Nurtured over the years, the father's hatred eventually burst forth from the breasts of his sons into a war of revenge. Yet in the end this hatred for Rome would consume not only all the Barca family but destroy Carthage as well.

In the year 238 B.C. the Carthaginian senate appointed Hamilcar to head a large expeditionary force to Spain. Before he departed, Hamilcar sacrificed to his gods for a safe journey and success. As he made his libations and finished the sacred rituals, he called his eldest son, Hannibal, then only nine, to join him at the altar. Hamilcar commanded the boy to swear an oath that he would always be an enemy to Rome and to anyone who stood with Rome. Hatred, the father taught his young son, was appeased only with the blood of one's enemy. Until he was old enough to draw that blood, the boy would let his hatred sustain him. As the years passed, Hannibal proved willing to sacrifice anyone who might stand in the way of his plan to destroy Rome. With that childhood oath, the hatred of Rome passed from the father to the son—a hatred that would bring to the ancient world a long and costly war which would change forever the course of Western civilization.

Sometime between 238 B.C. and 237 B.C., Hamilcar Barca crossed the Mediterranean Sea from North Africa by the Pillars of Hercules and entered Spain. There he proceeded to establish the power of Carthage. His sagacious combination of force and diplomacy brought the various Celtic cities, towns and tribes under his domination and began the systematic exploitation of the natural wealth of Spain.[3] Over a twenty-year period, from 238 to 218 B.C., Hamilcar and his successors established a larger and richer empire in Spain than Carthage had ever possessed in Sicily. Spain would become, as Hamilcar planned, not only the trove of the new Carthaginian empire but a political and military base for the next war against Rome.

As Hamilcar consolidated his power, the country became the private domain of the Barca family. By securing and exploiting the two most valuable resources of southern Spain—minerals and manpower— the Barca family grew even richer than it had been in Carthage. As the gold and silver mines of Spain yielded their wealth to the efficiency of their new African masters, Hamilcar's power in Spain and influence in Carthage grew stronger. No one in the Carthaginian senate would dare oppose him as long as a good portion of the wealth of Spain flowed into the city on a steady basis. The second resource exploited by the Carthaginian was a large pool of native manpower. The Celts had been the original occupants of the central and western areas of the country and over the centuries had been largely displaced by the Iberians. Some mixing of the two groups had occurred and resulted in the evolution of a wild and warlike people called the Celtiberians.

Warriors from these tribes were impulsive and knew little fear in the face of their enemies. In spite of their strength and courage, however, they were undisciplined, took direction poorly and were unable to cooperate with one another. They were capable of fierce resistance against the Carthaginians, especially when they defended their homes, but they were incapable of joining forces in a coordinated effort to defeat a sophisticated enemy. These tribes were distinguished by their bravery in battle and by the quality of the weapons produced by their craftsmen and artisans. The finely tempered blades of Iberia were unsurpassed in the ancient world and remained the standard for quality in Europe until well after the end of the Middle Ages.

The Carthaginians exploited the military potential of these native tribes as systematically and efficiently as they exploited the gold and silver mines. The Spanish tribesmen under Carthaginian commanders were eventually trained and transformed into excellent troops. They did much to expand the political power of the Barca family in Spain. In the areas under Carthaginian control native recruits were conscripted directly into the army, while from the outlying areas they were enticed to join by Hamilcar's agents. Supplementing his Spanish forces with seasoned African ground troops and cavalry, Hamilcar established an army in Spain such as Carthage had never possessed before.

The financial condition of Carthage improved as the empire in Spain was exploited. Within a generation the ancient city of North Africa had regained much of its former greatness. But this only raised Roman suspicions and fears. The Romans were allied with the Greek city of Massilia at the time. This city early in its history had been a Phoenician colony. Now it was a Greek city and controlled numerous smaller colonies along the Mediterranean coast of France and Spain. Among the Greek allies along the southern coast of Spain was the city of Saguntum (Sagunto, north of present-day Valencia). The Greeks became concerned about Carthaginian activity near this city and they complained to the Romans.

The Romans inquired of Hamilcar and he seemed always to be able to put their ambassadors at ease with his assurances that his intentions were peaceful. Hamilcar maintained that he was content to remain in the southern half of Spain and exploit the resources there in order to pay the war indemnities due Rome. As long as the payments to Rome were timely, and often made in greater amounts than specified in the treaty which ended the First Punic War, the Roman Senate seemed content to accept his explanations and not challenge his actions.

During this period, Rome was occupied with the responsibilities, costs and problems of administering her new empire in Sicily and establishing her presence in Sardinia and Corsica. There was also a threat of rebellion developing among the Gauls in northern Italy, which did eventually erupt into a short but fierce war between 225 and 222 B.C. The Romans had been worried about these Celtic tribes who inhabited the Po Valley ever since they had sacked Rome in 390 B.C. Anxious that this never happen again, the Romans established two sizable colonies at Cremona and Placentia (modern-day Cremona and Piacenza) to keep a watch on things. Roman forces were also involved in a police action against the pirates of Illyria (the former Yugoslavia and Albania) along the eastern Adriatic coast. They were also keeping a watchful eye on Greece, specifically Macedonia, which was becoming unsettled under a youthful and aggressive king, Philip V.

Hamilcar's second in command in Spain was his son-in-law, Hasdrubal "the Handsome."[4] Hasdrubal had married into the Barca family and would eventually succeed Hamilcar upon the latter's death. From many years of close collaboration there developed between them a consistency of policies and direction that enabled the two men to establish what became in effect a dynasty in Spain. The consistency, stability and strength of their rule in the years from 238 until 221 B.C. resulted in their "de facto" independence from the government at Carthage and established the unopposed succession of Hannibal in 221 B.C.[5]

Hamilcar and then Hasdrubal depended upon the army that they had built and united around their charisma to rule in Spain. They were able to remain independent of Carthage, and eventually the soldiers in Spain came to owe their allegiance more to the Barca family than to the North African capital. This gave Hamilcar and then Hasdrubal the power to pursue a course independently of the Carthaginian senate. The senate accepted that the two men had become practically monarchs but, because of the enormous wealth they kept flowing into Carthage, the senators made little protest and were willing to look the other way.

Hamilcar was killed in 229 B.C. while he and two of his sons, Hannibal and Hasdrubal "the Younger," were in the field.[6] The father and his sons were cut off from their own forces by enemy tribesmen. With only two avenues of escape open, Hamilcar ordered his two sons to take the safer route while he drew off the pursuing tribesmen in a more hazardous direction. Hamilcar attempted to ford a dangerous river and as he entered the torrent he was swept from his horse and drowned.[7]

When Hamilcar Barca died, none of his sons were of an age to succeed him so the army elected Hasdrubal "the Handsome" to assume command. Their choice was quickly ratified by the senate at Carthage and Hasdrubal's first action was to avenge the death of his father-in-law and mentor. The Carthaginian army showed little mercy to the Spanish tribes who had driven Hamilcar Barca to his death in the river. Those who were not killed in battle, including women and children, were crucified in the Carthaginian fashion as an example to any other tribes which might be considering resistance to the Barca dynasty. This was a scene that had been played out many times before with a callous indifference to human suffering, and that would be played out again many more times in the decades to come. As well as avenging the death of Hamilcar, Hasdrubal added considerable territory to the Carthaginian holdings in Spain.

Hasdrubal devoted most of his efforts in the years that followed to consolidating the power of the Barcid dynasty in Spain and in strengthening his autonomy from Carthage. Hasdrubal continued the policies of Hamilcar, and his role in Spain gradually became more that of a governor than a commander. He built a capital on the southern Mediterranean coast and named it New Carthage or Carthago Nova (Cartagena). This new port city offered easy access to Carthage as well as a central location from which to administer the ever-growing Spanish empire.

Hasdrubal built a splendid palace at New Carthage and lived in regal luxury. Nearly a king, he ordered coins minted in gold and silver that bore his image with a divine countenance.[8] He also issued coins that bore the image of Hamilcar and it is from these that we have some idea of the appearance of these two leaders. The tribal chiefs of Spain paid tribute to Hasdrubal as they had to Hamilcar and they were often required to hand over their children as hostages to insure their good behavior and fidelity to Carthage. This was a practice that the Romans would quickly see the value of and later use effectively throughout their empire.

Large numbers of natives as well as slaves and criminals from Africa were forced to work in the mines of the Carthaginians, often under brutal conditions. This insured the uninterrupted flow of wealth into New Carthage and guaranteed the stability of the Barca dynasty in Spain. While discontent with Carthaginian rule might have been widespread among the proud Iberians and Celts, the discipline and organization imposed on the country by Hasdrubal, enforced by his army, ensured that order was preserved and that the wealth of the country kept flowing into the Barca treasury.

Concerned by developments in Spain, the Romans dispatched emissaries to New Carthage in 226 B.C. to negotiate a treaty with Hasdrubal and thus limit Carthaginian expansion. Hasdrubal received the emissaries and agreed not to venture north of a river believed to be the Ebro with any armed forces. He would recognize the area north of the river as a Roman sphere of influence.

There is some disagreement among historians about exactly which river in northern Spain was designated as the boundary between the Carthaginian empire and the Roman sphere of influence.[9] While many scholars have supported the idea that the Ebro River is that boundary, others have pointed out that the river is located a hundred or so miles north of the limits of the territory then controlled by the

Carthaginians. If the Ebro is accepted as the river designated in the treaty, that would have left the city of Saguntum, with ties to Rome, isolated deep within hostile Carthaginian territory and considerable territory north of Saguntum free for Hasdrubal to take. Saguntum, an independent city on the Mediterranean coast north of New Carthage, had strongly resisted Carthaginian encroachment over the years. Its inhabitants were probably able to maintain their independence for so long because they became allies of Rome, and both Hamilcar and Hasdrubal may have been careful during this period not to give Rome any cause to intervene in Spain. Hannibal would change all of that in short order.

There is a river south of Saguntum today named the Júcar and it is possible that this is the river referred to in the treaty between Hasdrubal and Rome. If the Júcar is taken as the northern boundary of Carthaginian territory, as specified in the treaty, then the Romans would have succeeded in limiting the territory controlled by Hasdrubal and protecting Saguntum. Hasdrubal probably agreed to the treaty because he was more concerned with consolidating power over his Spanish territories and exploiting their resources than embarking on further military conquests and risking war with Rome.

Hasdrubal's life came to a violent end in 221 B.C. when he was murdered by a Celtic slave working in the palace. The motive appears to have been revenge, since Hasdrubal had recently crucified a kinsman of the assassin for plotting against him.[10]

Hannibal was twenty-five years old when he took command of the army and political control of the country. In spite of his youth, he had already won the confidence of the army in field operations and had learned the art of politics at the side of Hasdrubal in the palace. The army must have seen in him their ancient commander Hamilcar restored in all the vigor and enthusiasm of youth. Hannibal had spent years in the camps and had trained with the common soldiers. He was held in high regard because of his royal lineage as well as his demonstrated ability to command.

There is an allegory related by the French novelist Gustave Flaubert[11] (in his novel about Carthage entitled *Salammbô*), about a young boy, who, while hunting in the mountains around Carthage, caught an eagle by surprise. The great bird struggled and dragged the boy in a desperate attempt to escape. The boy would not let the eagle go and the trapped creature, in its fury and fear, clawed at the boy with its talons. Undaunted by the pain of the struggle, he clasped it ever tighter to his chest until the exhausted bird gave up the fight and began to die. The boy burst forth with a cry of joy that resounded through the valley. (The eagle is symbolic of Rome and the young boy is Hannibal, driven by his hatred to endure any pain to defeat his enemy.)

Hannibal was born at Carthage in 246 B.C. toward the end of the First Punic War. As a child he lived through the turbulent years of the mercenary wars (240–237 B.C.) and then followed his father to Spain. Exactly when Hannibal went to Spain is unclear, although it is probable that he went when still very young, say in 237 B.C., and stayed at least until his father's death in 229. How long a period he remained in Spain after that or how often he traveled between there and Carthage is difficult to determine. It is known that Hannibal was with his father when he died in 229 B.C. and that he returned to Carthage shortly thereafter. Hasdrubal sent for him a few years later in order for him to commence his military training.

The request to send Hannibal to Spain was important enough to be debated by the Carthaginian senate, and that may be interpreted as an indication of how determined the Barcas were that they would continue their dynasty and have their war on Rome. The faction in the senate opposed to the move argued that the boy should remain at Carthage to be schooled in "proper subjection to the law and its officers."[12] Hanno, the leader of that faction, warned that should the young Hannibal be allowed to live in Spain he might be corrupted once he saw the power that his father and now his brother-in-law wielded. Hanno knew the hatred of the Barcas for Rome and he worried that the young boy, "a small spark" he called him, might one day "kindle a great fire." While many of the nobility in the senate supported Hanno, in the end Hasdrubal prevailed and the boy was sent to Spain.

When Hannibal arrived at New Carthage the troops celebrated

with unbridled enthusiasm. Old veterans saw in this young boy their old commander Hamilcar, while the new soldiers quickly fell under the charismatic spell of the next generation of Barca leadership. As the years passed Hannibal matured in the camps of the army and learned the tactics of war.

Hasdrubal favored Hannibal above all his other officers, not so much because of their relationship but because of ability. Hannibal learned the arts of politics and statecraft quickly through spending time at Hasdrubal's side, and the tactics of war came naturally to him. Under his leadership soldiers showed their best in the field and strove to excel. He inspired them by his example and he showed time and again that he could endure with equal ease any of the elements while on the march. Hannibal was a young man who, according to ancient commentators, ate and drank in moderation. He consumed only as much as he needed to sustain his strength and slept only when he had completed his work.

Hannibal often slept upon the bare ground in the company of the common soldiers and stood his turn on guard duty throughout the night. His clothes and armor were simple for his rank and did not reflect his royal lineage. He developed into a skilled fighter, either on or off a horse, and was always the first to attack in battle and the last to leave the field of combat. His popularity with the soldiers grew and eventually developed into a bond that would hold commander and troops together in the coming war with Rome. Physically, in that age of cut-and-thrust weapons and close combat, he must have been impressive, both strong and agile, and we can assume he possessed a commanding air. As the years in Spain passed, Hannibal developed his own charisma and no longer needed to depend on the memory and glory of his father. Hannibal had become a force in his own right.

Hannibal had been well educated during his early years at Carthage. While his native language was Semitic Punic, it is known that his second language was Greek, and that as a child his parents had provided him with Greek tutors. As a man, he surrounded himself with Greek scholars and learned Latin, the language of his enemy, in order to better understand the people he had devoted his life to fighting. He also developed a natural curiosity about the customs of Spain, and married the daughter of a Celtic chieftain rather than a woman from the Carthaginian aristocracy. Her name was Imilce and she bore him a child.

Hannibal had a dark side to his personality. The ancient sources describe a man who harbored within his heart a hatred for his Roman enemy that consumed him. This hatred grew with the passing of years and was never tempered even up to the last days of his life. He had within him a burning to avenge the wrongs done to Carthage. The First Punic War was fought by Carthage to defend an empire, while the Second was fought by Hannibal for revenge. The ancient sources are clear that the cause of the war was the anger of the father which lived in the heart of the son.[13] The second war between Rome and Carthage was caused by the legacy of a man who had died ten years before the first battles were ever fought.

It was alleged that Hannibal in war was capable of an almost inhuman cruelty if circumstances warranted it.[14] As a ruler and a general he often evidenced a total disregard for the truth as well as a willingness to sacrifice honor and religion if they conflicted with his interests at the moment. Such was the complex character of the man who became the leader of the Carthaginians and the nemesis of Rome. He had an irresistible will, a singleness of purpose and the ability to inspire unquestioning loyalty in his men-at-arms. All these qualities he embodied in a mind that in terms of military strategy and tactics bordered on genius. His qualities, both good and evil, would drive him to wage a war that the ancient sources regarded to be "in defiance of not only reason but even of justice."[15] Cities by the hundreds would crumble before Hannibal's army—first in Spain, then in France and finally in Italy, even as thousands of people died.

After the assassination of Hasdrubal in 221 B.C. the senate of Carthage confirmed Hannibal as his successor, and the next generation of the Barca dynasty continued on the path toward war with Rome. For the next twenty years Hannibal was to dominate events throughout the western Mediterranean and come closer to bringing down the Roman Republic in Italy than his father had ever dreamed of doing in Sicily.

Hannibal's first act as commander in Spain was to lead an expedition against some tribes which had decided to test the resolve of the new Carthaginian commander. The hostile tribes occupied the highlands of Spain in the area known today as La Mancha. After a quick victory against these tribes, Hannibal subdued several neighboring towns as well and imposed a tribute upon them. Then he withdrew into winter quarters at New Carthage, distributed a generous bounty to the men who had served with him and awaited the spring and a new campaign.

In the summer of 220 B.C. Hannibal took up arms once more and defeated a large force of tribes which had congregated against him in the area of modern-day Salamanca. He cleverly avoided a pitched battle with a sizable force of enemy tribes and undertook a diversionary action. As he seemed to withdraw from the area, the enemy became bewildered by his actions, followed him and, in a preview of the tactics he would use so successfully against the Romans in the coming war, he drew them into a trap at the Tagus River.

Hannibal and his army stayed hidden as the enemy crossed the river on foot. Upon his signal the African cavalry cut down the enemy in mid-stream as they were hampered by their loads and the waters. Those who escaped were killed as they struggled up the steep river banks by a contingent of elephants that Hannibal had held in reserve by the banks. At the crucial moment in the battle Hannibal sent his main forces against the survivors. What Hannibal demonstrated at the Tagus was that he could utilize the element of surprise to his advantage and that he would always retain the initiative. Throughout his long military career Hannibal would always determine where he would fight, how he would utilize the terrain and maintain the initiative in fighting his enemy. Hannibal would always choose under what conditions to fight his battles. This was something he would never leave to chance or the enemy.

Following his victory at the Tagus, few tribes south of the Ebro River would challenge his authority or dare to face his army in battle. During the three years that he presided on the peninsula, 221 to 218 B.C., Hannibal extended the limits of the Carthaginian empire north to the Ebro and controlled virtually all of Spain. Only the city of

Saguntum remained outside the Carthaginian sphere of influence, and only for a brief period. The people of Saguntum feared Hannibal and relied on their alliances with the Greek city-states of southern France and with Rome to keep the Carthaginians at bay. They sent delegations to Italy to warn the Senate of the growing strength of the new Carthaginian leader. The Greeks also warned Rome that Hannibal could become a dangerously destabilizing force in south-western Europe and a serious threat to the security of the area.

The Romans eventually sent a delegation to New Carthage to confront Hannibal and demand that he abide by the conditions in the treaty between Rome and Carthage signed by Hasdrubal some years before. The Romans insisted that Hannibal guarantee the con-tinued independence of Saguntum and pledge that he would restrict his military activities to the territories south of the Júcar River.

Though Hannibal was only twenty-seven at the time of his first meeting with the Roman emissaries, he showed no fear of Rome. He advised the Roman delegation that there were tribes living around Saguntum who were allies of Carthage and that some of these groups were being persecuted and even executed. Hannibal warned the Romans that the people of Saguntum should not think that their alliance with Rome would protect them as they persecuted others who were under the protection of Carthage. The Carthaginians, Hannibal lectured the Romans, had an ancestral tradition of taking up the causes of the victims of injustice and he would continue to honor that tradition in Spain.[16]

The Roman delegation left New Carthage convinced that Hannibal was impossible to reason with and that war was inevitable. The ambassadors reported to Rome by dispatch that Hannibal was obsessed by his hatred for all Romans and that they found him to be in a state of "unreasoning and violent anger."[17] His accusations that the citizens of Saguntum were persecuting allies of Carthage were without merit and only being used to justify a course toward war with Rome. The Roman delegation sailed directly to North Africa to discuss the situation with the leaders of Carthage. Hannibal in the meantime laid siege to Saguntum.

While the Roman delegation addressed the senate of Carthage,

Hannibal stormed the walls of Saguntum. As the Romans demanded that Carthage force Hannibal to honor the treaty they had signed with Hasdrubal, the Carthaginian battering rams worked mercilessly night and day against the Spanish city's walls. The Carthaginian senate listened and then debated the matter. There were those who praised Hannibal's actions and even advocated war with Rome. These factions argued that Carthage had recovered from its defeat in the First Punic War largely because of what the Barcas had done in Spain. A war against Rome now would restore Carthage to her former position of power in the Mediterranean and allow her to recover her lost colonies. Gone were the days when Rome could dictate terms to a defeated Carthage. Others in the senate counseled a more moderate course and advised that Hannibal should be ordered to withdraw from Saguntum.

From the party opposed to the Barca dynasty and in favor of peace with Rome, Hanno spoke.[18] He reminded the senators that he had warned them years before not to allow the son of Hamilcar Barca to go to Spain. The "spark" was now very close to lighting the fires of war throughout the Mediterranean. The ghost of the father possessed the son, he warned, and so long as one Barca lived there would never be peace between Carthage and Rome. Even now the son was leading them toward another war with Rome. But Hanno and his party could effect only a partial compromise in the senate. The final resolution was to support Hannibal and recommend to the Romans that they not let their concern for Saguntum take precedence over their longstanding treaty of friendship and cooperation with Carthage. The Roman delegation left Carthage and sailed to Rome to report what had transpired to the Senate there.

The siege of Saguntum took eight months.[19] The defenders used every means to drive the army of Hannibal from their city walls. They poured burning oil and a combination of pitch and tow upon the Carthaginians, setting fire to the men and machines below. Still the forces of Hannibal kept up a relentless assault against the city walls. Finally a section of the main wall and two towers came down and left a large gap in the defenses. The Carthaginian assault troops flooded in. The defenders of Saguntum fought with all the courage and strength they could muster, knowing full well their fate and that of their city should they fail. Hannibal was at the forefront of the action. He was wounded in the leg when he led a rash and frenzied attack against one of the most fortified and heavily defended portions of the city.[20] As a result he was forced to withdraw from the fighting for a period and leave direction of the assault in the hands of his brothers.

The city of Saguntum finally fell and the army of Hannibal unleashed its full fury on the inhabitants in an orgy of rape, murder and looting. What happened at Saguntum was a preview of the horror that would be repeated time and again in cities all over Italy during the Second Punic War. Many of the survivors threw themselves into the fires that raged everywhere in the city rather than surrender to Hannibal's men.[21]

When the fighting and slaughter ended, the city lay open and Hannibal took its treasures and divided them, giving equal amounts to his soldiers and sending the considerable amount that remained, plus a large contingent of the defeated, as slaves back to Carthage. When the wealth that came to Carthage from the fall of Saguntum was displayed, it impressed everyone in the city and disposed the senate favorably toward the young commander. Thus Hannibal had ensured the fullest support of the Carthaginian leaders for his next step by appealing to their most basic instinct: greed.

It was important to Hannibal that the old hostility that had existed between his father and the senate during the First Punic War not hamper him in the second. Hannibal was as much an astute politician as he was a brilliant military commander, and he was intent on beginning the war with the full support of the Carthaginian senate. If the treasure and slaves taken from Saguntum could assist in that, so much the better. With the fall of that unfortunate city, Hannibal now controlled nearly all of Spain, and the base of support that his father and brother-in-law had sought from which to launch the war on Rome was now firmly established.

The Romans sent another delegation to Carthage and demanded that Hannibal be turned over to them to be transported back to Rome for trial as a war criminal.[22] Hanno suggested as a compromise that Hannibal should be removed from command in Spain and banished to some remote island—banished, Hanno argued, to a place so remote that not even the sound of his name would ever reach Carthage again and disturb the peace of the Mediterranean world.[23] Nothing succeeds like victory, however, and with the fall of Saguntum and the spoils of war that flowed into Carthage, the senate went solidly behind Hannibal and voted him its full support. The Carthaginians blamed the people of Saguntum for bringing their demise upon themselves and they urged the Roman ambassador to remind the Roman Senate when he returned that their longstanding treaty of friendship and peace with Carthage should take precedence over this insignificant, and provocative, Spanish city.

The Roman ambassador addressed the senate of Carthage with the folds of his toga grasped tightly about his chest. "I hold here both peace and war," he warned. "I will let fall from my hands which ever of the two you choose."[24] The leader of the Carthaginian senate dismissively replied, "Let fall whichever one you want." With that the Roman ambassador relaxed his grip and said, "war has fallen." The senate of Carthage accepted his pronouncement with a cheer. In such a seemingly casual manner began the greatest and most destructive war the ancient world had ever seen.

When word reached Hannibal that Carthage and Rome were at war, he moved to secure the sea routes between Spain and North Africa. While the politicians of the two empires argued the finer points of their treaty violations, and debated who was to be blamed for starting this next round of slaughter and destruction, Hannibal was busy preparing for his war. With the sea routes between Spain and Africa secured by the Carthaginian navy, Hannibal turned to address the fears of the people at Carthage. Many of the older and more influential generation remembered the Roman invasion of North Africa during the First Punic War some thirty years earlier, and they feared another and more forceful assault. To alleviate their fears Hannibal sent a large force of recruits from Spain, together with a small naval force, to protect them and the surrounding countryside. He purposely sent recruits from the Spanish tribes to guard Carthage, and African troops to guard Spain. This method of cross posting—

that is, sending soldiers from newly conquered territory to garrison provinces far from their homes—was used to minimize the chances of revolt among the soldiers. The Romans would later adopt this method and use it successfully in the garrisoning of their empire from Britain to Palestine. From Africa Hannibal brought more troops to Spain and he placed the entire force under the command of his younger brother Hasdrubal.[25]

He developed a plan by which his brother would govern Spain and deal with the inevitable Roman invasion there while he himself marched on Italy. With these strategic moves Hannibal had secured Africa and Spain and could now concentrate on his preparations for the invasion of Italy.

No one knows precisely when Hannibal first determined on an invasion of Italy by crossing the Alps. It is possible the idea originated with his father Hamilcar, when the elder Barca first began to carve out the extension of the Carthaginian empire into Spain. Neither do modern scholars have access to the maps available to the Barcas at this time; however, Hannibal must have been acutely aware from at least the moment he took command in Spain that Rome was only a march away. Of course, the exact difficulty of that march through the Alps may have eluded him during the years he imagined leading his powerful army to the very gates of Rome.

Whoever first suggested the crossing of the Alps, the idea was predicated upon the Carthaginian assessment of Roman strength in Italy. Not yet a unified country, Italy was a land of semi-autonomous city-states and tribes loosely held together in a confederation only recently dominated by Rome. Hannibal believed that this confederation would dissolve in the face of a challenge to Roman authority and that many of the member states might even join him in the war. Rome would lose its hold over Italy and the Roman legions would be tied to the mainland, suppressing insurrections.

Hannibal's crucial conclusion was that the Second Punic War could not be fought like the first if Carthage were to succeed. The new war would have to involve a drastic, innovative move on his part, a reversal of roles among the major combatants. Since the end of the

First Punic War the Romans had built a formidable fleet and controlled much of the Mediterranean Sea around Italy and Sicily; and Carthage was no longer the naval power it had been during the first contest. If Hannibal were to risk an invasion of Italy by sea and the Roman navy were to intercept his slow transport ships, his entire invasion force could be destroyed in an instant and the war lost before the first battle on land could be fought.

Instead he believed that by following a land route he would avoid many of the logistical problems encountered by his father in Sicily during the first war. Hamilcar had been isolated on the island of Sicily and dependent on the ships of Carthage both for reinforcements and supplies. The Carthaginian navy had failed him through a combination of natural disasters, poor strategy and the strength of the opposing Roman fleet. This, coupled with the lack of support from the politicians in Carthage, had caused his ultimate defeat. Hannibal would not allow his forces to be dependent on supply by sea and the good will of the senate at Carthage. Once the war began, Hannibal intended to remain as independent as he could, both from Carthage and supply via the sea lanes. He would take a bold, new initiative and control the land route just as Rome had done in the first war. Whether this was a strategy that came to him one day, or if it was a concept that had germinated within the entire Barca family ever since the First Punic War, remains a matter of speculation.

The Romans never suspected that Hannibal planned to carry his war to Italy. Their leaders and military strategists calculated correctly that Hannibal would never risk coming by sea given their naval superiority. For him to attack Italy by land would be equally unlikely, they reasoned, given that he would first have to make a journey of a thousand miles over hostile territory and cross two mountain ranges. The Pyrenees and the Alps were formidable barriers, especially the latter, which was the highest mountain range in Europe and was inhabited by the uncivilized Gauls, whom even the Romans had been unable to subdue. The Romans knew little about the Alps at this period in their history and they somewhat naively regarded them as an impenetrable barrier for all but barbarians.

The Romans believed the Second Punic War would be fought in

Spain and in North Africa, for which contingency they had built up their navy. They were convinced that Hannibal would wait for them to invade Spain. Their transports would ferry troops from Italy to the peninsula, and then control the sea lanes while Roman legions would defeat Hannibal on land. Spain would fall and become another addition to Rome's growing empire. The second war would be a simple replay of the first, the Romans establishing naval and ground superiority over Hannibal and then invading Carthage. What the Romans did not anticipate was that Hannibal, against all odds, and with amazing speed, would succeed at accomplishing the impossible and bring the war to Rome itself.

Hannibal assembled his army in the early spring of 218 B.C. and announced to his men that a state of war now existed between Rome and Carthage. He recounted to his soldiers how the Romans had demanded that he be taken to Rome and tried as a war criminal and how the Carthaginian senate had rejected these demands. Then he announced his bold plan to cross the Alps and carry the war to Italy. The army, ignorant of what lay ahead, was swept up by the passion of the moment and the eloquence of the speaker, and roared its approval.

Hannibal described to his army the wealth of the lands through which they would be passing on their march, the spoils to be had and the fierce Gauls who waited on the other side of the Alps to join them in their war against Rome. He assured them that the route to Italy would be difficult but passable, and he said that the Gauls would assist them along the way. He praised the fighting spirit of his army and their resolve to conquer Rome. Hannibal fixed their departure for a day in the late spring of 218 B.C. Then he gave his army leave to go home and see their families. For some of these men it would be seventeen years before they would again see their loved ones, but for most it would be the last time.

Hannibal was confident that the Gauls who inhabited both sides of the Alps and the Po Valley of northern Italy would join him. The tribes which inhabited that valley had recently fought a war with Rome and they deeply resented Roman attempts to subjugate them. He had sent his agents into the Alps months before the march began, to reconnoiter the route, scout the mountain passes and establish contact with the natives. He had instructed his emissaries to seek out the Gauls and make alliances with their most important chieftains along the route, ensuring their cooperation through bribes. The success of his venture depended on the cooperation of these chieftains and their willingness to guide him over the Alps, even to the point of joining his army in its war on Rome.

When these agents returned to New Carthage in the winter of 218 B.C. they reported that the Celts were favorably inclined toward Hannibal and that many of the tribes on the Italian side of the Alps eagerly awaited his arrival and the opportunity to wage war on Rome. They also reported that the passage over the Alps, though arduous and in places difficult, was by no means impossible if done at the right time of year. Not all the mountain tribes, however, could be counted on to help him. There would be those who would attempt to block his passage—not because they were allied to Rome but because they were naturally warlike. The success of Hannibal's plan depended on his ability to cross the Alps quickly, organize the Celtic tribes under his leadership and attack the Romans before they realized what he had done and had a chance to organize their resistance.

From his scouts, Hannibal collected considerable information about the route through what is today France and what he could expect in the mountains. Always in his mind as he planned the march in the spring of 218 B.C. must have been the uneasy knowledge that he had to cross the French Alps before the onset of winter. Were he to be delayed too long in any one place along the route, his army would arrive in the Alps too late to cross the snow- and ice-covered passes. They would then be stranded and most of his men would probably die of starvation and exposure in the barren valleys.

The men who assembled to follow Hannibal that spring were recruited from many parts of the ancient world. Some had served with him, as well as with Hasdrubal and even Hamilcar. There was a loyal veteran corps that formed the heart of the army to be sure, but the majority were probably mercenaries who owed no allegiance to anyone. These were men who fought for plunder. Murder and rape were their stock-in-trade, and the prospect of unlimited spoils must have been the only tie that bound them together. Hannibal's achievements in the Second Punic War were all the more extraordinary because he was able to mold these men into a disciplined and loyal fighting force.

His army was composed of Africans, Spaniards, Ligurians, Phoenicians, Gauls and Greeks. It was a polyglot force of many races and spoke in many tongues. While the mercenaries were a far smaller force than the Romans they would confront, the devastation that they wrought on Italy, both physical and psychological, proved to be far greater than could have been imagined from their small numbers.

According to the ancient sources, the army that Hannibal assembled in the spring of 218 B.C. at New Carthage numbered nearly 100,000 men.[26] It was a force of mostly infantry, with about 12,000 cavalry from Africa and a contingent of war elephants and their handlers. The largest groups of soldiers were Iberian and Celtiberian tribesmen from Spain, many of whom had fought Hamilcar, Hasdrubal and even Hannibal over the years. While details of their arms are lacking, they were probably lightly armed troops carrying the famous short Spanish sword, a spear and shield, and wearing light body armor. The officers were all Carthaginian, as required by the military tradition of Carthage.

The cavalry was composed of African horsemen recruited from the ancestors of the Berber tribes who today live in Algeria, Tunisia and Libya. Of these the most formidable were the Numidians. They were skilled riders and fighters who would become the backbone of Hannibal's army. As well, there were Ligurians and Gauls from southern France, and heavily armed Greek infantry. From the Balearic Islands off the Mediterranean coast of Spain came "slingers" who demanded payment not in gold but in captive women.[27]

To further augment his army when he arrived in Italy, Hannibal hoped to raise a force equal to his own among the Gauls. Along the route he was confident the mountain tribes would be swept up in the grandeur of the moment and join the march to Rome the way pilgrims would join a crusade. The campaign was in fact Hannibal's crusade to recover from the Romans the greatness of Carthage and the honor of his father.

Historians are of the opinion that the elephants which Hannibal had with him on the march were probably of the African variety.[28] The consensus developed from detailed studies of coins issued about 220 B.C. is that these elephants came from areas near the forests in the foothills of the Atlas Mountains in North Africa and along the coast of Morocco. While Indian elephants are larger and fiercer and would have been available to the Carthaginians via the trade routes linking North Africa with Egypt, Syria and India, the elephants portrayed on these coins bear an unmistakable resemblance to the African variety.

The back of the African elephant, as can be easily seen from the coins minted in Spain at the time of the Second Punic War, shows a dip between the hump of the shoulders and another hump further back over the hindquarters. The Indian elephant is depicted on other coins from the same time period from other lands as having an unbroken convex dome over the back, stretching from the shoulders to the hindquarters. The hindquarters of the African elephant are nearly flat, whereas the hind quarters of the Indian elephant project backwards at a fairly sharp angle. The head of the African elephant is carried high on these coins, whereas the head of the Indian elephant is in a low position. The forehead of the African elephant is flat while the profile of the Indian is concave. The elephants used by Hannibal probably stood about eight feet high from the shoulder and were the type used by the Egyptian pharaohs. These elephants were considerably smaller than the African bush elephants found in central Africa, which average about eleven feet from the shoulder, and the Indian elephants, which could range as high fourteen feet.

There are historians who believe that Hannibal may have had some Indian elephants on the march as well.[29] There are references in Polybius to handlers of these beasts known as the "*indoi.*" The first inclination is to assume that the word means Indian and the conclusion drawn is that the handlers and their elephants came from India. The name "*indoi*," however, must be taken in a broader context. Based on what modern historians have learned about the war elephants, Indians were considered to be the experts in training and handling elephants for war. They may have been utilized in many armies in the ancient world over the centuries since Alexander the Great first encountered them when he fought King Porus of India at the Battle of Hydaspes in 326 B.C.

No doubt Hannibal had hired Indians to train and drive his elephants on the march, but there is no indication that they trained only Indian elephants. The word "*indoi*" may also have been a generic term meaning elephant driver rather than specifically an Indian. The elephant which Hannibal rode over the Alps was named "Surus," meaning "the Syrian."[30]

It is well documented in the literature that Syria was the country from which the Egyptians were known to have obtained their elephants and that those elephants probably came from India. Carthage and Egypt were close geographically and maintained friendly relations during the period of the Punic wars. Hannibal might well have obtained Indian elephants through the Egyptian trade channels with Syria.

Finding sufficient amounts of food for the army must always have been a concern for Hannibal, as the specter of starvation on the march was always a real and frightening possibility. An army the size of Hannibal's must have consumed tons of food each day. Each soldier burned four to five thousand calories a day marching, and more during combat. That would translate into nearly two pounds of food per day per man to function at peak efficiency. Hannibal's army would have consumed a hundred tons a day of food and been able to drink small rivers and streams dry as it went. Some of the food could have been carried but most would have to be foraged from the countryside. An army the size of Hannibal's would have left a wasteland of desolation and human misery behind as it moved forward. The unfortunate natives in its path would have lost everything: their crops, their livestock, possibly their lives to the foraging soldiers.

While Hannibal was planning the logistics of the march and discussing the problem of food, one of his generals, Monomachus, told the war council that he feared starvation in the Alps more than he feared the Romans. He proposed that because of the length of the march, and the often barren nature of the terrain through which the army would pass, the soldiers should be conditioned to eat human flesh.[31] He suggested that small amounts be cooked into the daily rations and then increased as the army moved farther into the Alps. The army could thus consume its dead and dying, feeding upon itself as it moved or upon its enemies if that were possible.

Hannibal allegedly could not bring himself to accept this idea and the matter was dropped. At least no further mention of it appears again in the ancient sources. Perhaps the story is true or perhaps it was Roman propaganda. It is interesting to note that the ancient historians have commented that many of the atrocities committed in Italy later in the war and attributed to Hannibal might really have been the work of this general Monomachus.[32]

In addition to the horses and elephants used in combat, a multitude of pack animals also accompanied the column and had to be provided for. These animals were necessary to carry the vast amount of supplies needed for the army to sustain itself on the march and prepare for the battles that lay ahead. Thousands of mules and oxen dragged the ponderous siege engines, battering rams and catapults needed for storming the fortified cities that lay in the path of the army on its way to the Alps and throughout Italy.

At the end of the column would have been another group, perhaps a fourth as large as the regular army. In this group would have been merchants who sold goods at the end of each day, ranging from cooking utensils to blankets, as well as cobblers to mend the soles of the soldiers' boots and blacksmiths to repair their equipment. There would have been opportunists eager to exploit the misfortunes of others by buying anything of value stripped from the dead on the field of combat or looted from the many cities and towns that would inevitably fall before the onslaught of Hannibal's army.

Then there would have been the final pathetic elements of humanity who have historically followed in the dust and filth behind advancing armies. These were slaves, captives from earlier wars or people snatched up along the route, who were there to do the bidding of the soldiers. Prostitutes from Spain and Africa and captive women either followed the column willingly or were dragged behind it to be worn out while they were young, and then left to die by the roadside when they were old and useless, like so many lame pack animals which could no longer carry their burdens.

The ancient world must not have seen such a concentration of force as Hannibal had assembled on the day he left New Carthage since the time when Alexander the Great prepared to march from Greece into the Persian Empire nearly a hundred and fifty years earlier. With a fire burning in his heart and a torch blazing in his hand, Hannibal mounted his massive elephant, Surus, in the faint light of dawn. As the sun slowly rose over New Carthage he turned the long column north toward Gaul. As the army began its march toward the Pyrenees Mountains on that spring day in 218 B.C., Hannibal turned his back on a wife and child he would not see again for seventeen years. The army and its charismatic commander took their first steps toward Rome in the firm belief that they could effect the destruction of a proud enemy. Ultimately, their conviction would be proved correct.

NOTES

[1] T. Livius. *Ab Urbe Condita,* Bk. XXI, Sec. 1.
[2] Sir Gavin deBeer, in his early work *Alps and Elephants,* refers to the four sons as "the lion's brood," p. 2.
[3] Polybius, Bk. II, Sec. I.
[4] Not to be confused with Hamilcar's youngest son, who was named after him.
[5] Polybius, Bk. II, Sec. I.
[6] Polybius, Bk. II, Sec. I.
[7] *Cambridge Ancient History*, p. 23.
[8] *Cambridge Ancient History*, p. 25.
[9] Cary and Scullard, *A History of Rome*, p. 125; *Cambridge Ancient History*, p. 30; Cottrell, *Enemy of Rome*, p. 14; Bradford, *Hannibal*, pp. 33–34; Lancel, *Carthage: A History*, p. 380.
[10] Polybius, Bk. II, Sec. 36.
[11] Gustave Flaubert, *Salammbô*, p. 109, Penguin, translated by A.J. Krailsheimer, London (1977).
[12] Livy, Bk. XXI, Sec. 3.
[13] Polybius, Bk. III, Sec. 10–11.

[14] Polybius, Bk. III, Sec. 13; Livy, Bk. XXI, Sec. 14–15.

[15] Polybius, Bk. III, Sec. 15.

[16] Polybius, Bk. III, Sec. 15.

[17] Polybius, Bk. III, Sec. 15.

[18] Livy, Bk. XXI, Sec. 10.

[19] Livy, Bk. XXI, Sec. 15.

[20] Polybius, Bk. III, Sec. 17; Livy, Bk. XXI, Sec. 8.

[21] Livy, Bk. XXI, Sec. 14.

[22] Livy, Bk. XXI, Sec. 10.

[23] Ibid.

[24] Livy, Bk. XXI, Sec. 18.

[25] Livy, Bk. XXI, Sec. 22.

[26] Livy, Bk. XXI, Sec. 23.

[27] Livy, Bk. XXI, Sec. 21; Polybius, Bk. III, Sec. 33. The name Balearic comes from the ancient word "slinger," a weapon made famous by David in his renowned biblical encounter with Goliath.

[28] deBeer, p. 6.

[29] deBeer, p. 94.

[30] Cottrell, p. 27.

[31] Polybius, Bk. IX, Sec. 24.

[32] Ibid.

CHAPTER III

THE ANCIENT SOURCES

A story about an event that occurred in ancient times is always difficult to tell with a high degree of certainty. The most valuable sources of information have usually been lost over the centuries, or what exists has been rendered suspect by alteration, fragmentation or corruption. While ancient historians generally wrote about events in considerable detail, often what the modern writer has left to examine is not always sufficient to support the story fully, or the sources are themselves subject to so much controversy, contradiction and doubt that they are useless. The story about how Hannibal crossed the Alps is no exception, for it has many of these same problems when it comes to the source material.

Far and away the most convincing proof a writer can offer his readers that an event occurred in history is hard archaeological evidence. Unfortunately, evidence regarding Hannibal and the crossing of the Alps does not exist. No one has ever found a single piece of archaeological evidence to prove conclusively that Hannibal ever even set foot in Italy. So, how do we know that Hannibal crossed the Alps and that his story is not just another legend? First, a number of ancient Roman historians and writers tell us that Hannibal invaded Italy in 218 B.C. and that he came very close to destroying their republic. Second, numerous Greek writers confirm this when they also wrote about the wars between Carthage and Rome, and especially about Hannibal's invasion.

It is an accepted fact that the city of Carthage existed and that it controlled a vast empire in the western Mediterranean in the centuries between 800 and 200 B.C. The ruins of that once magnificent city still stand on the shores of North Africa for anyone to see, and evidence of Carthaginian colonies can be found throughout Sicily, Sardinia and Spain. There is enough evidence to enable archaeologists to accurately date many of these ruins and formulate an image of what the city must have looked like.[1] Traces of the Carthaginian legacy are evident in modern-day place names such as the Spanish cities Cartagena (New Carthage) and Barcelona ("camp of the Barcas"). Examples of Carthaginian art and literature, unfortunately, are rare. There is limited archaeological evidence that points to Hannibal's being in Spain and Italy, but it is often inconclusive and the historical context can be difficult to establish.

The majority of the evidence that exists about Hannibal is derived largely from coins, and indirectly from a few inscriptions and carvings. Coins have always provided an important source of information about people and events in the ancient world. There are many fine examples from the time of the Punic Wars and these are helpful in establishing approximate dates and some degree of chronological relationship with other objects and artifacts. Coins have been discovered in Spain that bear the likeness of men who experts believe could well have been Hannibal, his brother-in-law Hasdrubal, one or more of his brothers and even his father, Hamilcar Barca.[2] Evidence such as this yields important yet limited information about these rulers— such as when they lived and died, significant events that occurred in their reigns and how long they ruled. The quality of the silver and gold in many of the coins is a reliable guide to the prosperity of an area at the time they were issued, however, and can be an indication of how peaceful or warlike the period might have been.

The designs on these coins often represent political or religious themes and the symbols found on them can be guides to the policies that certain rulers followed. Often the symbols reflect a persona that a particular leader wanted to promote among his subjects. However, to extract this information and apply it to events in the Punic Wars, or to specific historical figures like Hannibal, requires a degree of specialization that is beyond the scope of this book. Numismatic evidence has to be formulated with considerable care and caution, and the drawing of conclusions must be left to specialists.

Inscriptions and carvings taken from columns and monuments are another valuable, if limited, source of information about Hannibal and the Punic Wars. Most examples that have survived are Roman and yield considerable information on both public and private affairs in the ancient world. These inscriptions were written, carved and displayed mostly on stone and metal such as bronze. Some of the inscriptions and carvings were erected by individuals in the form of epitaphs or dedications, while others were expressions of thanks to the gods for completion of a long and potentially dangerous trip or perhaps a prosperous business venture. Other inscriptions were made by public authorities in the form of regulations, decrees and resolutions. Some inscriptions are found on rock walls or milestones. Carvings found on columns and monuments usually depict battle scenes and military campaigns. From these carvings specialists are able to extract considerable information about everything from the size of the soldiers to the types of military dress and weapons they used.

Many inscriptions, however, are not closely dated, and when lettering and carvings are worn away by the elements over the centuries they become difficult if not impossible to read. Many are so damaged or worn that they are indecipherable. While many inscriptions and carvings contribute substantially to the understanding of historical events, they have their limitations, and often require, like numismatics, the application of special expertise to understand and utilize.

There is a great deal of archaeological evidence about Rome available to scholars that reveals everything from the construction of military fortifications and civilian habitats to the manufacturing and use of a multitude of artifacts necessary to everyday life. There are the remains of Roman roads (some with wheel-ruts), foundations of buildings (many with inscriptions), rock-cuttings, utensils, weapons, furniture, votive offerings and a variety of other antiquities. The evidence from these findings throws light on many aspects of Roman life and history but unfortunately tells us precious little about Carthage and Hannibal.

One area of fairly recent promise, nevertheless, is a series of archaeological excavations being conducted in central Italy that indicate a Carthaginian presence there.[3] These are excavations of incineration pits and burial grounds located in the area of Lake Trasimene, the site of one of Hannibal's greatest victories. Archaeological work at these sites has shown that large-scale battles between the Romans and the Carthaginians or a similar people took place there, but no evidence has yet been found that points conclusively to Hannibal's presence.

Another interesting source of information, perhaps more amusing and intriguing than informative, comes from a number of contemporary stories that relate to Hannibal and the crossing of the Alps. They are tales of archaeological objects that were allegedly found by chance in the Alps and then lost. Among the more interesting of the stories is one from the eighteenth century about a farmer in France who found elephant bones while plowing in his field. The bones were buried in a ritual manner with an unusual copper medallion at a place where Hannibal could well have passed on his march to the Alps.[4] Unfortunately, both the bones and the medallion have become lost, so have been of no help to modern scholars.

There are also scattered reports in the literature of the nineteenth century about elephant bones found in an Alpine pass.[5] Yet again, nothing has survived to be examined and authenticated except the stories. Finally there is the interesting tale of a tablet allegedly inscribed with the name of Hannibal and found on a high and remote Alpine pass toward the end of the nineteenth century. This tablet, if it had survived, would have been the strongest proof ever that Hannibal crossed the Alps. Yet it was lost when its enraged finder, a local inhabitant concerned more with profit than history, threw it into a glacier when he could not extort a high enough price for its sale.[6]

The story of Hannibal has captured the imagination and inspired people up to our own century to try a number of stunts to prove that he went over the Alps. In the early 1960s someone attempted to take an elephant over the Alps simply to prove that it could be done. There have been scores of expeditions, from the professional to the amateur, that have combed the mountains looking for Hannibal's pass. Generations of scholars from ancient times down to the modern era have fixated on the story of Hannibal and devoted some of their best efforts to proving it. Emperors and generals from Julius Caesar, Pompey and Constantine to Napoleon have taken armies over the Alps in attempts to duplicate Hannibal's feat.

The last and most dangerous place to search for evidence on Hannibal is in the French Alps themselves. Largely unchanged over time and standing as silent witnesses to the events of history, they hold somewhere among their summits the answer to the question. All that is necessary is for someone to be persistent enough, brave enough and lucky enough to find it. Two thousand years is not a long time in the context of Alpine history and scientists are sure that the terrain over which Hannibal passed and the climatic conditions he endured have not changed significantly in that period.[7]

The main passes over the Alps today are essentially the same that have been in use for thousands of years. Throughout the Middle Ages, the thousand-year period from the fall of the Roman Empire to the beginning of the Renaissance, the only routes over the Alps were the ones established by the Romans.[8] There were, from the records that exist, few new routes opened over the Alps in this medieval period, probably because the local governments lacked the financial resources and a large pool of cheap labor comparable to that of the Roman army and the slaves of the Empire. Engineering skill during the Middle Ages may have been severely lacking as well. Evidence of the Roman Alpine routes is reflected in the various milestones that they carefully placed along their roadways to mark the distances between towns. Inscriptions made by the Romans and others on walls of rock, on the remains of Roman roads and on buildings can still be found on or near some of the routes to the passes. One only needs to go into the Alps and, with a great deal of patience, caution and time, look for the evidence.

The possibility of discovering one conclusive piece of archaeological evidence is not as remote as one might think. For the Alps, once so inaccessible and remote, have now become winter and summer vacation spots for thousands of tourists each year. As these vacationing hoards descend on the mountains each season, someone, given the right set of circumstances and a little luck, may come upon the physical evidence of Hannibal's passing.[9]

During no other period in history have scholars had the access to the Alps that they have today. While still dangerous,[10] modern conveniences and technological advances have made them accessible even to amateurs for research purposes. Satellites, helicopters and airplanes have allowed aerial surveys to be conducted that give views of the valleys, ridges and peaks never before available on such an accurate and detailed scale. Developments such as metal detectors, inexpensive and portable, allow professionals and amateurs alike to undertake investigations of more remote areas that heretofore would have been deemed too difficult, inaccessible or expensive for traditional methods of archaeological excavation.

However, until the remains of an elephant or a Carthaginian soldier are found on some remote Alpine pass, scholars will have to rely on sources other than archaeological to make their case. What remains is what the ancient historians wrote about Hannibal: the literary evidence. The works of these writers are the most reliable sources of information available, yet they have their problems as well. The task is to examine and evaluate what they had to say about Hannibal, and how that information can be of use today in helping to determine his route over the Alps.

Nearly everything we know about Hannibal and his march over the Alps comes to us by way of ancient Greek and Roman historians. Some of them lived during and shortly after the time of the Punic Wars, but most lived years and even centuries after the events. Yet they were close enough to the events that their sources of information can usually be accepted as reliable. While references to Hannibal show up in many places and by various authors, they must all be viewed cautiously since most of the works that have survived the centuries have a pronounced Roman bias.

While the earliest examples of physical manuscripts dealing with Hannibal and the Punic Wars date from the tenth and eleventh centuries A.D.,[11] the greatest quantity of them date from the fifteenth and sixteenth centuries. These are transcriptions of the original Greek and Roman texts made during the Dark Ages by medieval monks and scholars. The original manuscripts were lost or destroyed centuries earlier. All of what the ancient historians wrote about Hannibal and the Punic Wars has been passed down to us over the centuries in the form of these medieval transcriptions.

The problem with using these manuscripts as evidence is that over the centuries they were transcribed by first one medieval editor, then another. Modern scholars, unable to go directly to the original sources, have had to rely on the accuracy of the transcriptions. For centuries the accuracy of the medieval editors in preparing their transcriptions was accepted by later scholars with little question. Recently, however, some scholars in the field have voiced concerns that the medieval transcriptions may contain serious errors that have impacted the research conclusions of generations of scholars.[12] With these warnings in mind, we can now turn to an examination of the ancient sources and what they had to say about Hannibal and the passage over the Alps.

The most reliable account of Hannibal's crossing would have been provided by someone, preferably a historian, who was actually with the Carthaginian mercenaries and made the climb. Hannibal supposedly provided for just such an account of his march across the Alps to be written, literally each day as it unfolded. The account was allegedly written by a Greek who accompanied the Carthaginian army as its official historian. His name was Silenus and we know about him through the writings of the later Romans who made references to his work.[13] The account of Silenus, however, was lost or destroyed centuries ago.

We also know that Hannibal studied Greek and possibly Latin from another historian and teacher, Sosylus. This Greek wrote a biography of Hannibal but unfortunately it too was lost long ago. We know of its existence only because, like the work of Silenus, Roman and Greek historians referred to it in their own later works.[14]

A young Roman officer, Lucius Cincius Alimentus, provides another source of information on Hannibal and the crossing of the Alps. Though he was not an eyewitness to the crossing, he was taken prisoner after one of the first battles between Hannibal and the Roman legions in Italy. This Roman officer subsequently spent several years in the Carthaginian camp. There were many periods in the course of the Second Punic War when the armies of both sides were inactive because of poor weather conditions or other problems. During one or more of these periods of inactivity, Hannibal apparently had the leisure to discuss with Alimentus, at length, the circumstances of his long march from Spain and the suffering his army endured when it crossed the Alps. Hannibal allegedly described to Alimentus how the Carthaginian mercenaries had struggled over the hostile terrain of the Alps, fighting against both the mountain tribes who lived there and the elements.

Alimentus was eventually freed and allowed to return home, but so far as we know he did not write an account of his captivity by the Carthaginians. He did pass on to others some of what he had learned from Hannibal, and that information eventually made its way into the writings of some of the later Roman historians.[15]

The most comprehensive and accurate history of the wars between Rome and Carthage was written by a Greek who was born at the end of the Second Punic War and lived throughout the Third. Polybius (c. 200–118 B.C.) was a native of a mountainous region of southern Greece called Arcadia. After the Romans conquered Greece, Polybius was arrested along with a number of others because he had been active both politically and militarily in this region. He was sent to Italy in 168 B.C., where he remained in Rome under a loose form of house arrest for nearly sixteen years, though he was never formally accused of a crime.

While in Rome he had the good fortune to met Publius Scipio, an aristocrat who admired the Greeks and appreciated their civilization. Both men shared a love of learning and this became the foundation for a lasting friendship. Eventually Polybius was invited to live in the household of Scipio, head of an influential Roman family, that was involved in the politics of the Republic at the highest level and in the struggle against Carthage. Members of this patrician family had led the fight against the Carthaginians for generations, both from the floor of the Roman Senate and on the battlefields of Italy, Spain and Africa. Through his long association with both sides of Scipio's family, the Aemilii Paulli and the Cornelii Scipiones, Polybius came to know many of those who had made Rome the most powerful city in the ancient world.

Fifty years after the end of the war with Hannibal, Polybius began to write his comprehensive history of Rome. He drew upon a variety of sources, many of which are no longer clearly identifiable. We know that he used a wide range of documentary evidence, such as the important treaties between Rome and Carthage, and that he also had access to memoirs, minor treaties and other important documents in the government and private archives of Rome. He must also have made extensive use of the many conversations he had with some of the leading men of the time. All these sources gave him important information and a unique perspective on the course of historical affairs in the ancient world.

During the lifetime of Polybius, Rome became the most powerful and sophisticated capital in the ancient world, and as a result was visited by nearly everyone of importance. Thus Polybius had opportunities to interview many of those who had played key or crucial roles in the events that he would later write about. Polybius relied on personal inquiry as his most important research tool and interviewed eyewitnesses to many of the events. He drew, in addition, on written sources such as what other authors and historians had recorded as well as the numerous treaties and correspondence between the Romans and the Carthaginians. He also used published speeches of senators. Further, Polybius visited many of the battlefields in Italy and used information from an inscription that he found at the Temple of Hera on the Lacinian promontory in the southeastern tip of Italy (Cape Colonna).[16]

Polybius was eventually released from house arrest by the Roman authorities, probably because of his close association with the family of Scipio. He was allowed to leave Italy and he visited Africa, Spain and Gaul. The Roman war with Hannibal had aroused great interest in the ancient world and Polybius, as a historian, traveled to many of the battle sites abroad to investigate for himself what had happened. We know that while in Africa he met with the aged King of Numidia, Masinissa. This tribal king had once been a close ally of Carthage and had fought with Hannibal in Spain. Toward the end of the Second Punic War he saw the handwriting on the wall and joined with the Romans. The Numidian king fought against Hannibal at the Battle of Zama in 202 B.C., so there is little doubt that Polybius discussed this climactic Carthaginian defeat with him at length when they met.

On his return from Africa, Polybius traced Hannibal's footsteps over the French Alps in order to see for himself what the terrain was like and the circumstances of the march.[17] He reconstructed the route of Hannibal from Spain, through France and into Italy for use in his history of Rome. In the sections on the Punic Wars Polybius recounted the distances covered by the Carthaginian army as it moved through Spain and France and he provided time frames for sections of the march which enable us to reconstruct much of the route with a high degree of probability. He interviewed witnesses to the events and carefully recorded what he learned from them. He wrote in his histories that he sought out eyewitnesses and personally inspected the Alpine route Hannibal followed, which at that time probably still contained physical evidence of the march.[18] All these factors taken together make this Greek historian probably the most valuable and accurate ancient source available on Hannibal.

Moved by the events of the epic struggle between Carthage and Rome, Polybius went to North Africa toward the close of the Third Punic War to watch this historical drama play out it last act. Aemilianus Publius Scipio, his former pupil and the son of his close friend, had been given charge of the Roman army at Carthage, with the task of besieging the city. Polybius was present when, after a three year siege, the Romans finally breached the walls and began to obliterate both its people and its structures. He recorded the thoughts of his friend Scipio as the two men watched the magnificent city burn throughout successive nights. A city which had flourished for over seven hundred years was coming to its tragic end and both men saw in this the inevitable march of history and the poignant decline of civilizations.

The era of Carthage had come to an end and the city of splendor and luxury which had ruled a vast empire for so long was being reduced to rubble and ashes. Scipio wept and lamented the fate of his enemy, for he saw in their misfortune the same fate for Rome. He turned to his friend and tutor Polybius and commented on how, in spite of the glory of the moment for Rome, he was seized within by a fear and foreboding that someday the same fate would befall his own city.[19] Scipio could not have realized how true his words would prove, when six hundred years later Rome suffered the same fate at the hands of invading barbarians.

As a historical source on the ancient world Polybius is unequaled because of, among other things, the balanced perspective he brings to his work. Polybius presented both the Roman and Carthaginian perspectives during the Punic Wars. The theme of Polybius in his *History of the Roman Republic* is simple and straightforward. He wanted, as a historian and philosopher, to understand how the Roman people had succeeded in less than fifty years in bringing almost the whole of the inhabited ancient world under their control. This was an accomplishment that he found to be without parallel in history.[20]

Polybius believed that the expansion of Roman power throughout the Mediterranean during those critical years was the product of a conscious desire on the part of the Roman people to extend their domination over the ancient world. Polybius was convinced that decisions were made and policies formulated at Rome specifically toward that end. What is sometimes in dispute is whether his view is correct and accords with the facts that he provides. Because he was a Greek, a captive of the Romans, albeit in a gilded cage, there is the question of whether he really understood the Roman people and to what degree his own nationalistic predilections colored his perspective on events. After all, Greece had been conquered by the Romans during that same period and in some cases Greek cities had suffered the same treatment as Carthage—burned to the ground and their survivors enslaved.

Polybius believed the Romans brought the ancient world under their domination in such a short space of time because they were a tenacious people gifted in the art of government. They could discipline others, Polybius wrote, because they had learned to discipline themselves. The Romans were a people who, once they set their mind to something, would not quit no matter how high the price of eventual victory. Polybius believed that civilizations were like men: they went through periods of infancy, vigorous manhood and old age. Carthage was thus destroyed simply because her time had come. An "old man" by the Third Punic War, Carthage had to make way on the stage of international politics for a younger and more vigorous challenger.

Polybius had devoted himself to the study of a time period that began with the Second Punic War, about 220 B.C., and ended in 146 B.C. with the destruction of Carthage. His work originally comprised forty books, although only a fraction of that number still survive. Fortunately the books that deal with the Punic Wars, Volumes I to V of his history, are intact and available to scholars.

From the fall of the Roman empire in about 400 A.D. until the early fifteenth century, the work of Polybius disappeared, as did many other ancient literary, scientific and historical works of the Greek and Roman period. Little is known of what happened to the history of Polybius and his other works; his writings simply fell into the abyss that was the Dark Ages. Copies of his texts began to surface and circulate again only at the end of the medieval period, in the first light of the Renaissance. The books initially appeared at Florence, then gradually over large parts of Italy. With advances in printing, editors began to publish the Latin transcriptions of his history in the fifteenth century. The sixteenth century saw a great flowering of interest in the writings of Polybius, with translations from the Greek and Latin appearing in French, Italian and German. The first English translation appeared in 1568.

The works of Polybius became popular in the Renaissance and were studied not only as a history of the ancient world but also for the insights they contained into the philosophies of politics, war and human nature. Polybius was regarded as an ancient teacher who could offer valuable advice to medieval princes in the organization of their armies as well as in the conduct of their lives.

Following Polybius, the next historian of importance for scholars interested in the subject of Hannibal is Livy (c. 59 B.C.–17 A.D.). A Roman, living at the apex of Roman power under the Emperor Augustus, Livy devoted his life to the writing of a massive history of the Roman Republic.

Livy was born at Patavium (Padua) and then moved to Rome. There he started on his history at about the age of thirty and continued to work on his magnus opus for the next forty years. When completed, the work came to number 142 volumes. Of that number 35 survive. Ten of the surviving books are devoted exclusively to the Second Punic War between Rome and Carthage, which is essentially the story of Hannibal. These ten have come down to us intact and they are important because they provide descriptions of the route Hannibal followed on his march from Spain to Italy, complete with the names of places through which he passed. Livy gave a detailed physical description of the pass by which Hannibal went over the Alps, which we will examine in greater detail later.

From what we can determine, Livy was a reclusive scholar who devoted nearly his entire adult life to the creation of his history of Rome. Little is known about his personal life other than that he lived in the relative stability of the golden age of Augustus and that he was well known in Rome as a literary figure. In spite of his notoriety, Livy was not active in public or military affairs but devoted himself entirely to scholarly pursuits.

The account that Livy wrote about Hannibal's crossing of the Alps is a dramatic narrative, written by a scholar who believed that there are lessons to be learned from history and that the lives of men like Hannibal and his opponents provide important practical examples for the conduct of our own daily lives. Livy was able, more so than Polybius, to bring the past to life and recreate the spirit of the period in history when Rome faced her greatest challenge. This history of Rome is among the more imaginative, patriotic and creative historical writings, and there are few ancient historians who can compare with Livy in this regard.

In assessing the value of Polybius and Livy in advancing our knowledge of Hannibal's crossing, it is important to note that there has been throughout the centuries a tendency among scholars to view Livy with a degree of caution, even somewhat suspiciously. This has been largely because of the fear that this ancient Roman historian might have been too heavily influenced by the earlier work of

Polybius. While comparison of passages from the two histories may cause one to suspect that Polybius was the main source for large amounts of the material used by Livy,[21] his history is still of exceptional importance. The primary importance of Livy is that he verifies much of what Polybius wrote and provides information on the lost sections of Polybius' history.

As a historian Livy has always been read in the shadow of his Greek predecessor. Even though Livy wrote long after the events he described, he had access to good firsthand sources in Rome. There were records of senatorial decrees kept in the archives at Rome, as well as the *annales maximi* (the annual records of state elections, ceremonies, state visits, etc.) which he no doubt utilized in writing his history.

In spite of the tendency to regard Livy in a dimmer light than Polybius, there have been periods in history when his work has been preferred to that of the earlier historian. The current trend, however, is to view both sources as substantially in agreement on the details of Hannibal's march and to use the them together to advance research on the subject, especially concerning its geographical aspects. It must be noted that there are contemporary historians who view the two ancient authors as being at odds, and that their writings cause scholars to follow distinctly different routes over the Alps. A key question to resolve is whether Polybius and Livy are writing about the same route in their manuscripts or two different routes. We are fortunate because the sections of both histories dealing with the Punic Wars are intact and allow for comparisons to be made.

A Roman poet occupies the next place in the chronicle of ancient sources on Hannibal. Silius Italicus was born in A.D. 26 in the same town from which Livy had come, Patavium. He wrote an epic piece on the Punic Wars[22] and used many details from Livy's history. His primary value to a modern scholar is that Silius serves as a check on readings in extant manuscripts of Livy.

In addition, a Greek geographer named Strabo, born in 64 B.C., mentioned in his work the pass which Hannibal used to cross the Alps, as did a Roman historian, Marcus Terentius Varro, born in 116 B.C.

The impact of Hannibal was so great in Italy that no Roman historian could ignore the Punic Wars. References to Hannibal are found in the works of such ancient authors as Diodorus, Dio Plutarch and Cornelius Nepos in the first century B.C., Trogus Pompeius in the first century A.D., Justin, and Appian in the second and Eutropius in the fourth. Timagenes of Alexandria, a skilled historian and geographer, came to Rome in 54 B.C., where he caught the attention of the young man who would become Emperor Augustus. Little of his work has survived except some interesting fragments quoted by other Roman historians such as Ammianus Marcellinus. Timagenes included in his work a brief description of Hannibal's march through the Alps, which is important because it gives the names of the tribes through whose territories Hannibal passed.[23] Unfortunately, what these ancient authors had to say about Hannibal and his march across the Alps is slight and does little to shed additional light on the subject.

Another interesting source of information about Hannibal, though indirect, comes from a number of archaeological finds of itineraries or lists of towns and way-stations on specified routes through the ancient world.[24] Among the most important are the *Gaditanian Vases*, dating from the first or second century A.D., the *Itinerarium Antonini Augusti*, the *Itinerarium Burdigalense* and the *Tabula Peutingeriana*, from the third century A.D. The *Tabula* is the most complete of all the ancient lists and is virtually a road map of the ancient Roman Empire. The itinerary was based on surveys carried out in the reign of Augustus and dated as far back as a map system drawn up by a Greek geographer, Eratosthenes, during the time of the Second Punic War.[25] These itineraries are valuable because they mention a number of passes in the French Alps and from them we learn of at least thirteen that were known at the time of the Roman Empire. It must be remembered, however, that Hannibal crossed the Alps some three to four hundred years before these itineraries were written and that his passage over the Alps was probably one of the major factors that caused the Romans to explore the area. Prior to Hannibal's coming over the Alps, the Romans knew little of the mountains that separated Italy from Gaul. The itineraries nevertheless enable researchers to confirm that many of these routes and Alpine passes were probably well known in Hannibal's time and that he could have followed one or more of them on his march from Spain into Italy.

NOTES

[1] Serge Lancel. *Carthage: A History.*

[2] *Cambridge Ancient History,* Vol. VIII, p. 14.

[3] Mark Healy, *Cannae 216 B.C.,* pp. 56–57.

[4] Sir Gavin deBeer, *Hannibal's March.* Report of elephant bones found buried in a ritual manner in a farmer's field near the village of Maillane in 1777 were noted by deBeer. The village is near the Rhône River, where Hannibal might well have passed on his way to the Alps.

[5] R. Bosworth-Smith. *Carthage and the Carthaginians.* Bosworth-Smith reports on elephant bones found in the Little St. Bernard Pass in 1828.

[6] R. Vaccarone, *Ball del club Alpine Italiano.* The magazine tells of a tablet found on the Col d'Arnas and thrown into a glacier by an angry local who could not get his price for its sale.

[7] *Washington Post,* August 13, 1997, report of the Intergovernmental Panel on World Climate Change.

[8] W.W. Hyde, *Roman Alpine Routes,* p. 30.

[9] *Washington Post,* October 15, 1992. The paper notes the discovery of a man who had died over five thousand years ago preserved in a glacier.

[10] The French authorities report that as many as two hundred people die in the Alps each year from falls, exposure or other accidents.

[11] deBeer, *Alps and Elephants,* pp. 10–11.

[12] deBeer, *Hannibal's March,* p. 33.

[13] Cicero, *De Divinatione,* Bk. I, Sec. 24, and Lucius Coelius Antipater as quoted in Livy, *History of Rome,* Bk. XXI, Sec. 38.7.

[14] Cornelius Nepos, *Vie d'Hannibal,* Sec. 13.3.

[15] Livy, *History of Rome,* Bk. XXI, Sec. 38.3, as found in the manuscripts by Jacques Gronovius, *Titi-Livii Patvini Historiarum,* 1670, Paris, and Carlo Sigonio, *T. Livii Historiarum,* 1555, also at Paris.

[16] Polybius, Bk. III, Sec. 33.

[17] Polybius, *The Rise of the Roman Empire,* Bk. III, Sec. 48.12, as found in the manuscripts by Isaac Casaubon, *Polybii,* 1609 and 1617, Paris, and Vincent Obropaeus, *Polybii Historiarum,* 1530, also at Paris.

[18] Polybius, Bk. III, Sec. 48.

[19] Appian, *Libyca*, p. 132.

[20] Polybius, Bk. I, Sec. l.

[21] *Cambridge Ancient History,* Vol. VIII, p. 9.

[22] Silius Italicus, *Second Punic War.*

[23] Ammianus Marcellinus, *Rerum Gestarum Libri.* Bk. XV, Sec. 10.11

[24] F. d'Urban, *Recueil des itinéraires anciens,* Paris, 1845.

[25] Hyde, p. 32.

CHAPTER IV

⋖⊰⊱⋗ · ⋖⊰⊱⋗

FROM SPAIN TO THE ALPS

During the months before he marched on Italy, Hannibal planned his strategy for the war with Rome and carefully studied the route he planned to take through the Alps. He dispatched envoys to the chiefs of the Celtic tribes that inhabited the area of the Po Valley to induce them to join him as allies in his war and to augment his forces. He had prepared his ambassadors to exploit the hatred that the Celts bore toward Rome, and their fear of Roman expansion. These envoys had been given the latitude to make lavish promises of Carthaginian friendship and aid to the Celtic chiefs and to ply them with gifts of gold.

At the same time Hannibal sent scouts to Gaul to survey the routes through the Alps. He knew that his only chance for success depended on being able to cross the mountains quickly by the most direct route and catch the Romans unprepared for his attack. Everything depended on a combination of planning, timing and an element of luck.

The envoys returned to New Carthage during the winter months of 219–218 B.C. to inform Hannibal that the Celts eagerly awaited his arrival in Italy and were anxious to begin the war on Rome. The scouts reported that the route over the Alps was difficult but by no means impossible, so long as the army crossed before the onset of winter. Hannibal understood that if the army were delayed in reaching the Alps and caught on the passes when the snows began to fall, it would be defeated by the mountains before they ever engaged a Roman legion in combat.

Hannibal set out from Hispania (Spain) in the late spring of 218

B.C. with a force of Carthaginian officers, mercenaries of various nationalities, Spanish troops and African cavalry. The size of the army has been estimated as high as 90,000 foot soldiers, 12,000 cavalry and a large contingent of elephants and their Indian handlers.[1] More conservative estimates have placed the force at between forty and fifty thousand men. In any case it must have been a considerable collection of all types of men, animals and baggage.

As part of his general strategy for the war Hannibal placed his brother Hasdrubal in command of Spain, North Africa and Sicily with a sizable army and navy to protect those areas from a Roman invasion. African troops were posted in Spain while Spanish troops were stationed in Africa, in the belief that the service by each in a foreign country would provide a mutual guarantee of dependability. For psychological and political reasons Hannibal further strengthened the garrison at Carthage. Many of the Carthaginians in the city were old enough to remember the Roman invasion of the First Punic War, and so to alleviate their fears and guarantee continued political support for his campaign in Italy he placed a large contingent of troops around the city. A sizable fleet of some fifty quinqueremes, two quadremes, and five triremes was dispatched to patrol the waters between Sicily and North Africa and to provide for the coastal defense of southern Spain. When Hannibal left New Carthage, he had provided for nearly every political and military contingency that could develop while he was away so that he could focus his attention on the march to the Alps and the war in Italy.

During the first phase of the campaign Hannibal marched north along the Spanish Mediterranean coast for several hundred miles, subduing a number of hostile Celtic tribes that stood in his way. The march was grueling and the fighting savage and frequent, as many of the Celtic tribes of northern Spain put up fierce resistance when he tried to pass through their territories. After several weeks Hannibal finally came to the Pyrenees, at which point he had completed more than half the distance of his march to Italy. He crossed the Pyrenees by the Col du Perthus, a relatively low pass near the eastern end of the mountains near the Mediterranean Sea. The Col du Perthus is less than 800 meters high and even in ancient times was an easy passage over the mountains. Hannibal left a contingent of infantry in the Pyrenees under the command of his other brother, Hanno, to secure the pass and several others in the mountains as well.

Now that the initial excitement and euphoria of the early stages of the campaign had subsided, and the reality of the long march and nearly constant fighting had set in, some of the soldiers became disgruntled and others were fearful of what lay ahead. The army had been marching for weeks over difficult and hostile terrain, often fighting nearly every mile of the way. As the column crossed the Pyrenees and came down into southern Gaul, a group of about 3,000 Spanish mercenaries called the Carpetani threatened to mutiny and made it evident to Hannibal that they wanted to return home. The fear of what lay ahead, and especially the danger of crossing the Alps, had unnerved them. Their fear began to spread throughout the army and resulted in the first challenge to Hannibal's authority.

The leader knew that he had to contain the situation and defuse it quickly in order to prevent a demoralization of his entire force. Most of his soldiers were mercenaries and among them were many who were difficult to keep disciplined and motivated. They tended to be wild and follow their impulses rather than orders. Hannibal could have reverted to the traditional response of commanders faced with rebellious troops and executed the leaders as an example to the rest.

Instead he assembled his army and explained to them that he sensed some were losing their heart for the campaign and wanted to return home. Hannibal contended that he needed to send some of the army back to Spain to reinforce the garrisons there and so constructed an acceptable pretext by which he was able to dismiss several thousand men whose loyalty and dependability he questioned, including the Carpetani. In this manner he avoided inflicting harsh punishments on soldiers who had already endured weeks of hard marching and fighting, and the risk of a potentially violent confrontation with discontented elements of the army that could spread. Hannibal had been willing to ignore the insubordination of the Carpetani by pretending that they were being dismissed for the same reason as the regular soldiers[2] in order to defuse a situation which had the potential to escalate and compromise his entire campaign.

Hannibal would prove time and again that he was as astute a judge of human behavior as he was a brilliant strategist and tactician. He recognized the complexities of human behavior, especially among men under stress, and knew that sometimes more than strength is needed to command. In this case he was willing to find an accommodation rather than risk a show of force by which he could win the battle and possibly lose the war. Leadership, Hannibal understood, was a judicious mixture of power, psychology and politics.

With the loss of this group, and the casualties and desertions that would have been an expected part of any military campaign of this magnitude, Hannibal must have had about 50,000 infantry and 9,000 cavalry left when he finally marched through Gaul in the summer of 218 B.C.[3] The army he commanded at that point, though significantly smaller than before, was more effective by virtue of its resolve, loyalty and experience. While its numerical strength had been cut in half, it was well trained and experienced by the long march through Spain and the almost continual fighting against the Celtic tribes there.

Hannibal may also have trimmed the size of his force for logistical reasons. He knew that weeks and possibly months of difficulty lay ahead before the army would reach Italy. Food, always a consideration, would become increasingly hard to find the farther they penetrated into the Alps, and he may have believed his chances for success were better with a smaller, though more mobile and motivated army. The men who accompanied Hannibal into Gaul that fateful summer were the best of his forces.

Through his envoys and scouts Hannibal made the Gauls who inhabited the territory between the Pyrenees and the Rhône River aware that his army was only passing through their lands on its way to Italy and that he meant them no harm. Nevertheless, these tribes had heard how the Carthaginians had subjugated the Spanish, and some of them feared that if they allowed Hannibal to pass they too might become Carthaginian slaves and be forced to work in the gold and silver mines. The prospect of losing their freedom alarmed many of them and impelled a number of the tribes to join together at the town of Ruscino (Castel-Roussillon) near Perpignan to resist Hannibal's advance.

The danger from a violent encounter with this large group of Gauls was not so much the number of casualties Hannibal might suffer but the valuable time he would lose in a protracted siege of their city or in fighting them in a series of battles. A delay of several weeks here could mean that he would arrive at the Alps too late in the season and find the passes already sealed by snow and ice for the winter. To try to avoid a battle Hannibal sent a delegation to these tribes and offered to receive their leaders in his own camp or to come to them as a friend in order to find an accommodation. He assured the Celts that he had no intention of fighting against them unless they compelled him to do so. The message was delivered and the Gallic chieftains came to the Carthaginian camp. There Hannibal showed such hospitality and lavished so many gifts upon them that they allowed the Carthaginian army to move through their territory without resistance.

By the time the army was approaching the Rhône River it had already been on the march for two months or more and had covered nearly 700 miles. Another 200 miles were left before the column would reach the final pass into Italy. While the longest part of the march was over, the hardest and most dangerous was still to come.

The Romans had meanwhile received word that Hannibal was moving north toward the Pyrenees, but did not realize he was already in Gaul. They believed the Carthaginian army was still in Spain and that Hannibal was probably preparing to meet their invasion from the sea. Nor did they imagine that his objective in this war was to plant the Carthaginian standard on the ruins of their city itself.

The Roman Senate formulated its strategy for the opening phase of the war with Carthage under the assumption that Hannibal was still in Spain. In standard fashion they appointed the two consuls for that year and gave them command of separate armies. The first consul, Publius Cornelius Scipio, was ordered to Spain with a force of about 25,000 to engage Hannibal and stop any further Carthaginian advance to the north. The second consul, Tiberius Sempronius Longus, was ordered to Sicily with a larger army and instructions to

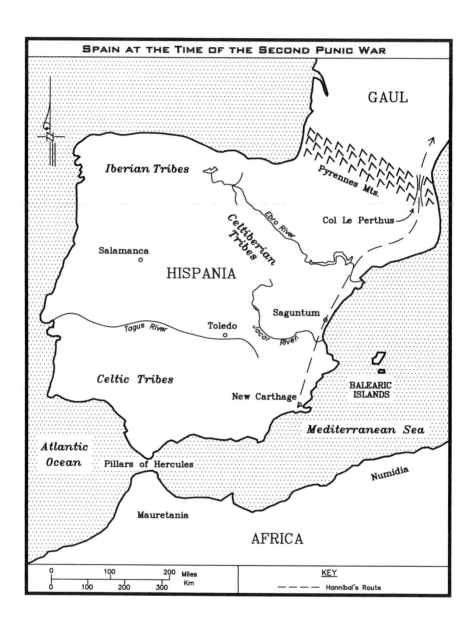

SPAIN AT THE TIME OF THE SECOND PUNIC WAR

GAUL

Iberian Tribes

Celtiberian Tribes

Ebro River

Pyrennes Mts.

Col Le Perthus

Salamanca

HISPANIA

Saguntum

Toledo

Tagus River

Jucar River

Celtic Tribes

BALEARIC
ISLANDS

New Carthage

Mediterranean Sea

*Atlantic
Ocean*

Pillars of Hercules

Numidia

Mauretania

AFRICA

| 0 | 100 | 200 | Miles |
| 0 | 100 | 200 | 300 | Km |

establish a base there for the eventual invasion of Africa. This was the Roman strategy for the beginning of the Second Punic War and it was well formulated, based upon the information that was available to the Romans at the time.[4]

Unanticipated events in northern Italy, however, changed everything and caused the Romans momentarily to divert their attention from Carthage. Two Gallic tribes, the Boii and the Insubres, joined together in an attack on the new Roman settlements of Cremona and Placentia. The reason for the attack was their resentment over the establishment of these two Roman colonies in the area of the Po River. The Gauls saw the settlements for what they were: an attempt by the Romans to gain a foothold in northern Italy and eventually bring the entire area under their domination.

The Gauls' unexpected attack on these colonies caused alarm and considerable confusion among the Romans in northern Italy. Many of the colonists, including the officials sent from Rome to administer the colonies, abandoned the settlements and fled south to the more secure Roman city of Mutina (Modena) for safety. The Gauls followed them south, devastating the area in their path. A column of legionaries was sent from Rome to aid the colonists but fell into an ambush because the commander was so contemptuous of his Gallic adversaries that he did not send out scouts to reconnoiter the road ahead of his army. The legion was badly mauled before it managed to extricate itself from the ambush and retreat to a fortified town nearby.

The Roman Senate now had a small war with the Gauls on its hands as well as the larger war with Carthage looming. Additional troops were conscripted from throughout Italy and dispatched to the north to deal with the problems there while the Senate once more turned its attention to preparations for the war with Hannibal. From Hannibal's perspective the revolt of the Boii and the Insubres was an unwelcome development. The Gallic uprising was premature and only served to draw attention to northern Italy, causing the Romans to further fortify the area. The presence of additional Roman troops near the Alps could blunt the Carthaginian attack when it came. Still, the Romans had no idea that Hannibal was moving rapidly through Gaul and on his way toward Italy. They thought their only problem in the Po Valley was with the Gauls and had no idea of the storm that was developing on the other side of the Alps.

The consul Cornelius Scipio sailed from Rome in August, bound for Spain with a fleet of sixty warships that carried his legions. The fleet followed the northwestern coast of Italy and sailed across the Ligurian Sea until it reached the Greek city of Massilia. There the fleet put in for provisions and rest, for many of the legionaries on board the transport ships had been sick for days as the result of an unusually rough voyage. Shortly after he landed, Scipio, in a routine move, sent out a party of some three hundred horsemen to scout the area around Massilia.

Hannibal meanwhile had quickly arrived at the Rhône River. He bribed most of the Celtic tribes to let him pass without resistance through their territories, and his army forced its way through those whom gold could not buy. He had marched through southwestern Gaul with the Mediterranean Sea always to his right, passing by the sites of the modern French towns of Narbonne and Béziers, then past Montpellier and finally into the most desolate country in all of France—the Camargue.

The Rhône flows south as a single river from the center of France until it reaches the Camargue, about thirty miles from the Mediterranean. There the river divides into a number of tributaries and flows through this vast expanse of flat land filled with desolate areas of marsh and scrub and home to wild horses and bulls. The tributaries continually divide into a multitude of sluggish streams that often spill over into broad lagoons. Much of the area is still as wild today as it was when Hannibal passed two thousand years ago. On the eastern side of the Camargue, some fifty miles away on the coast, is the site of the ancient Greek colony of Massilia and the modern city of Marseilles.

After passing through the Camargue, Hannibal came to the main tributary of the Rhône. Where exactly Hannibal crossed the river is subject to considerable speculation and has been a point of debate among scholars for centuries. The ancient sources specify that the crossing place was four days' march from the sea, "where the river is still single." This means that Hannibal and his army crossed at a location where the river had not yet broken into the hundreds of tributaries and lakes that abound in the Camargue and some thirty or forty miles from the sea. In addition, there are indications in the writings of both Polybius and Livy that the river at this point was wide, fairly shallow and not too swift.

A number of locations conform to some degree to these descriptions in the ancient sources, the most probable being a point just above today's Arles, called Fourques.[5] Here the river has not yet begun to divide. At this location the river is perhaps a half-mile wide, not too deep, and indeed slow-moving. A number of other possible sites between Arles and Orange, to its north, have been suggested by scholars. Among these crossing points are Tarascon,[6] just a few miles farther north along the river than Fourques, and Roquemaure[7] just south of Orange. While all of these are possibilities, there has been no archaeological evidence discovered so far at any one of them that proves definitively that Hannibal crossed there.

The strongest case for a crossing point can only be made by correlating the distances Hannibal traveled from Spain over a given period to known geographical reference points in France. Polybius wrote that Hannibal traveled a distance of 1,600 *stadia*, or approximately 170 miles, from the Greek colony of Ampurias, at the foot of the Pyrenees on the northeastern coast of Spain, to his crossing point at the Rhône River. The actual distance from the site of Ampurias to just above Arles at Fourques is 170 miles. Tarascon, only about ten miles further north along the Rhône than Fourques, is just as strong a possibility. Roquemaure, however, is a considerable distance farther north, just below Orange, and is not as likely for this reason to have been the crossing point.

When Hannibal came to the place at the Rhône River where he intended to cross he found it was inhabited by a particularly aggressive Celtic tribe called the Volcae. The Volcae had sizable settlements on both sides of the river, and in order to cross at that point Hannibal needed to come to terms with them. The natives were anxious for a fight, however, and rebuffed his overtures of peace and friendship. The aggressiveness of the Volcae might be accounted for as nothing more than a manifestation of the bellicosity that generally characterized most of the Gauls of central and southern France. The Volcae were a naturally warlike people who were probably excited by a fight and the prospect of the spoils they would find in Hannibal's baggage train.

Like many of the tribes that Hannibal would encounter as he marched farther into the Alps, the Volcae knew little of what went on in the more developed and sophisticated areas of the ancient world. These tribes were isolated from what was happening and they neither knew nor cared about the epic struggle then beginning between Carthage and Rome. They could not have comprehended the changes which were beginning to take place and which would affect their lives over the next two centuries as Rome came to dominate and transform all of Gaul.

These tribes probably did not know who Hannibal was, where he was heading or what he was planning to do, unless he sent envoys ahead to tell them. Even then they might not have understood. Their hostility toward him was not motivated by any sense of alliance with Rome or a particular dislike of Carthage. They probably resisted Hannibal because they regarded the Carthaginian army as a threat to their villages and hamlets, their crops and livestock, and their women.

The Carthaginian column that came to the banks of the Rhône River that day must have stretched from five to six miles in length and been a rolling ecological disaster at least a half-mile wide. As the column cut a swath through the countryside it consumed everything in its path and must have left acres of cropland devastated and stripped of anything useful. In its wake must have been a wasteland devoid of most life, and polluted beyond modern comprehension by vast quantities of human and animal waste, garbage, discarded materials of every description and the bodies of the dead and dying.

As always when an army moves through foreign territory there is the predisposition for abuses to be perpetrated on the defenseless local inhabitants, be they allies or enemy. Hannibal's army of mercenaries might have been worse than usual and as it moved it must have left behind hundreds of locals who had been robbed, beaten, raped or killed. An army the size and composition of Hannibal's must have had little compassion for anything in its path like a small village or hamlet. No doubt the soldiers took what they needed from the countryside and continued to move forward at severe cost to both people and nature.

Some of the Celtic tribes on the western bank of the Rhône, for one reason or another, accepted Hannibal's offers of peace and friendship when he arrived. In fact, they made considerable sums of money selling him supplies as well as their boats, canoes, rafts and anything else that would float for his crossing of the river. These tribes must have been only too happy to reap the profits from these sales, and then move the Carthaginian army off their lands as quickly as possible.

While one of the logistical problems of the crossing had been solved by the purchase of large numbers of boats, Hannibal now had to focus his attention on the next problem: he had to transport his fighting forces across the river and at the same time devise tactics for dealing with the Volcae on the opposite bank. They had massed in large numbers on the eastern bank of the Rhône and they let Hannibal know by their shouting and ritual posturing that they intended to resist his crossing. Hannibal was too competent to attempt forcing a crossing under such unfavorable conditions. The logistical problems of transporting large numbers of soldiers, civilians, thousands of horses, tons of baggage, and thirty-seven elephants over a wide stretch of the river, even with a sluggish current, must have been enormous. All this was made more dangerously complicated by the prospect of fierce resistance from the Celts on the other side.

Hannibal, however, formulated a plan for both crossing the river and fighting the Volcae. He sent one of his best commanders, Hanno, out of the camp under the cover of darkness with a sizable contingent of Spanish and African cavalry. Hanno proceeded north along the Rhône for about twenty miles to a crossing spot known by the Gallic guides, probably near Avignon. At that point Hanno crossed the river at dawn and then rested his troops in the woods and brush during the remainder of the day. The next day Hanno sent a smoke signal to indicate that his forces were ready to descend along the river's east bank and move into position behind the camp of the Volcae. There they would wait for the moment when their scouts saw Hannibal and the army coming across the river, at which time they would attack the Celtic camp.

When he saw the smoke signal from Hanno, Hannibal launched his first flotilla of boats filled with soldiers. As the flotilla slowly made its way across the wide expanse of the river it was protected in part by a line of larger craft that were stationed at points upstream and used to break some of the force of the current. Most of the cavalrymen entered the river and swam beside their mounts, which were tethered by lines to the sterns of the boats that carried the infantry. Other horses were ferried across the river on rafts with their riders, already saddled for use when they arrived on the far shore and the combat began.

As Hannibal's force began crossing, the Volcae came surging to the riverbank howling and shouting, as was their custom before engaging in battle. They shook their shields above their heads in Celtic fashion and brandished their spears at Hannibal's army in preparation for the fight. The din of the crossing must have been deafening. The noise from thousands of the Volcae shouting and screaming in anticipation of the coming battle was mixed with the cries and shouts of Hannibal's soldiers as they struggled to overcome the current and urged each other on. All this noise was further amplified by the shouts of encouragement coming from Hannibal's men who lined the western riverbank and were anticipating their turn to cross the river and fight.

Just as the Volcae prepared to attack the first of Hannibal's forces landing on the riverbank, Hanno and his cavalry charged into their camp and began to burn it. When the Volcae turned to see their camp in flames they were momentarily diverted from the landing. They became confused and did not know whether to concentrate on resisting the landing or return to the camp to save their families from Hanno's attack. The psychological impact of this surprise momentarily wrested the tactical advantage from the Celts. The diversion allowed enough time for Hannibal's advanced landing force to secure a foothold on the riverbank, and in short order thousands of Carthaginian troops were on the east bank of the Rhône ready for battle.

Now the Volcae were caught between the charging cavalry of Hanno behind them and thousands of Carthaginian soldiers in front. After a brief attempt at resistance the Volcae abandoned the battle. Many ran in panic to seek refuge in their villages, while others disappeared into the forests. For the remainder of that day Hannibal continued to ferry his soldiers and supplies across the river without further resistance. That night the Carthaginian base camp was firmly established on the eastern bank of the Rhône and the Volcae were nowhere to be seen.

The next day Hannibal was faced with another problem in logistics. He had to get the elephants over the river.[8] When the animals were led to the edge of the water they refused to enter the river no matter how hard they were prodded by their drivers. While the elephants had been trained to obey their mahouts, the "*indoi*," under no circumstances could the drivers prod the beasts to enter the river.

The engineers attempted to solve the problem by constructing a series of rafts which they lashed together to a width of about fifty feet and extended into the river about two hundred feet from the bank. When this main pier was stabilized, additional rafts were placed at its end and held in place by ropes attached to trees growing along both sides of the riverbank. The rafts at the end had been placed so that they could be easily cut loose from the main structure and then pulled to the opposite bank by the ropes that served as towing and guide lines. Smaller boats were positioned along the sides of the rafts to provide additional support and to prevent the rafts from being carried downstream. By a system of ropes and pulleys, the rafts were held against the current and could be pulled and towed to the opposite shore.

The elephants, however, would not walk onto the structure. They would walk as far as the edge of the water and then stop. The engineers tried to fool the beasts by spreading dirt and grass on the structure to make it look like the continuation of a path they were used to traipsing to the river's edge to drink. But again, when the beasts were driven down the path by their mahouts they stopped at the edge of the river and would not venture onto the rafts no matter how inviting and natural the engineers had tried to make them appear.

In exasperation at the stubbornness of the elephants, one of the more aggressive mahouts relentlessly goaded and taunted a notably ferocious bull elephant on the path. The enraged beast turned on the mahout, forcing him to leap into the river and swim for his life. The elephant would not give up the pursuit and in an effort to catch the mahout plunged into the water. A few of the other elephants, goaded as well by their handlers, followed the bull. Terrified when they found themselves in deep water, the beasts struggled at first but eventually allowed the current to carry them to the far side.

The majority of the elephants, however, still would not move from the riverbank. So the mahouts brought two particularly docile females to the front of the line and gently enticed them down to the edge of the river and onto the rafts. The males immediately followed and that aspect of the problem was quickly solved. As soon as the last of the thirty-seven elephants was aboard, the rafts were cut loose from their moorings and allowed to drift out into the middle of the river. At this the elephants became so terror-stricken that they began to move around the rafts and caused them to capsize. The elephants fell into the river, drowning or crushing most of the mahouts on their backs. Some elephants eventually recovered, found firm footing on the river bottom and were able to continue to the opposite bank. A variation of the account of the crossing relates that when the elephants found firm footing on the river bottom they were able to extend their trunks above the water line so that they could breathe and walk safely to the opposite shore.[9] While most of the elephants survived the crossing, most of their handlers were drowned or trampled.

At the time this operation was in progress, Hannibal sent a scouting party of some five hundred Numidian horsemen to reconnoiter the area beyond the river. The Numidians moved in a southeasterly direction away from the Rhône and within a few miles encountered the cavalry detachment of Romans that had been sent out from Massilia as scouts by Scipio. Despite the small numbers involved, the fight that ensued proved to be particularly savage and the casualties were high on both sides. After several hours of fighting the Numidians finally broke off the encounter and returned to their camp.

When Hannibal learned that the Romans were nearby, his instinctive reaction was to assemble the army and move to fight them. Hannibal, however, was a brilliant strategist as well as an effective battlefield commander. At this point he needed to think in terms of the overall strategy of the war and not to react to developments in the field too rashly. Keeping in mind his ultimate objective, the invasion of Italy, he decided to avoid a confrontation with Scipio and alter his course to the Alps accordingly.

By fighting Scipio now, in southern Gaul, Hannibal risked his entire campaign and all the efforts he had gone through to bring the army this far. A battle with the Romans at this point could have compromised his strategy for the war. His soldiers were already tired from the crossing of the river and the battle with the Volcae. Hannibal could ill afford additional casualties, and even worse the psychological consequences of a defeat on his men and on the allies who waited for him in Italy. Moreover, he reasoned, what would a victory over Scipio in Gaul gain him other than a brief moment of euphoria. Hannibal had much to lose by fighting the Romans at this point and little to gain, so he decided to check his emotions and not allow himself to be distracted from his original plan.

A delegation from the Boii, the Celtic tribe fighting the Romans in the Po Valley, arrived in Hannibal's camp as the news of the Roman presence at Massilia and the cavalry skirmish was being reported. This group had just crossed the Alps, led by a chieftain named Magalus, to tell Hannibal that their tribes had begun the war with Rome and to guide his army over the mountains. Magalus reinforced Hannibal in his decision to avoid a battle with Scipio and proceed directly toward the main objective, Italy.

As Hannibal prepared to break camp and resume the march, stories about the dangers of the route ahead spread through the army. The prospects of the long march into unknown territory, the fear of ambushes, the dangers of climbing the Alps, the prospect of numbing cold and the specter of starvation all began to have a psychologically adverse affect on some of the mercenaries. Soon a general discontent began to manifest itself throughout the army and threatened to stop Hannibal from moving forward.

Hannibal assembled his troops, and with Magalus and the other Boii by his side, he addressed the assembled soldiers:

> What sudden panic is this which has entered your hearts, where fear was never found before. You followed me from Spain bent upon destroying Rome and setting the world free. Now, when you have already completed the greater distance, when you have made your way over the passes of the Pyrenees and fought the wild tribes there, tamed the violence of the mighty Rhône and crossed its waters in the face of the countless Gallic warriors who awaited you on the other side, finally when you have the Alps nearly in sight and know that on the other side is Italy, now at the very doors of the enemy you stop!
>
> What do you think the Alps are? They are nothing more than high mountains. No part of the earth touches the sky there; no height is insurmountable to men of determination. Common men live in the Alps, they till the soil, they herd their animals there. Look at these men [pointing to Magalus and the other Boii], how do you think they got here, you think they flew over the Alps? They are simple country people from Italy. Many times, with women and children, they crossed the Alps. Surely then, you, soldiers with nothing more than your weapons to carry, can cross these mountains. You came to conquer Rome, the mightiest city in the world. Steel your hearts, march forward and halt only when you have scaled the walls of Rome.[10]

When the army heard his speech the men recovered their resolve. Hannibal had spoken and dispelled their fears and given them the enthusiasm and courage to continue. Then the Celtic chieftain Magalus spoke to them about how his people, already at war with Rome, awaited them on the other side of the Alps. Magalus acknowledged that sections of the route over the mountains would be difficult and many of the approaches to the passes dangerous. Still, the route, he assured them, would be passable and there would be ample supplies of food and water along the way as well as experienced guides to lead them.

In the weeks ahead the words of Hannibal and Magalus would ring hollow as the army, often lost, struggled to find its way through the countless valleys, gorges and defiles of the Alps. Many of the guides would be killed along the route while others would lose their way and lead the column for miles and days without direction. The army would suffer the ravages of nature and endure the savage ambushes of mountain tribes. Starvation, cold and exhaustion would take a terrible toll and when the crossing was at last completed and the army finally descended into Italy, Hannibal would have lost more men to the mountains than he had in fighting all the battles and crossing all the rivers on the long march from Spain through France.

After the speeches and the cheering had ended, Hannibal ordered his men to rest for the remainder of the day and prepare to break camp early the next morning. The route Hannibal and Magalus had plotted for the column was designed to avoid any confrontation with the forces of Scipio. It was decided that the column would march north along the Rhône toward central Gaul and then move east toward Italy. Hannibal was sure that by now Scipio knew Italy was the Carthaginians' objective. Time was more important than it had ever been; Hannibal had to cross the Alps quickly and join the war in Italy before the Romans had time to assemble their forces and prepare for him. As always, he noted that the days and weeks had passed quickly and it was now mid- or late summer.

How Hannibal would have gotten over the Alps under normal circumstances is not difficult to figure. The Alps form a range of high and steep mountains nearly a hundred miles wide stretching from the southeast of France to the frontier with Italy. They begin as relatively low mountains (1000–1500 meters) near the Rhône River and then extend east, gradually building in height and steepness until they attain their full measure (4500 meters) on the Italian frontier. Not a solid wall between France and Italy, the Alps have a series of depressions between their highest ridges or peaks which in modern terms we call passes. The word itself comes from the Latin *"passus"* which means a footstep or track. While the word was used in the time of Julius Caesar mostly to indicate the stride of a soldier on the march, we have adapted it in modern usage to designate these depressions.

The Romans referred to the passes as *"montes"* or *"alpes"* because of their altitude. They found that these depressions made for convenient divisions of the mountains into sections along the Alpine range, many of which still keep their Roman names. The Alpes Maritimae, or Maritime Alps, for example, extend north from the Mediterranean Sea between Nice and the Italian Piedmont and are the official departmental name for that section of France. The second range, the Alpes Cottiae, were named by the Romans after King Cottius, a loyal regional ally, and the Cottians extend from Mt. Cenis to west of Turin, separating the Italian Piedmont area from French Savoy. The Alpes Graia, or Greek Alps, are farther north, between Mt. Cenis and Mt. Blanc. The Greek Alps were allegedly the range crossed by Hercules on one of his legendary adventures in antiquity. The final range are the Alpes Penninae, or Pennine Alps, which extend from the Swiss border and the Upper Rhône to the extreme upper portions of northwestern Italy. For our purposes we are most concerned with the Cottian Alps.

In the Middle Ages special names were given to the Alpine passes, but still in the Roman fashion such as Mons Cenis and Mons Genevre. As a result the word *"mons"* came to mean individual peaks or mountains. The word for pass then became *"col"* in French and *"collo"* in Italian derived from the Latin word *"collum,"* or neck.

From the north the Alps begin in Switzerland and extend south for nearly two hundred miles, all the way to the Mediterranean Sea. In this direction the southern Alps contain two distinct ranges of mountains: the Alpes du Dauphiné and the Hautes Alpes, separated by a series of parallel valleys. There are also a number of smaller and steeper transverse valleys that lead directly to the highest mountains of the Alps.

For Hannibal to have crossed the Alps from the Rhône Valley he would not simply have turned east and then marched uphill all the way to Italy. First, he would have had to climb over a ridge of relatively low mountains (1000–1500 meters), the Alpes du Dauphiné. From there he would have descended into a series of valleys before starting a second and final climb over higher mountains (3000–4500 meters), the Hautes Alpes, on the frontier with Italy.

The only way to get over these mountains traveling from west to east is to follow the large valleys that parallel the mountain ranges and then find the smaller transverse valleys that usually contain small rivers and lead to the mountain passes. These rivers, which begin as streams on the highest slopes of the mountains near the border with Italy, then cut their way through the Alps along the transverse valleys and eventually flow through the parallel valleys to the Rhône.

The rivers are the only way through the Alps because they afford reasonably level footing along their valleys, ample supplies of water and eventually lead to the passes. The passes are the only way over the high peaks and into Italy. Even following the rivers it is easy to become confused and then lost in any of the hundreds of blind valleys along the way, or be trapped in gorges and swept away by the torrents of water, mud and rocks that periodically surge from the mountains and destroy everything in their path.

There are only five main rivers that flow from various points in the Alps west to the Rhône. The farthest north and the longest is the Rhône itself; this river flows southwest from Lake Geneva in Switzerland and passes through Lyon on its way to the sea. The next is the Isère, which flows from the glaciers of the high Alps near the Val d'Isère and enters the Rhône at Valence. The Drôme is the third. Not as long as the Rhône and the Isère, this river begins in the pre-Alps, the Alpes du Dauphiné, and flows into the Rhône just south of Valence. The Aygues, several miles south of the Drôme, begins, like the Drôme, in the pre-Alps and enters the Rhône at the city of Orange. The last major river and the one of the five farthest south is the Durance. It is a long river that begins on the slopes of the highest Alps of the Italian frontier and flows along a broad valley into the Rhône just south of Avignon.

The easiest and most direct route for Hannibal to have utilized in crossing the Alps would have been to cross the Alpes Maritimae near the Mediterranean coast. A short distance inland there are a number of passes by which he could have crossed into Italy. Today the same route forms the bed for the modern superhighway through Provence to Italy. In fact, the French autoroute and the Italian autostrada were constructed following the original Roman coastal road from Italy to Spain. This route, however, entailed the risk of encountering the Romans, as well as groups of particularly savage mountain people, the Ligurians. So terrible were the Ligurian mountain tribes that the Romans did not succeed in pacifying the Alpes Maritimae until the reign of the Emperor Augustus, nearly two hundred years later.[11] This route would have had to be avoided at all costs, not only because of the Ligurian tribes, but because the Romans had a naval advantage over Hannibal and they could have intercepted the Carthaginian army virtually anywhere along the coast.

After the coastal route, Hannibal's next possibility would have been to leave the Rhône just north of Arles and march due east following the Durance River all the way through the Alps and then over the Italian frontier. Yet this route, in its initial stages, was also fraught with risks because it would have taken Hannibal and his army perilously close to the Greek city of Massilia and a possible confrontation with Roman forces there.

What Hannibal had to do was find a route farther north along the Rhône so as to avoid the Romans and then, by following the valleys, make his way to the upper reaches of the Durance. Once Hannibal could reach this river—well away from any possible confrontation with Scipio—he could follow that valley past the sites of the modern French towns of Sisteron, Embrun, Guillestre and Briançon, and move his column over the Alps by the Col du Montgenèvre or, by a slightly more southerly deviation along the Ubaye River, over the Col de Larche.

Either of these two passes, the Montgenèvre or the Larche, would have afforded his army a rapid and reasonably safe passage over the mountains and into Italy. Both of the passes are low (2000 meters) by Alpine standards, and were traveled in ancient times. The Col de Larche is considered the "lowest, safest, and most accessible pass in the Alps, lying over gentle slopes and pleasant pastures."[12] The Col du Montgenèvre is almost as easy to cross as the Larche, even under winter conditions.

Hannibal knew that he had to find an easy, quick and direct route over the mountains. He had been delayed at the crossing of the Rhône and by the battle with the Volcae. Now he looked apprehensively at the late-summer skies and thought about what lay ahead. As his army moved through the mountains he knew the constant effort of marching and climbing, becoming lost and then having to find the way again, suffering from the effects of cold, heat, wind, rain and ice would consume valuable energy and require enormous supplies of food. Supplies in the mountains were not readily available. They had to be carried with the army on baggage trains or foraged from the local inhabitants, who often had little with which to sustain themselves. Starvation and exposure were very real dangers in the mountains and in the end Hannibal would lose more of his men to these two elements than he had lost in battle.

The sudden appearance of the Roman army at Massilia compelled Hannibal to abandon any plans he had to follow a direct and easy route through the Alps. Instead he was forced to move his army farther north along the Rhône River than he had first planned and follow a different and more difficult route than he had intended. The ancient sources indicate that after Hannibal left his crossing point on the Rhône he marched four days north along the river in an attempt to avoid the Roman army.[13] Allowing that his army covered eight to ten miles a day[14] under good conditions, this would have brought them to a point along the river somewhere near the modern French city of Orange.[15]

The marching distances of eight to ten miles per day for the army are reasonably accurate since we know that at the time of Hannibal's invasion there existed in Gaul a usable system of roads. Most of these roads followed the wider river valleys that run parallel to the mountains or they cut across the ranges by following the transverse valleys. They course through a system of wide detours and sharply graded narrow pathways until they reach the passes over the highest mountains. Land travel, especially in the interior regions of Gaul, was well developed for a considerable period before the coming of the

Romans. Thus, much of Hannibal's journey, except along some of the transverse passes and in the most difficult reaches of the Alps, may have been along fairly established roadways.[16]

When Scipio learned from his scouts that Hannibal had crossed the Rhône, the Roman commander could hardly believe the reports. Scipio expected that Hannibal was still in Spain and never imagined that the Carthaginian army could have covered so much territory so quickly. Scipio knew that he had underestimated Hannibal and appreciated that the situation demanded immediate action. Hannibal had crossed a vast amount of territory under adverse conditions in an amazingly short space of time and Scipio sensed almost intuitively that he must adjust his own movements to the actions and strategy of his adversary.

It was apparent that the Carthaginians were headed to Italy, so Scipio assembled his army and immediately set out to find Hannibal in order to inflict as many casualties as possible and delay his march. The Romans reached the site of Hannibal's camp at the crossing of the Rhône too late. Hannibal was gone. Ready for battle, all Scipio found was a deserted campsite and confirmation of his worst fear. Hannibal was moving quickly toward the Alps and could well be in Italy within weeks.

Scipio knew that Hannibal had too much of a start to be overtaken, especially given the uncertainty of which route he might be following. Nor was Scipio prepared to follow Hannibal into the Alps without adequate provisions and equipment. So he returned to Massilia and made preparations to sail back to Italy. There he would raise a new army and await Hannibal as he came down from the Alps. At the same time, Scipio was unwilling to leave Spain without establishing a Roman presence there. He therefore sent his army on to Spain under the command of his brother, Gnaeus, while he sailed alone back to Italy.

After four days marching north along the Rhône River, Hannibal came to a piece of land called in the manuscripts simply "the island."[17] This area was described as triangular in shape and lying between two rivers, the Rhône and a river which Polybius, writing in Greek, named the "Iskaras" or "Skaras" and Livy, writing in Latin, called the "Arar." The area is described as similar to the Nile delta in that it was a low-lying region, subject to periods of flooding, densely populated and very fertile. Polybius used the ancient Greek word "*nesos*" to describe the area; the word can mean, in addition to island, a land flooded by the Nile.[18]

When Hannibal reached the "island" he found it inhabited by a large tribe on the verge of internecine warfare.[19] Two brothers, descendants of a deceased king, were disputing the right to the throne. The elder brother, Brancus, had taken the throne by right of primogeniture, and the other brother was seeking to depose him with a cabal of younger nobles. Brancus appealed to Hannibal to mediate the dispute; however, the ancient sources are contradictory as to how aggressive a role Hannibal played.

According to the accounts of Polybius, Hannibal sided with Brancus because it was to his advantage to do so, and helped drive the younger brother and his supporters from the area.[20] Livy, on the other hand, maintains that Hannibal played a much less aggressive and more mediatory role.[21] Hannibal, Livy contends, served as arbitrator in the dispute at the request of both brothers, and with the advice and support of the leading men among the tribe.

Either way, Hannibal settled the dispute in favor of the elder brother, Brancus.[22] Both Polybius and Livy are clear that Brancus was beholden to Hannibal for the role he had played, and to show his gratitude he gave Hannibal new weapons for his soldiers to replace those that had been damaged and worn out by the recent fighting. He also had his people provide clothes for the soldiers that were suitable for the mountains, and boots. As well, Brancus furnished Hannibal with experienced guides and a cavalry escort as far as the foothills of the Alps.

The question of the "island" highlights the first of three major controversies among scholars interested in the route that Hannibal followed over the Alps. The first controversy concerns the location of the "island" somewhere along the Rhône River. The second concerns the question of what river Hannibal followed when he left the "island" and began his ascent toward the Alps. The third concerns which pass Hannibal used to cross the Alps and descend into Italy.

According to the classical or traditional view, the Isère River is the one which is identified with the river "Iskaras" or "Arar" in the manuscripts and which Hannibal later followed to the Alps.[23] The Isère is the accepted version of Hannibal's route to the mountains and it has prevailed in the literature, with few challenges, for well over two hundred years. It is the story of the crossing of the Alps found in almost every general textbook on ancient history.

The Isère River begins among the glaciers of some of the highest mountains of the Alps in the area of the Col de l'Iseran (3000 meters high). From its watershed on the frontier with Italy, the river winds its way west through the mountains for nearly two hundred miles until it reaches the Rhône. By following this riverbed eastward, against the flow of the river, the Carthaginian army would have marched along a relatively direct and easy route to the Alps. Eventually Hannibal would have come to a point by which he could have crossed into Italy by any one of three possible passes, the Col du Clapier, the Mt. Cenis or the Little St. Bernard.

Looking at a map of the Alps, it becomes evident that this is an eminently logical route for Hannibal to have followed. Throughout the centuries proponents have buttressed the validity of their claims by emphasizing the strong similarity between the words "Iskaras" or "Skaras" in the ancient Greek and Isère in the French. Upon closer examination, however, the arguments of logic and convenience in this case are not necessarily persuasive.

The first problem with designating the Isère as the location of the "island" is that the area at the confluence of the Isère and Rhône does not form a triangle, nor is it today a particularly fertile area given to seasonal flooding. Another problem is the distance from where Hannibal crossed the Rhône at Fourques to the Isère, which is nearly a hundred miles away. It is doubtful that Hannibal and his army could have marched that many miles in four days. In order to reconcile this discrepancy, proponents of the route offer a crossing point of the Rhône at Roquemaure considerably farther north than Fourques and within the four-day marching range of the Isère.

Perhaps the most serious question about the Isère route centers on controversies over the reliability of medieval transcriptions of the ancient manuscripts. While the earliest manuscripts that deal with Hannibal and the Punic Wars date from the tenth and eleventh centuries,[24] the greatest quantity of them date from the fifteenth and sixteenth. These are not original manuscripts but transcriptions of transcriptions made during the Dark Ages by monks and scholars, the originals having been lost or destroyed centuries earlier. What we have to work from today are these transcriptions done by the medieval editors. Critics of the Isère route have contended that the medievalists made mistakes in their transcriptions which have caused the word "Iskaras," from the original manuscripts, to be replaced over the centuries in translations of Polybius and Livy by the word Isère. These errors in the transcriptions, handed down century after century have caused generations of scholars to accept Isère as synonymous with "Iskaras."[25]

Polybius, writing in ancient Greek, named the river that bordered the island the "Iskaras," while Livy, writing in Latin, called it the "Arar." The confusion apparently began with medieval editors, who could not reconcile the Greek "Iskaras" and the Latin "Arar" with the medieval names of the rivers that flow into the Rhône. There are cases where transcribers, unclear about what names corresponded with what rivers, even took out "Iskaras" from the manuscripts of Polybius and substituted "Araros."[26] Nicolas Perotti, as an example, published a Latin translation of Polybius in 1530 and substituted the Latin "Arar" for the Greek "Iskaras."[27]

The Latin name for the Isère River was Isara, and because it had many letters in common with Arar the two were frequently interchanged. Philip Cluver in 1624 substituted Isara for Arar in his manuscript and then altered the Iskaras of Polybius to read Araros and then Isaras. The result of these "changes" in the manuscripts is that the editions and translations of Polybius and Livy available to scholars today contain the names Isaras, Isara or Isère. They give little or no indication of the fact that these changes are not what were in the early works of either Polybius or Livy and that accepting them as authentic could affect the direction and outcome of a scholar's research.[28] Thus, a number of modern translations of Polybius contain references to the Isaras and indicate that it was the Isère, while modern translations of Livy show a reading of Isara for what should be Arar.

Another theory along these lines places the location of the "island" several miles farther down the river from the Isère, at the Ile du Colombier near the city of Orange.[29] At this location the Aygues River enters the Rhône from an obtuse angle and forms the second leg of a triangle such as Polybius and Livy described. The area between these two rivers is broad, low-lying, subject to periodic flooding and even today is very fertile. (It is the site of a French nuclear power plant at Marcoule.) The Aygues is located approximately forty miles north from where Hannibal crossed the Rhône just above Arles, a distance his army could easily have covered in four days.

The question now is whether there is any connection between the French name Aygues and the ancient Greek name Iskaras. Polybius wrote in Greek and we know that the ancient Gauls used the Greek alphabet. So it is possible that Polybius, when he noted the name of the river, copied it directly from the Gallic name written in Greek as well. The river Aygues had many names during the medieval period. Among the names found in some of the early documents are the Araus, Icarus, Aigarus, Escaris, and Equeris.[30] The ancient Greek name "Iskaras" is readily apparent in some of these forms.

To further strengthen the claim that the Aygues is really the Iskaras and the location of the island,[31] proponents of the theory rely on a portion of the manuscript written by Livy in which he noted that after Hannibal left the "island" he did not march directly toward the Alps but "turned left" and marched to "the territory of the Tricastini."[32] If one stands on the eastern bank of the Rhône River at its juncture with the Aygues, facing east in the direction of the Alps, and then turns left one is headed north along the Rhône. We know from Polybius and Livy that Hannibal marched ten days along a river and covered a hundred miles before he arrived at the foothills of the Alps. The river Hannibal followed is unnamed but it must have been initially the Rhône and then either the Drôme or the Isère. If the river Iskaras were identified as the Isère and the location of the island, then a left turn by Hannibal at this point would have taken him along the Rhône all the way to Switzerland. This would have been too far north.

From Livy we know that Hannibal and his army passed through the territories of certain Celtic tribes when they left the "island," because he named them and Polybius confirmed at least one of them. These territories can be located with a fair degree of accuracy and they are valuable markers for those who are seeking to establish Hannibal's route two thousand years later. According to Livy, Hannibal left the island and marched first into the territory of the Tricastini, then skirted the far edge of the territory of the Vocontii, entered the territory of the Tricorii and fought the Allobroges in the Alpes du Dauphiné. Other ancient historians also mention the territory of the Tricastini and the Vocontii as marking the line of Hannibal's march.[33] Where are these regions located today?

When the Romans conquered southern France, they named it Provence. To organize the region for administrative purposes they kept the names of the various Celtic tribes who lived there. They established continuity in name between the areas under their control and the particular Celtic tribes who had occupied the lands long before the Roman conquest. With the end of the Roman Empire, the church of Gaul retained the Roman names with some minor changes in spelling to delineate their dioceses. As a result, a survey of the ecclesiastical districts of southern France reproduces with a degree of accuracy the territories of the Celtic tribes of pre-Roman Gaul.[34] For example, the territory of the Tricastini, mentioned by Livy, is represented by the diocese of St. Paul-Trois-Châteaux just a few miles to the north of the river Aygues.[35] The connection between the Latin Tricastini and the French Trois-Châteaux is too close to have been merely a chance occurrence. The dioceses of Die and Vaison-la-Romaine represent the territory of the Vocontii, while the territory of the Tricorii is represented by the diocese of Gap, which encompasses the area around the middle course of the Durance River.

After Hannibal had settled matters between the two brothers on the island and provisioned his army, he turned left and began his march along the banks of "the river." Neither Polybius nor Livy mentions in the manuscripts which river Hannibal followed, but it may be inferred from the texts that for the first part of the march it had to be the Rhône. We know from both sources that Hannibal, "still avoiding the most direct route to Italy,"[36] was concerned about the Roman forces at Massilia and moved still farther north along the Rhône to avoid them. There are the only two major rivers in this stretch of the Rhône that flow from the Alps and correlate with the distances as specified by Polybius. These are the Isère and the Drôme.

Hannibal set out from the "island" and marched along the banks of the unnamed river, either the Isère or the Drôme, for ten days and covered a hundred miles. With every mile, his army moved deeper into the territory of more hostile mountain tribes known as the Allobroges. The march was uneventful and relatively easy until the column reached the foothills of the Alps. At this point the escort provided by Brancus left the column and headed for home.

As Hannibal's army began to advance into more difficult country, and without the escort of Brancus, the Allobroges began to shadow the column from the heights above the riverbed. These tribes may have been under the command of the younger brother of Brancus, who had been driven from the "island" by Hannibal and would have had a reason for revenge. While there is no mention in either manuscript of this possibility, Polybius points out that the hostile tribes were named the Allobroges and Livy specifies in his manuscript that the tribe of Brancus was also called the Allobroges. It is possible that the name Allobroges encompassed a large number of different tribes who inhabited the area from the Rhône to the Alpes du Dauphiné and were loosely bonded by connections of language and custom.

Hannibal had now come to the Alpes du Dauphiné, the foothills of the Alps. Even though these are formidable mountains of from four to five thousand feet high, behind them, miles and days ahead, loomed the most difficult part of the march at even higher altitudes and over more dangerous roadways. For the soldiers who marched for mile after mile, these mountains seemed to go on forever, always growing higher and more treacherous with each passing day. The footing became more difficult, the journey more tiring and the surrounding cliffs steeper and more menacing.

As the column entered the mountains it slowed, and as it passed through a narrow valley Hannibal began to notice more mountain tribesmen shadowing them from the heights above. Each night when the column halted, the soldiers had to encamp in the best stretch of level ground they could find. Even so, they were usually hemmed in on all sides by rocks and cliffs. Hannibal became apprehensive and sent his guides forward to reconnoiter the area.

When the guides returned they reported that the column would have to cross the mountain range by following a particularly difficult and narrow gorge ahead and then climbing over a pass. Rumors and exaggerated reports of the dangers ahead spread quickly through the column. The soldiers bemoaned the fact that they were in difficult and dangerous terrain already and they imagined that what lay ahead must be far worse. With each passing mile the confines of the valley walls only increased, as did the soldiers' fear of ambush. They became concerned and even fearful as the shadows and figures moving quickly and furtively along the ledges above them seemed to grow in number.

The army was apprehensive the morning when Hannibal gave the order for camp to be broken and the column to move into the gorge. Hannibal was most concerned about an ambush at the point where most of the column would be well into the narrow gorge ahead and many along the line would have begun the climb to the pass. Each day more and more tribesmen could be seen in the heights above and in the last few days Hannibal could not help but notice that they made little effort to conceal themselves.

The Celtic scouts reported that they suspected the mountain tribesmen only shadowed the column during the day and that at night they returned to their villages. According to Livy, the scouts that Hannibal used spoke the same language as the tribesmen who were preparing the ambush, so that they were able to listen in on some of the conversations to gain valuable information.[37] As the column approached the gorge Hannibal knew he had to take every precaution to avoid an ambush. Late that afternoon the army made camp just at the foot of the gorge at a spot where they were still out of range of the weapons of the tribesmen in the heights above. Hannibal ordered his officers to make it appear that the army was preparing to camp there for the night. Large numbers of campfires were kept burning throughout the night to give the tribesmen the impression that the entire army was in camp.

The mountain tribesmen watching from the heights above were confident that Hannibal's army had settled in and would not try to enter the gorge until dawn. As darkness settled over the gorge the tribesmen abandoned their posts and withdrew to the comfort of their village huts. In the early hours of the next morning, Hannibal assembled a force of lightly armed infantry and left camp under cover of darkness. Over the several hours that followed Hannibal and this force climbed to the heights overlooking the pass, but at a higher level than the positions normally held by the tribesmen. There they established themselves and settled in to await the dawn. At daybreak, as the Allobroges made their way to the heights above the pass, they discovered what Hannibal had done. With the infantry force in position and covering the heights, the army entered the gorge and began the climb along the narrow road to the mountain pass.

Some of the tribesmen occupied the ledges and cliffs below Hannibal while others were following the column at a distance. At first they did nothing but watch the long column of infantry, cavalry and pack animals slowly and painfully make its way along the gorge and then up the narrow track leading to the pass. By the time most of the column was in the gorge, the vanguard had begun the climb to the pass, where footing became difficult. As the situation on the roadway became more and more dangerous, the column began to lose its cohesion. From the narrow ledge that formed a very rough roadway up to the pass the men saw a precipitous drop to the raging river below. As the army moved along, often in single file, there was confusion, excitement and fear among the men. They were unsure whether the mountain tribes would attack and fearful of the exposed position in which they found themselves.

The horses and pack animals became nervous on the narrow ledge and were often on the verge of panic. The road leading up to the pass was not only narrow and uneven but flanked with precipices so the

The painter J.M.W. Turner's famous visualization of the construction of Carthage. By the time the Punic Wars ended, few traces of the once-great city remained. (Courtesy of the National Gallery, London; the photos on the following pages are by the author.)

A view of the gorge where the second ambush took place, a day's march from the Alpine pass. Celtic warriors lined the heights on either side, throwing boulders and logs and then charging down amidst Hannibal's men. Other Celtic forces attacked from both ends of the gorge to seal the Carthaginian troops within.

Today a paved road has replaced the path trod by Hannibal's column inside the gorge; nevertheless the site still resonates with danger.

After the ambush, those Carthaginians who survived gathered and rested around a huge, "cathedral-like" rock that rose in the center of a valley.

After his troops had regrouped, Hannibal had one day of relatively easy marching before he reached the pass on Mt. Viso.

The ancient sources record that the army rested for a day near the top of the pass on a broad, flat camping ground. Arguments against the Col de la Traverseette have stated that it contains no such area— but it does, as proven by this photo!

The Carthaginians began to suffer as they made the difficult climb to the pass. Although this photo was taken in mid-summer (it being otherwise too treacherous to climb this terrain) the reader must picture the slope covered with ice or snow, or, if you were a Carthaginian far back in the column, slippery, trampled slush.

This photo of the path to the Col de la Traversette depicts exactly what the ancient sources so vividly described. Covered with ice at the time of year of Hannibal's crossing, literally thousands of Carthaginians fell to their deaths over the steep precipices. Once a man lost his footing and slid, there was little that could be done to save him.

One of the highest passes in the French Alps, parts of the Col de la Traversette along Mt. Viso are covered with snow year-round.

A view from the top of the pass. Hannibal stood on a ledge, and as his men passed by he bade them look at Italy spread out below them.

This photo, taken from the top of the pass, helps convey the magnitude of what Hannibal and his Carthaginian army achieved in their dangerous trek to launch a surprise offensive against Rome.

least disorder in the column caused some of the animals to be forced over the edge with their loads. The slightest slip or miscalculation sent men and animals off the ledge and into the raging torrent thousands of feet below. One man's error on the ledge could result in the deaths of three or four others and as many pack animals and horses.

As they watched the Carthaginian column slowly and laboriously moving through the pass, the mountain tribes could no longer contain themselves—despite Hannibal and his men holding the heights above them. The tribesmen charged impulsively down over the rocks and cliffs, screaming their war cries and hurling their weapons.

The Carthaginian column now found itself literally between a rock and a hard place. The narrow track was dangerous enough to begin with, but after thousands of men and animals had walked along it and the Gauls had attacked, parts of the path were becoming unstable. By this point the column was spread out nearly single file along the narrow ledge, where the slightest mistake could mean a fall over the side. From above the column was under attack by the mountain tribes whose battle cries echoed and re-echoed through the valley, only adding to the panic and confusion among the Carthaginians on the narrow ledge below.

The tribesmen hurled rocks and rolled boulders down upon the column that caused the panic to intensify among the animals. Horses were purposely wounded by arrows shot by the Gauls. As they reared out of control because of their pain they often lost their footing and fell over the ledge. As one horse slipped it pulled others tethered to it, as well as men. Some of the horses and pack animals in their panic pushed ahead along the ledge and shoved men and other animals to their deaths. Great numbers of soldiers and noncombatants as well as animals were flung over the sheer cliffs that bounded the pass and fell to their deaths below.

The Celts had only to keep up the barrage on the column below and let fear, panic and confusion take their toll. Hannibal, watching from above, strove to keep his troops on the upper heights of the pass restrained. The loss of so many men and animals on the ledge was a shocking sight even to these experienced warriors. They pleaded with Hannibal to allow them to charge down upon the Celts and relieve the pressure on their comrades below. Yet Hannibal feared that to allow them to join the fight would only add to the confusion on the ledges below and increase the casualties.

Finally the Carthaginian column began to break apart and casualties increased to the point where Hannibal realized that he had to attack the Celts or risk losing all of the supplies he would need for the passage over the higher and more difficult mountains that lay ahead. Hannibal ordered his men to charge down upon the enemy from the heights and their charge quickly scattered the mountain men; but as he feared, this attack only increased the lethal disorder among his other men pinned down on the track below. The casualties in the column increased even more while his relief forces killed many of the tribesmen and drove off the rest.[38] Once the enemy had fled from the heights and the situation was stabilized, the officers were able to restore order in the column and the rest of the army was able to move through the pass without further difficulty.

As the remaining elements of the army climbed the ledge to the pass they walked in silence, perhaps out of fear or shock at what they had seen happen to those who had been on the path just ahead of them or out of respect for their dead. When the last of the soldiers and supplies had been brought through, the elephants were carefully led along the ledge without a loss. After the entire column had come over the pass, Hannibal regrouped his forces.

A short distance away from the location of the ambush there was a sizable town that belonged to the mountain tribes which had attacked the column. Hannibal assembled his troops and led them to attack the town, but when his army entered they found it nearly deserted. Most of the inhabitants had been on the heights joining in the ambush, and afterward had fled into the mountains to hide.

In the town Hannibal was able to recover much of the baggage that had been plundered from his column during the attack and earlier, and his men discovered to their surprise some of their comrades who had been captured by the Gauls in the preceding days. It was a Gallic tactic when they shadowed the column to wait in hiding around dusk, when small groups of Hannibal's soldiers would go off into the forests to forage for kindling or food. They would kidnap these unfortunate men and take them back to their villages to be tortured for information or amusement. Hannibal found many of these men bound but unharmed in a number of the town's huts. They were promptly freed and able to rejoin the column. The town must have been sizable, for Hannibal found enough grain and cattle to supply his army for the next three days. News of his victory over this mountain tribe and his capture of their town spread quickly through the adjoining valleys, and inspired such fear among other tribes in the vicinity that none would dare to attack him as he continued his march through their territory.

Where was Hannibal first ambushed? While the Isère River offers a relatively easy route to the Alps in terms of hiking, there is a problem in finding an ambush site along it that fits the descriptions given by Polybius and Livy. The Isère leads to the Alps by a reasonably direct route, at least for mountainous terrain, without any particularly difficult gorges to march through and no passes to climb. From the accounts of Polybius and Livy concerning this ambush, we know that the Carthaginian column had entered rugged mountain territory and eventually had to reach a dangerous pass at the end of a narrow gorge. The army had to march along a difficult and treacherous ledge to the pass, make its way over the top and then descend the other side. It is unlikely that this ambush could have occurred anywhere along the Isère River because of the terrain along its valley. No place anywhere along the valley corresponds closely to the descriptions of the rugged pass where Hannibal and his column were first ambushed.

A site suggested by scholars supporting the Isère route is located in the Gorges de la Bourne.[39] To reach this gorge, however, Hannibal would have had to leave the Isère River at St. Nazaire-en-Royans and follow the Bourne River due east. The gorge through which this small river flows is admittedly an ideal site for the ambush. The problem is that from the Gorges de la Bourne he would have had to pass through a second gorge, the Gorges du Furon, a few miles farther along the route. There is no mention in the ancient sources of a second gorge. Nor is there a pass along this route. Eventually the narrow gorges lead back to the Isère at Grenoble.

It does not make sense that Hannibal would have left the Isère, a relatively easy and straightforward route to the Alps, to detour through two narrow gorges and risk an ambush. Was Hannibal seeking a shortcut from one location on the Isère to another farther upriver? This is possible because we know he had guides who understood the local mountain dialect and thus must have been familiar with the area. And the Isère River at this stage does make a long loop around a low (1500 meters) and heavily forested mountain range called the Vercors (today part of a national park).

Tracing the distances on a map, it becomes evident that taking this "shortcut," given the difficulty of the terrain and the distance involved, actually would have made the march longer. It would have been shorter, simpler and easier for Hannibal to have followed the Isère directly to Grenoble. Furthermore, it is doubtful that an experienced and cautious commander like Hannibal would have left a secure route like the Isère to enter a series of long and narrow gorges with often treacherous footing and multiple locations for an ambush. We also know that at this point the escort furnished by Brancus had turned back and it is questionable whether Hannibal had local guides with him to show him the way. If he did have guides provided by Brancus, they would have known how treacherous and dangerous the Bourne gorges were.

Another site favored by scholars is the Bec d'Echaillon, which is located along the Isère River near Moirans.[40] The problem with this site is that while it has a cliff of about 600 meters on one side there is a wide expanse of valley on the other, making an ambush very unlikely. Hannibal and his men could have avoided the dangers here by simply crossing the river and marching on the other side out of range of the Gauls.

The Drôme River is a route that offers more possibilities as the route followed by Hannibal. The river enters the Rhône only a few kilometers farther south than the Isère and it is located close to the area identified as the island. The Drôme does not lead to the higher mountains of the Alps and the Italian frontier like the Isère. The riverbed leads east only so far as the first range of mountains, known as the pre-Alps. It does, however, eventually bring one into close proximity to the Durance river valley farther north. Livy wrote that Hannibal eventually reached another river on his march that he named the "Druentia." Druentia could be the Latin equivalent of Durance.[41] Polybius makes no mention of another river.

While Hannibal would have avoided the Durance River where it flows into the Rhône near Arles for fear of encountering the Romans nearby, farther north, however, it would have led him to one of two low passes over the Alps, the Col du Montgenèvre or the Col de Larche. This route has been suggested in the literature several times over the centuries but has generally been dismissed either in favor of the Isère or for "lack of evidence."[42] It remains to re-examine this route to the Alps, for there are convincing arguments in its favor.

Reconstructing Hannibal's route by the Drôme River, a number of factors fall into place. First, the distance from where the Drôme enters the Rhône to where the ambush could have occurred is about sixty miles. Hannibal could easily have covered this distance in the ten days that Polybius says it took him to reach the point where he was ambushed. There are two possible ambush sites along this route. The first is the Col de Grimone, which is reached by leaving the Drôme by a tributary and walking through a narrow and treacherous gorge called the Gorges des Gas. After following the gorge for a few miles one comes to the Défilé du Charan near the village of Glandage. Through this narrow defile one walks to begin a long climb to the Col de Grimone. The pass is at 1300 meters and the descent is by an easy path down toward the small town of La Faurie. From La Faurie one follows an easy roadway to a larger town, Veynes, then to the town of Gap and finally into the Durance Valley. The distance from the Col de Grimone to the Durance is about 30 miles and within the three-day time frame specified by Polybius for the portion of the march following the ambush. The second possible site is a little farther south at the Col de Cabre and is not as persuasive. This pass at 1200 meters does not have the narrow defile before it like the Grimone. It is a few miles from the Col de Cabre to Veynes and the passage to the Durance Valley. Either pass is suitable for the ambush as described by Polybius and Livy, and both lead to the Durance valley.[43]

At this point Hannibal and his army had succeeded in crossing over the first and lowest barrier of mountains on their march to Italy and they had survived the first ambush. None of the tribes in the area bothered the column any further after it came down from the pass and took the town of the Allobroges. Following a march of three more days, Hannibal and his army came to the wide valley of the Durance River. They had come upon a route to Italy that follows the river and passes today by the towns of Embrun, Guillestre and Briançon directly to the frontier. Hannibal and his army were now in view of the highest and most difficult mountains of the Alps and on a direct and easy route to Italy. The column was within two or three days of crossing this last barrier of difficult mountains by an easy pass, the Col du Montgenèvre. Fate and circumstances, however, intervened to deal them a more difficult turn of events. The tribulations of Hannibal and his army were far from over. Unbeknownst to them, the worst was yet to come.

NOTES

[1] Livy, Bk. XXI, Sec. 23; Polybius Bk. III, Sec. 35. Both sources are in agreement about the numbers of soldiers and horsemen, yet neither source makes any references to the numbers of elephants Hannibal took with him. Polybius emphasizes the accuracy of his figures by commenting that he found a bronze tablet upon which Hannibal had written these figures in the extreme southeast of Italy, near the modern Cape Colonna.

[2] Livy. Bk. XXI, Sec. 23.

[3] Polybius, Bk. III, Sec. 38.

[4] Polybius, Bk. III, Sec. 40.

[5] W.W. Hyde, *Roman Alpine Routes*, p. 207; G. deBeer, p. 26.

[6] H.L. Long, 1831; R. Ellis, 1853; T. Montanari, 1890; C. Torr, 1925.

[7] Napoleon, 1816, deLuc, J.A., 1818, Larauza, J.L., 1826, Law, W.J., 1866, Hennebert, C., 1878, Ollivier, 1889, Dodge, T. 1891, Fuchs, J. 1893, Hall, W.H. 1898, Freshfield, D. 1914, Ferrand, H. 1925.

[8] Polybius, Bk, III, Sec 42. First reference to the number of elephants Hannibal took with him. Polybius says thirty-seven.

[9] Polybius, Bk. III, Sec. 46.

[10] Livy, Bk. XXI, Sec 30.

[11] Augustus erected a massive temple, La Turbie, on the pass above modern-day Monaco, as a monument to the subjugation of the Ligurian tribes and the pacification of the Alpes Maritimae under Rome. The remains of the temple are still there and from the heights there is a magnificent view over Monaco, the sea and the mountains.

[12] D. Freshfield, Alpine Pass of Hannibal, p. 38.

[13] Livy, Bk. XXI, Sec. 31.

[14] Polybius, Bk. III. Sec. 50. Eighty Greek stadia a day, the rough equivalent of 14–15 kilometers, or 8–10 miles.

[15] Livy, Bk. XXI, Sec. 31, and Polybius, Bk. III, Sec. 49.

[16] M. Cary, *The Geographic Background of Greek and Roman History*, Oxford: 1950, p. 251.

[17] Livy, Bk. XXI, Sec. 31, and Polybius, Bk. III, Sec. 49.

[18] Polybius, Bk. III, Sec. 49. In the manuscript of Nicolao Perrotto, 1473, the name of the river in Latin is "Arar"; Causaubon, 1609, and Gronovius, 1670, use the Greek word for the river; the geographer Phillipi Cluver, 1624, refers to the river as the Isara.

[19] Polybius makes no mention of their name, while Livy calls them the Allobroges.

[20] Polybius, Bk. III, Sec. 49.

[21] Livy, Bk. XXI, Sec. 31.

[22] Livy, Sec. 31.

[23] Dennis Proctor, *Hannibal's March in History*, p. 203.

[24] Codex Colbertinus, 10th century; Codex Mediceus, 11th century; Codex Vaticanus, 11th century.

[25] Gavin deBeer. Professor deBeer did the pioneering work in this area during the 1940s and 1950s. The former director of the British Museum of Natural History, he had a lifelong interest in the story of Hannibal's passage over the Alps and devoted a considerable portion of his personal and professional life to produce some excellent scholarship on the question of mistakes in the medieval transcriptions and their effects on the scholarship of subsequent generations of scholars.

[26] Isaac Casaubon. *Polybii*, editions 1609 and 1617, Paris.

[27] Nicolas Perotti. *Polybii Historiarum*, 1530, Paris.

[28] Gavin deBeer, *Alps and Elephants*. Chapter III, pg. 14, has the best discussion of this problem and contains the highlights of deBeer's work. While the author consulted the original sources in Paris, he was guided throughout his research on this phase of the event by deBeer's work.

[29] Ibid.

[30] Joanne Paul. *Dictionnaire Géographique de la France*, Paris: 1894, Vol. 3, p. 1436.

[31] deBeer,1955, Cottrell,1960, Bradford, 1981.

[32] Livy, Bk. XXI, Sec. 31. "Sed ad laevam in Tricastinos flexit . . ." "but toward the left he turned toward the Tricastini . . ."

[33] Silius Italicus, *Punica*, Bk. III, pp. 442–76, gives a description of Hannibal's route. Timagenes describes Hannibal's march in Bk. XV, Sec. 10, of *Ammianus Marcellinus*.

[34] deBeer, *Alps and Elephants*, p. 36.

[35] Etienne Clouzot. "Pouilles des provinces d'Aix, d'Arles, et d'Ebrun" and "Pouilles des provinces de Besançon, de Tarentaise, et de Vienne," *Recueil des Historiens de la France*, Paris: 1923 and 1940.

[36] Livy, Bk. XXI, Sec 31.

[37] Livy, B. XXI, Sec 32.

[38] Polybius, Bk. III, Sec. 51.

[39] J.F. Lazenby, *Hannibal's War*, 1978.

[40] J. Colin, 1904, Spenser Wilkinson, 1911, H. Ferrand, 1925.

[41] Livy, Bk. XXI, Sec 31. "Pervenit ad Druentiam flumen."

[42] deBeer promoted the pass in his three books: *Hannibal*, 1969, *Hannibal's March*, 1967, and *Alps and Elephants*, 1955. The pass was first mentioned in the literature by a Frenchman, Denina, in his work *Tableau historique, statistique, et moral de la haute Italie*, Paris:1805.

[43] deBeer. *Hannibal's March*. deBeer was the most adamant proponent of this route and supported his assertion with extensive and painstaking research.

CHAPTER V

❧ · ❧

THE EYE OF THE NEEDLE

The mountains were a dreadful sight before their eyes,
high peaks, covered with snow and stretching to the sky,
and all around them everything was stiff with cold.
Shaggy, unkempt men perched on the crags above,
more horrible to look upon than words can tell.
All this renewed the fear of the [Carthaginian] column[1]

After Hannibal and his army had fought their way out of the first ambush and captured the town nearby, they marched for three days and finally came within sight of the Hautes Alpes, the highest and most difficult mountains in the French Alps and the last barrier that stood between them and Italy. The first range of mountains they had passed through, the Alpes du Dauphiné, was relatively low by alpine standards. They rose to a height of only four to five thousand feet. Now the Carthaginian column stood on the valley floor and gazed in awe at the giants that lay before them. The peaks of these mountains soared into the sky and touched the clouds. These were mountains whose summits rose to thirteen thousand feet, and stood like an unassailable wall guarding Rome and daring the mercenaries to try to scale their heights.

As Hannibal and his army moved forward they were approaching the last and most difficult leg of their march to Italy. There would be no bucolic meadows or picturesque village hamlets with scenic mountain backdrops here. The people who inhabited these mountains and valleys, according to the ancient sources, were only "half-civilized."[2] They pulled a meager living from the rocky land and sup-

plemented what little they had by attacking and plundering other villages and towns. The ancient Greek geographer and historian Strabo
has left us a disturbing image of their brutality, especially toward the
people who lived on the other side of the mountains in Italy, where,
thanks to nature, life was a little more bountiful and a little less
harsh.

"When they capture a village or even a small town," wrote Strabo,
"they not only murder all the males but they also kill the male
infants. Nor do they stop there either, but in their frenzy also kill all
the pregnant women who their priests say carry within them male
children."[3]

We learn even more about these mountain people from another
Greek historian, Diodorus, who wrote in the 1st century B.C.:

> Here in this rough country, men and women live a toilsome
> and luckless life. Because of constant climbing, heavy work
> and insufficient food they are generally a thin but muscular
> people. They hunt and trap wild animals and drink only water
> and milk. Most of their diet consists of the meager vegetables
> which they cultivate in some plots on the stony ground and
> the flesh of the animals they hunt. They have no wheat or
> vineyards. They live either in huts with their cattle, or in hol-
> low rocks and caves, yet they possess the strength and courage
> of wild beasts.[4]

We know from the Roman historian Pliny the Elder that many
people living in the mountains suffered from goiter, a condition they
contracted from a lack of iodine in their diet. The condition left
many of them disfigured and remained a problem in the Alps until
the beginning of the twentieth century. As a result, mountain women
for centuries wore amber necklaces as an ineffective talisman against
the malady.[5]

From Polybius and Livy we learn that, surprisingly, the Alps at the
time of Hannibal were fairly well populated and that many of the
people who lived there were settled in fortified villages and sizable
towns as well as in the more primitive accommodations described by

Diodorus. The tribes that inhabited the areas through which Hannibal passed must have been quite large to dare to attack, even from ambush, a force of some forty thousand veteran soldiers, fully armed, with elephants and cavalry.

When Hannibal came down from the mountains of the Dauphiné a delegation of elders from the surrounding tribes of the region came to greet him. They carried branches and wreaths with them as symbols of peace and they came to Hannibal, they said, as envoys from the sizable numbers of tribes that lived in the fortified villages near the pass toward which he was headed. When the elders presented themselves to Hannibal they related to him how they had heard the news of his victory over the Allobroges and his capture of their principal town. They assured Hannibal that their tribes preferred reaching an accommodation with the Carthaginian rather than risk suffering the same fate as those in the neighboring valley who had attacked his column. They were not so stupid, the elders contended, that they were unable to learn from the examples of other men. They gave Hannibal repeated assurances that he had nothing to fear from them and made numerous proffers of peace and friendship. Hannibal acknowledged their words and in return demanded from them hostages to insure their good behavior, provisions to feed his army and guides to lead the column over the mountains that lay ahead.

The elders readily agreed to his demands and over the next several hours selected from their villages men and women, and probably children as well, and turned them over to Hannibal as hostages. They provided his army with cattle and large quantities of supplies. Then they brought forth the men they had selected to guide Hannibal and the column over the last and highest range of mountains and into Italy.

Hannibal was skeptical of these tribesmen and their offers of friendship. He suspected that their generosity had been too quickly forthcoming and that there might be treachery afoot. He had just survived a particularly difficult time in the last valley and was reluctant to accept overtures of peace and friendship from mountain people at face value. At the same time he was desperate for supplies. His troops badly needed provisions; those they had looted from the town three days before had been consumed on this last stage of the march.

While Hannibal was suspicious of the mountain tribesmen, he was reluctant to reject their offer of friendship outright for fear that he might offend them. A perceived slight to these warlike tribes could be all the excuse they needed to attack his column. Thinking that if he accepted their offers, they might be less inclined to attack, Hannibal took the supplies and thanked them for their generosity. It was now late September, or perhaps even early October, and conditions in the higher elevations of the mountains were becoming more unsettling and dangerous each day. Hannibal was anxious to press ahead and climb the final barrier of mountains. So he took their guides and when all was ready turned his column toward the peaks and headed toward Italy.

A question arises at this point about whom Hannibal had been using as guides along the march. The manuscripts make occasional references to guides and scouts and there may be an important differentiation between the two that is worth considering. The scouts were probably horsemen who would have been sent ahead of the column, perhaps by one or two days, to survey conditions along the route, gather intelligence for Hannibal and keep him generally headed in the right direction.

There is little doubt that Hannibal must have used the Boii as scouts from the time he crossed the Rhone River on, because of their general familiarity with the mountains. The Boii would have had a general idea of direction in the Alps and been knowledgeable about conditions in the mountains. They would not, however, have had the specialized knowledge of each area through which the army would be passing in order to act as guides. It is doubtful that these scouts were capable of actually leading the column along specific pathways, through gorges, along ledges and over passes. We know from Polybius and Livy that they came from Italy purposely to guide Hannibal over the Alps, but they probably had intended to lead him over the mountains by one of the easier coastal routes or lower passes. As things turned out, they were forced to follow a much more difficult route than the one they had probably intended.[6]

Polybius wrote that Hannibal engaged as scouts "natives of the country who were about to take part in his campaign." This can only mean they must have been the Boii or the Insubres from Italy since there is no indication in any of the sources that the mountain tribes Hannibal encountered along the way joined him in his march through the Alps and in the war with Rome. We surmise that guides must have been provided by Brancus at the "island," because we know he provided Hannibal with an escort for the first ten days as the column marched along the river. Furthermore, we know from the manuscripts that at the site of the first ambush the guides utilized by Hannibal understood the language of the Allobroges and were thus able to listen in on their conversations and learn their intentions. There is no indication in the manuscripts that Brancus provided guides any farther than the ambush point. The escort, in fact, turned back before the column was ambushed; and whether or not the guides who brought Hannibal to that point remained with the column after that is never made clear.

Guides, on the other hand, are different from scouts. They are people who know the specific routes through the mountains and they know how to reach certain destinations and avoid dangerous locations. Since only the peoples who lived in the areas he was traversing would have possessed this detailed knowledge, Hannibal must have had to utilize them at crucial stages in the march. From the Rhône to the foothills of the Alps we can be certain that Hannibal had reliable and trustworthy guides provided by Brancus, at the least in the form of the escort that accompanied the column.

Beyond that point Hannibal may have been blindly following the valleys. The ancient sources indicate that sometimes his column was moving through the mountains without any guides at all and was lost. By the end of the march, when Hannibal finally reached the pass by which he crossed into Italy, we know from Livy that his column had lost its way numerous times in the mountains.[7]

After only a short rest Hannibal reformed the column for the last and most difficult part of the march. He took the guides and hostages offered by the mountain tribes but, uneasy about what lay ahead, he tightened the formation of the column as it moved along the valley.

When it marched through territories where the scouts had determined they were safe from attack, or where the nature of the terrain was such that it afforded them a measure of protection from the tribesmen, Hannibal allowed the soldiers to march in a relaxed fashion. In times of danger or when conditions made him apprehensive he ordered the cavalry and elephants to be placed first in the line of march. Then he positioned the lighter infantry along both sides of the column to protect the baggage train and those civilians who had survived the last few months and still remained with the army. Last in the long line came a picked detachment of heavy infantry commanded directly by Hannibal and used to protect the column against attack from the rear.

For two days the tribesmen led Hannibal and the column toward the mountains and the Italian frontier. All the while, their elders were assembling fighting men from the surrounding fortified villages and hamlets, calling them in from their hovels, caves and forests. The tribesmen were formulating plans for an elaborate ambush of the column at the right moment. The prospect of all the goods in Hannibal's baggage train, his weapons and horses, the stores of food and clothing, the valuables his men had looted from cities and towns along the route of the march must have been too much temptation for these tribes. Perhaps, on the contrary, they planned the ambush because they resented Hannibal and the way he had come into their land and taken their provisions as winter approached, as well as many of their children and women as hostages.

They may have seen this new ambush as an occasion when nature gave them a slight edge over Hannibal and a chance to take back what was rightfully theirs—and perhaps a little more. It is possible they knew they were no match for the Carthaginians in a fixed battle on the valley floor, so they decided to wait for a more favorable moment when the terrain was more conducive to their style of fighting. Thus, in spite of what had happened to their brothers in an adjacent valley only days before, they decided to try their hand at the same treachery.

The Carthaginian column was led by the guides into a long, deep and narrow gorge. At its entrance the soldiers were forced to narrow their ranks in order to move into the gorge and this maneuver must have caused the column to extend itself to a distance of at least six or seven miles. Stretched out as they were within the steep walls of the gorge, they suddenly found themselves in a vulnerable position. They were marching along a narrow path with a steep wall on one side and a rapidly flowing river on the other. By marching his army through this defile, Hannibal had taken a grave risk. In the heights above them, spread out and concealed along the ridges of the gorge were thousands of tribesmen lying in ambush. Of the nearly 40,000 men who entered the gorge only half would survive the next five days and live to see the plains of Italy.

The Gauls waited patiently as the column below moved farther and deeper into the gorge and closer to their trap. Behind the column another, larger, group of Gauls shadowed at a distance, waiting for the right moment to attack. Several miles ahead, where the gorge opened into a valley, a third force of Gauls waited along the banks of the river to catch any survivors who escaped the massacre.

The Carthaginian column moved into the gorge silently and apprehensively. The Boii at the front followed the local guides but scanned the cliffs, continually looking for any sign of movement that might indicate an oncoming ambush. The tribesmen who were guiding the column, knowing full well what was to come, became increasingly restless and looked for an opportunity to escape before the carnage began. The hostages, like lambs being led to the slaughter, marched in line bound to their Carthaginian captors, meekly awaiting their fate.

Those Gauls who had positioned themselves in the cliffs above allowed the first part of the column to pass through the gorge while they patiently waited for the main body with the baggage train to move within their range. Large groups of boulders and rocks had been prepared at selected points along the ledges and positioned to be rolled down upon the column. At one place in the gorge the track became so narrow and the walls of the cliffs closed in upon the column so tightly that the mercenaries were forced to march no more than perhaps three or four abreast, often with "one foot in the river and the other on land."

The Gauls launched their first attack just as the middle of the Carthaginian column was moving slowly and painstakingly through this "steep and precipitous defile."[8] The initial attack came against the rear guard of the column as it was about to enter the gorge. Hannibal was neither surprised nor unprepared, for he had taken precautions early on. On his command, the heavy infantry turned in formation and positioned themselves to meet the charge of the mountain tribes.

Had Hannibal sent his heavy infantry into the defile first, at the head of the column, they would have been trapped immediately, isolated within the narrow confines of the valley walls and unable to protect the remainder of their comrades. The contingents of heavy infantry, placed as they were at the end of the column, however, were able to check the onslaught of the barbarians. However, they could do nothing to defend the column against the next and most devastating attack. This came from the cliffs on either side of the defile.

The tribesmen who had taken positions in the heights overlooking the pathway began rolling down huge boulders and hurling large quantities of rocks. It was almost a complete replay of the massacre in the first gorge.

Thunderous roars were heard time and again, often in quick secession, as tons of falling rocks and boulders came crashing down upon the column from various points along the gorge. Added to the roar of the rocks were the terrified shouts of men under attack, the triumphant cries of the attackers and the screams of the wounded. The moans and whimpers of the dying were buried in the noise and confusion among the living.

The column broke ranks as men ran desperately anywhere they could, seeking shelter against the walls of the gorge when none other could be had. Most had to stand their ground and endure the hail of death that rained down. Officers along the line, trying their best to maintain order, encouraged the soldiers to keep moving, but boulders, rocks, debris and the bodies of crushed and mutilated men and animals choked the narrow passage. As the river flowed through the defile, indifferent to the slaughter going on around it, its color changed from green to red.

After the boulders and rocks had done their damage the Gauls let loose an unrelenting hail of arrows and spears upon the column. As before, in the first ambush, animals were purposely wounded so as to be driven mad by their pain. Rearing out of control and thrashing out, they often caused as much injury within the column as did the weapons of the enemy. For hours the fighting raged along the gorge, sometimes intense and then intermittent, heavier in one area and lighter in another.

Yet through all this carnage Hannibal's soldiers kept pushing their way forward, over the boulders that had been rolled down from the heights to block their way, and over the dead and the dying. The only way out of this trap was to fight their way to open ground. The defile had become a killing ground of unimaginable horror as the column of nearly forty thousand was subjected to a murderous gauntlet from above.

In places the attack was so furious and concentrated that eventually tribesmen were able to establish themselves on the track and cut the column in half near the narrowest point of the defile. When Hannibal hesitated to send his heavy infantry into the gorge he enabled the tribesmen to deliver a flank attack—the most deadly maneuver in ancient warfare—against the weakest part of the column. For a short time the Gauls were able to control the pathway and separate Hannibal from his cavalry and elephants at the front of the column. The lighter infantry, civilians and the baggage train were now taking the brunt of the attack from the heights while Hannibal and the heavy infantry kept the rear defended. The situation became similar to the one earlier when Hannibal, during the first ambush, had restrained his covering forces on the heights from taking the pressure off the column. In both ambushes it was the weakest part of the column that bore the heaviest brunt of the attack.

Ahead of the column the elephants soon began to panic and some became nearly uncontrollable in the narrow gorge when the Gauls threw rocks and boulders down on them. Eventually their handlers were able to gain control over them, however, and the huge animals proved particularly valuable in the fight. When the elephants con-

fronted the Gauls on the track of the gorge they terrified the tribesmen, who had never seen such large beasts. When the mahouts
would drive the elephants head-on against the Gauls, they would
panic and run. The narrowness of the gorge somewhat limited the
elephants' effectiveness, but by the end of the battle the beasts in the
vanguard were being used by their handlers to clear the route ahead
of both debris and the enemy. The heavy infantry at the back of the
column were now able to keep the Gauls from flooding the gorge
with additional fighting men, and by late in the day only the middle
of the column was still being subjected to the heaviest attacks.

The Gauls positioned at the far end of the gorge, try as they
might, could not contain the column. Like a raging river forcing its
way past a temporary obstruction, the vanguard pushed and fought
its way through the wall of Gauls and debris blocking their escape.
Breaking free of the gorge, it was able to debouch into a wide expanse
of the valley. Once this happened, the greater part of the column was
gradually able to extricate itself from the ambush and regroup.
During the course of the day, Hannibal had been able to move along
the column and finally work his way forward where he took command of the vanguard trying to break out of the gorge. It took the
better part of the afternoon for most of the column to exit the defile.
In spite of heavy casualties and tremendous disorder, Hannibal and
his officers were able to keep most of the army intact.

It may seem curious, nevertheless, that an army that expected to
conquer Rome would have such enormous difficulties simply crossing
the territory of Gallic tribes. There is no way to ascertain the size of
the barbarian force that confronted Hannibal at the defile, although
it must have been considerable. A civilized column making its way
through their territory was a once in a lifetime event for many of the
Gauls, and thousands must have flocked to the scene for whatever
unique spoils could be won. The barbarians' prowess in combat
should also not be underestimated, particularly in ambush as opposed
to a battle favoring field tactics. Long after the Punic Wars had
ended, the Romans themselves would need to fight a protracted campaign to subdue the Alpine tribes, while able to call on far more
resources that Hannibal had at his disposal.

The main factor in favor of the Gauls was the fact that Hannibal had no wish to fight them. While the warlike tribes had every incentive to draw blood and seize what plunder they could from the Carthaginian army, Hannibal simply wanted to get through. After the first ambush, he had taken a day to destroy a barbarian city, by way of revenge, and as a signal of what he was capable of doing. However his primary mission was to get over the Alps and face Rome. The second ambush might have been a result of his single-minded determination to leave the Gauls behind and proceed to his true objective.

But why did Hannibal allow himself to be drawn into such an obvious ambush? Even some of the ancient commentators expressed surprise in their writings that a commander of his expertise would have allowed his army to be drawn into such a potentially fatal situation. In fact, Livy comments that Hannibal "nearly succumbed to the very tactics in which he excelled"[9]: outthinking and outmaneuvering his enemy.

Perhaps Hannibal erred because he was too anxious to get over the Alps before the passes were sealed by snow and ice for the winter. Or he may have simply underestimated the potential of the mountain tribes to mount such a concentrated and sustained attack along the length of the gorge. Perhaps, also, he had no choice since he may have been without guides and lost when he first encountered the tribesmen and had to turn to them for whatever help he could obtain. Perhaps because of his youth he simply erred. After all, Hannibal was not yet thirty years old when he led the column toward Italy, and he had been a commander for only a few years before that.

In the realm of speculation one must recognize, too, that tacticians of genius are not always members of the aristocratic families of great civilizations. What if the source of the Carthaginians' woes that day was a brilliant individual among the mountain tribes, an illiterate barbarian who nevertheless had an instinctive grasp of leadership, tactics and deception? If such an individual existed, his identity will never be known. In any case, and in the light of future events, we can assume that Hannibal Barca learned much from the Gauls that day, anonymous as they must remain.

When the vanguard left the gorge and came into the center of the valley they found, just a few miles away, an enormous rock. This rock was a massive dome, larger than a cathedral, and it rose out of the ground out of all proportion to the rest of its surroundings. Millions of years before it must have been dislodged from the heights above by some force of nature and hurled to the middle of the valley to await just this moment.

Now the rock became a sanctuary for those weary Carthaginians who escaped the slaughter in the gorge. They climbed over every part of it; they hid in its fissures and caves, and built themselves a defensive barrier against the Gauls at its top. Hannibal and most of the column spent the night here as they waited for their comrades still trapped within the gorge to find their way out. All through the night groups of soldiers, civilians and animals, many dazed and wounded, slowly made their way forward and found the rock. It was well into the next day before the stragglers finally stopped coming.

That same day Hannibal had the column once more on the move, heading east along the valley floor. The enemy had broken off contact with the column beyond the gorge except for small ambushes that still occurred on isolated sections of the baggage train as it moved slowly along. By a series of these brief surprise attacks the Gauls were able to carry off a number of the pack animals and any unlucky civilians and soldiers who happened to be near and could not defend themselves.

In the wider valley ahead Hannibal would be able to re-establish a greater degree of military order within the column and organize more effective perimeter defenses. Now, lost in the highest and most dangerous reaches of the Alps, and without guides, Hannibal began his next and perhaps most difficult move.

As the column left the protection of the great rock and headed east along the valley floor toward Italy, Hannibal had to turn his back on those of his soldiers who had remained in the gorge. He could not risk sending relief forces to rescue any who might still be alive. Among those left behind, the dead were the most fortunate. Their bodies would be looted by the Gauls, stripped of their armor and personal effects, and left to rot or be carried away by the river. More to be pitied were the wounded and those who had been captured, for they would be subjected to all manner of tortures as the Gauls used them to vent their frustration and anger at Hannibal's escape.

Where precisely was the location of this second ambush in the Alps? In order to help determine where it might have occurred we need first to turn to the ancient sources to see if we can find a physical description of the location, and then develop time frames for reaching that destination and the fighting. From that point we need to discover a location along one of the two possible routes identified by scholars that fits closely the description extracted from the manuscripts and that fits as well within the time frames.

Polybius is very clear that the column was ambushed as it was passing a "steep and precipitous defile." From his account we know that the mountain tribesmen held the heights above the column and were able to move along the slopes to position themselves for the attack. Finally, Polybius mentions that the column made its way out of a "gorge."[10] Livy describes the column marching along a "narrowing track" which on one side was overhung by a "precipitous wall of rock." Furthermore, we know from Livy that Hannibal hesitated to send his own division of infantry "into the pass." Finally, at the peak of the attack, Livy comments that the army made its way "out of the gorge."[11]

It is obvious from both sources that Hannibal and the column passed through a gorge or defile, and that the place was steep and precipitous. We know that it had to have cliffs above it low enough so that the Gauls could attack the column, but at the same time keep themselves well protected from a counterassault by Hannibal's forces. The track along the gorge was narrow, and we know that at a certain point the walls of the cliff on one side formed a "precipitous wall."

The next factor to help locate the gorge is to consider the period of time involved. We know from Polybius that Hannibal marched for three days after he sacked the town of the first mountain tribe that had ambushed him.[12] Livy confirms this and tells us further that the army made considerable progress because the march was made over relatively easy terrain, and that there were no further attacks by the local tribes.[13]

The first thing we need to calculate is how far Hannibal could have traveled in three days in the Alpes du Dauphiné. We know already that his army covered about a hundred miles when it marched ten days along the river to where the first ambush occurred. Based on figures taken from the accounts of Julius Caesar during the Gallic Wars (58–52 B.C.) we know that the Roman army, sometimes containing about the same number of men as Hannibal's, and moving over many of the same areas, was able to cover about twenty miles in a six- to seven-hour period, a day's march.[14] In the mountains and valleys of the Alps that figure could be cut in half depending on the terrain. Allowing that Hannibal's army, in the mountains, could have covered anywhere from 8 to 12 miles in a day, his marching distance of three days from the site of the first ambush and the captured town to the place where the elders of the second tribe came to greet him could have been anywhere from 25 to 40 miles.

Even though Livy mentions that the marching was "comparatively easy" at this stage and perhaps all downhill, it was still in the mountains, and, as any experienced hiker knows, going down the side of a mountain can be as hard on the body as the climb up. Thus, the maximum distance to expect the army to have covered in this terrain over three days should be restricted to 40, or at most perhaps 50, miles.

Following the Drôme River route and designating the Col de Grimone or the Col de Cabre as possible sites for the first ambush, we can plot a course within these distance limits. From the Col de Grimone, heading almost due east to the town of Gap, the distance is about 25 miles. While the terrain in this area is mountainous, the army would have marched nearly downhill all the way to the site of the small town of Veynes and then along the valley floor to Gap. The route from Veynes to Gap is very easy to walk and shows only a slight upward grade of less than a hundred meters over the distance of about 15 miles.

The mountains around this route range in height from 1200 to 1500 meters, but since Hannibal and his army would not have needed to cross any of them, they are of marginal consequence in establishing this particular route. The route by way of this valley all the way to Gap is direct and not particularly difficult to follow. Covering a distance of 25 miles in three days along this terrain is feasible for the army under the circumstances. From Gap the column could have moved south for an additional 8 or 10 miles and come directly to the Durance River. That would have been a total of some 33 or 35 miles covered by the army in three days.

In all probability it was at Gap or just south of Gap at the Durance River where Hannibal encountered the elders from the mountain tribe and obtained his guides. From this point he would have marched northeast along the wide river valley passing through what is today the lake Serre-Ponçon. This is a massive artificial lake caused by the damming of the Durance in this century. Following this route, the column would have passed by the modern-day site of the city of Embrun and then marched on to where the modern town of Guillestre is situated. The distance from Gap to Embrun and then to Guillestre is about 30 miles and could have been completed by the army in the two days specified by Polybius and Livy.

The floor of the Durance Valley is wide and level between these locations and makes for easy marching. There are no difficult places along the route and the valley eventually leads to the Col du Mont-genèvre by way of Briançon, a massively fortified city constructed by the French during the 16th and 17th centuries on the frontier with Italy. From this point Hannibal could have crossed over the Alps by the comparatively easy Col du Montgenèvre.

At Guillestre, however, the valley divides. To the left the larger portion of the valley continues past the fortified heights of Mt. Dauphin, another walled city constructed during the same time period as Briançon. To the right the valley ends within three or four miles at the entrance to the Combe (dale) du Queyras. This is a treacherous little gorge some six to seven miles long which contains a site that is promising as the location for the second ambush. After several miles the gorge eventually widens into a small valley. This valley continues for about fifteen more miles and ends in a cul-de-sac of very high mountains. The only way out of this cul-de-sac and over these mountains is by climbing the highest and most difficult pass in the southern Alps. The distance from the ambush site in the gorge, along the valley to the summit of the pass, is very short and could well have been completed in a day's march. The route from the end of the gorge to where the climb to the pass begins is level, wide and easily passable for an army the size of Hannibal's.

The Gauls probably led Hannibal into this particular gorge because they saw it as the best place to ambush his column. In the Combe du Queyras, the high cliffs on both sides would have trapped him. His only way of escape would have been along the valley floor and then over the pass. The Gauls planned their strategy well, figuring that any of the soldiers not killed in the ambush would be finished off on the treacherous snow-covered slopes leading to the pass. They were very close to being right, for Hannibal lost more of his men going over the pass than he had in all his battles with the Celts.

Certainly this was not Hannibal's intended route. If he knew where he was heading, and there is evidence he did not, it was probably along the Durance River to the much easier Col du Montgenèvre. This is a low pass by alpine standards (1850 meters) and can often be crossed even in winter. The approach to the pass by the valley of the Durance is easy to follow and because the valley is so wide and level nearly all the way to Briançon it affords an army on the move a route safe from surprise attack. There are no narrow gorges or defiles to pass through by this route. Yet this was not to be Hannibal's route, as he would be forced to cross the Alps by another difficult passage in the next valley.

The Guil River flows through the Combe du Queyras. The river begins in the melting snows on the slopes of Mt. Viso (3900 meters), the second highest mountain in the Cottian Alps, and then is fed by hundreds of streams that cascade down the slopes of the mountain until it becomes a torrent. It courses along the valley floor where it is quickly transformed into a swift and violent river that races through the gorge and eventually empties into the larger and slower Durance. So turbulent and violent is this little river that a number of times in this century it has devastated this small valley, destroying villages and hamlets along its banks. Some of the effects of the violent moods of the Guil are evident today in the ruins of once magnificent Victorian and Edwardian mansions which lined its banks in such remote villages as Ville-Vieille, Aiguilles and Abriès.

The valley through which the lower part of the river flows, the Combe du Queyras, starts as a long, deep and narrow gorge that begins a few miles outside the town of Guillestre and then widens into a small and pretty, yet ominous, valley. From the end of the gorge to the cul-de-sac of mountains, the valley is narrow compared to the Durance, yet wide enough for an army to move in relative safety and comfort. The valley is hemmed in on both sides by looming mountains that cast dark shadows over the road, but there are no dangerous places here where the column could have been subject to further ambushes like those in the gorge. The valley ends at a range of high and dangerous mountains that constitute the French border with Italy.

Even today, after decades of continuous and extensive work by the French government, the roadway along the gorge of the valley is still so narrow and difficult in places that two cars can barely pass between the walls of sheer rock on one side and the rapidly flowing river on the other. It is, indeed, says an old Baedeker guidebook, a "wild and narrow defile" with "lofty walls of rock, where road and river dispute the way."[15] The gorge is an ominous place, where it is speculated that Celtic priests, the ancient Druids, may have held ritual human sacrifices.[16] It is a place that easily lends itself to the type of ambush into which Hannibal was drawn, both from its physical appearance and the feeling it conveys to anyone who stands on its floor and looks above to the heights—which are often covered in dark shadows.

The narrow road today clings to the walls of the gorge as the swift and turbulent river forces its way through the narrow canyon below. At the beginning of the gorge and for a long part of the drive after, this road hangs precariously several hundred feet above the valley floor. It is suspended on a precipitous and narrow ledge from which one can stop one's car and look straight down into the gorge and the raging river below—a beautiful and at the same time frightening sight. The fragile road has a guard rail intended more to instill a false sense of security in the driver than to prevent a car from falling over the side. The road is frequently pitted with holes or blocked by boulders that have fallen from the heights above and it seems to survive year to year only by permission of the mountains that surround it.

The sheer cliffs that arch over both sides of the river and the long shadows cast by the mountains only deepen and heighten the sense of gloom within the Combe du Queyras. The light of the sun does not touch the floor of this gorge until late in the morning, and it becomes heavily shaded by early afternoon, even in the height of summer, when days are long and the sun is high in the sky. Streams cascade down the mountains from all sides and empty into the verdant waters of the river, whipping it into froth. The water rushing through the gorge is often the only noise resounding through the lonely defile. At points along the route the river floods sections of the road or streams cut channels under it and threaten its stability.

It was into this valley that the treacherous Celtic guides lured Hannibal. No doubt they led him there by convincing him that it would be a shorter and safer route over the Alps. The valley is surrounded on both sides by some of the highest and most dangerous mountains of the French Alps and is subject to raging floods and devastating avalanches. Once inside the valley, it would have been virtually impossible for Hannibal to turn his entire column around on the narrow pathway and march out the way they had come. The only way out for the Carthaginian column at that point would have been to move straight ahead along the valley floor for a distance of about twenty miles and then, at the very end of the valley, climb over the highest and most remote of all the southern Alpine passes.

While the Combe du Queyras is the most likely spot for the ambush to have taken place, it is necessary to consider for the sake of argument other competing sites along the Isère River route that have been suggested by scholars. Following the Isère, however, it was difficult for this author to locate a suitable site for either the first or the second ambush. Using the Gorges de la Bourne, which has been suggested by some scholars, and then plotting a course of between 25 and 40 miles, and allowing for three days' marching, would have brought Hannibal back to the Isère River near Grenoble. Since the Gorges de la Bourne is not located on the Isère but in a tributary, this route would have given Hannibal and his army 25 to 30 more miles of difficult hiking.

There have been scholars who suggested that Grenoble was the town sacked by Hannibal following the first ambush, but in this author's opinion that city is too far away from the only possible first ambush site in that vicinity, the Gorges de la Bourne. Other advocates of the Isère route have suggested that Grenoble might have been the place where the tribal elders greeted Hannibal, but this is equally doubtful since the distances and times do not coordinate.

Both Polybius and Livy specify that the three days that Hannibal marched east after the first ambush were days of easy marching and that the column covered a considerable distance. It would have taken Hannibal two days of difficult and slow marching merely to get through the Gorges de la Bourne. Then there is a second obstacle, the Gorges du Furon, through which Hannibal would have had to pass before finally reaching Grenoble. Given the difficulty of the terrain in those gorges, it is also unlikely he would have found a town large enough to sack anywhere in the area.

Another possible site that has been suggested along the Isère River route is the Bec de l'Echaillon,[17] which is about ten miles outside of Grenoble. That site, as has already been discussed, is not conducive to the first ambush either because the attack could have easily been avoided by crossing the river and marching along the other side out of range of the Gauls. Using this site just for the sake of argument as well, and having Hannibal march three days from there (covering 25–40 miles) along the Isère, would have brought him to the vicinity of Saint-Pierre. It is at Saint-Pierre that the Arc flows into the Isère and the valley leads to the Col du Mont Cenis and Col de Clapier. If Hannibal had obtained his guides here, and then marched two more days into the second ambush, he would have come to a location somewhere along the valley of the Arc. It is difficult to find a place anywhere along this valley that lends itself to the ambush as readily as does the Combe du Queyras.

If Hannibal had avoided the Arc River and continued farther along the Isère he would have arrived at Bourg-Saint-Maurice and the entrance to the Little St. Bernard Pass. It is unlikely that he followed this route since the distance from Grenoble to this town (50 miles) is simply too far to cover in two days and there are no suitable places for the second ambush that the author could locate in the area.

Of all the ancient sources, Polybius provides us with the most useful information regarding the distances for Hannibal's march and the times in which those distances were accomplished. That information can then be incorporated into a table and correlated with the distances plotted on a map of the south of France to identify possible ambush sites and passes over the Alps. From the accounts of Polybius we know that the entire march from Spain to the plains of Italy took five months to complete and covered a distance of nine hundred miles.[18] This means that the army averaged six miles per day on the march, but allowing for the fact that a good portion of that time was not spent on the march but in diverse tasks such as negotiations, battles with hostile tribes, mediating fraternal conflicts over inheritances, provisioning the army, crossing difficult rivers such as the Ebro and the Rhône, becoming lost in valleys and climbing over mountain passes, the army probably was able to cover substantially more ground in one day than the daily average would indicate.

We know that it took nearly a month for Hannibal to cover the distance from where he crossed the Rhône River near Arles to the point where he descended onto the plains of Italy. The first ten days of that month were spent marching along an unnamed river to the foot of the Alps. Fifteen more days were spent crossing the mountains and fighting the tribesmen there. The final three days of the period were used to descend the pass and arrive in the plains of Italy.

Polybius gives the distance from the Rhône crossing to the "foot of the final pass over the Alps" as 1400 Greek *stadia*, or about 150 miles. This becomes our most important reference point. From the pass to the plains of Italy we know it took Hannibal three days; however, the distance given by Polybius for that stage of the march is confusing. Polybius maintains it was 1200 *stadia*, or about 130 miles.[19] It is doubtful that Hannibal could have covered this distance in the allotted time. There must be an error here either on the part of Polybius or errors in the medieval transcriptions. The Greek manuscripts contain the phrase "from the length of the pass which

Hannibal was to cross to the plains of Italy was 1200 stadia."

Is Polybius writing here about the actual pass that Hannibal crossed or does he mean the pass that Hannibal may have been headed for before he was ambushed and lost his way? There is a crucial difference. The text at this point is confusing and the better interpretation might be that this was the distance between the plains and the intended pass, not the actual pass. While we know that Polybius, to trace the original route, crossed the Alps some sixty years after Hannibal, we are not sure that he actually crossed the pass used by Hannibal. We know he crossed a pass in the Alps, but the pass he crossed might have been the one that Hannibal had only intended to use, such as the Montgenèvre, or the Little St. Bernard. Polybius might have used either of these because they are a far easier and safer route than the pass which Hannibal actually crossed.

Polybius writes that the first stage of the march, from the "island," was along an unidentified river to the foothills of the mountains (the "ascent toward the Alps"[20]) and involved a journey of ten days and 800 *stadia* (90 to 100 miles). This river must have been initially the Rhône and then either the Drôme or the Isère, depending on which theory one subscribes to. Polybius specifies the distance from where Hannibal crossed the Rhône to the "foot of the pass" where he crossed into Italy as 1400 *stadia* (about 150 miles). If the distance from the crossing of the Rhône near Arles to the "island" at the Aygues River is some 80 miles, and then from there the distance "along the river" is another 100 miles, then the distances are close enough when compared with the suggested routes.

Regarding Polybius' figure of the final distance, "from the length of the pass to the plains of the Po River," as 1200 *stadia*, it is unclear what "from the length of the pass" means and there is little discussion of this phrase among scholars. Some have simply interpreted it to mean the entire distance from the first ambush, over the second pass, and onto the plains of Italy.[21] This distance, specified by Polybius, of about 120 to 130 miles is feasible and could have been covered in the fifteen days that the ancient sources say Hannibal used for crossing the Alps. It really is the only way this particular passage in the manuscripts can be interpreted if the distances are to come out right.

NOTES

[1] Livy, Bk. XXI, Sec. 32. From the 17th-century transcription by Johannes Fredericus Gronovius. Paris, 1670.

[2] W.W. Hyde, *Roman Alpine Routes*, p.17.

[3] Strabo, Bks. 4, 6, 8.

[4] Diodorus, Bk. 5.39, pp.1–8.

[5] H.N. Pliny, 37.44.

[6] Polybius, Bk. III, Sec. 44; Livy, Bk. XXI, Sec. 31.

[7] Livy, Bk. XXI, Sec. 35. "Per invia pleraque et errores, quos aut decentium fraus aut, ubi fides iis non esset, temere initae valles a coniectantibus iter faciebant." Or: "They had come over trackless areas and by round about routes, sometimes wandering, either because of the treachery of their guides, or when they could not trust the guides, to their own blindness, often guessing at the way."

[8] Livy, Bk. XXI, Sec. 35; Polybius, Bk. III, Sec. 52.

[9] Livy, Bk. XXI, Sec. 34.

[10] Polybius, Bk. III, Sec. 52–53.

[11] Livy, Bk. XXI, Sec. 35.

[12] Polybius, Bk. III, Sec. 52.

[13] Livy, Bk. XXI, Sec. 33.

[14] H.P. Judson, *Caesar's Army*, p. 63.

[15] Baedeker, *Southern France*, p. 419.

[16] Ibid., p. 420.

[17] Proposed by J. Colin, 1904; Spenser Wilkinson, 1911; and Ferrand, 1925.

[18] Polybius, Bk. III, Sec. 39.

[19] Ibid.

[20] Polybius, Bk. III, Sec. 50, has it: "anabole pros tas Alpeis."

[21] Gavin deBeer, *Hannibal's March*, p. 32.

CHAPTER VI

❦ · ❦

OVER THE PASS

After the near-catastrophe in the gorge, Hannibal and the column continued east along the valley floor. The march was surprisingly easy, given what they had just come through. The valley at this point was fairly wide, the terrain was not difficult and the distance to their destination was short. The only resistance they encountered came in the form of occasional raids by mountain tribesmen against the sections of the column containing the pack animals, or against any stragglers who lagged too far behind. The scouts encountered a few ambushes as they moved ahead of the column, but because of the nature of the terrain and the smaller numbers of barbarians in the attacking parties the scouts were able to drive the enemy off without suffering serious casualties. The Gauls were evidently more interested at this point in pack animals and any supplies they could steal from the column than they were in inflicting any type of military defeat on Hannibal. The elephants in the column were used effectively to repel attacking barbarians, who tended to run off at the first sight of them. There was open ground in which to maneuver in the valley, so the elephants could reach any sections of the column under attack and disperse the Gauls rapidly.

By mid-day the vanguard had already climbed the mountain at the end of the valley and reached the summit of the pass. Near this summit they established a base camp and awaited the remainder of the column. It had now been nine days since Hannibal and his forces had first entered the Alps and nearly three weeks since they'd left the Rhône River and the "island." For the better part of a month they had wandered through the Alps looking for the way into Italy and now they had found it. By late that same day most of the column were able to reach the base camp, and by nightfall the entire army was settled in. For the next two days the soldiers rested, as best they could, on the slopes of the mountain. A surprising number of the pack animals which had run off or were lost during the fighting over the past several days found their way to the camp. The animals, looking for food, had instinctively followed the track of the column and now wandered back to the army.

Hannibal's column had taken a terrible beating over the last several days. They had been ambushed twice and had been marching and fighting almost continuously to reach the pass. Exhaustion and despair were to be found everywhere, among both soldiers and officers. It could be seen in their faces and it affected their moods. Much of the supply train had been lost to the enemy and what little was left had nearly run out. The men were on short rations, which only added to their discomfort and despair. Bellies were empty and starvation was beginning to take its toll. First it moved among the wounded, taking a man here and a man there. Then it moved among the weakest; and finally it began to affect even the hardiest of the mercenaries. The soldiers had already eaten any of the animals that had died or that could be spared for slaughter.

Starvation, coupled with the harsh conditions in the mountains, took over where the hostile tribesmen had left off. Hunger and exposure were now the last and most fearsome enemies to be confronted, and they marched daily with the column—silent killers waiting their opportunity to snatch the weakest and most unsuspecting. All this suffering and adversity, with no end in sight, only made the mood among the soldiers darker and their countenances that much more somber.

The ground on the side of the mountain where the base camp was located was covered with snow. The soldiers first had to clear the area and then make themselves as comfortable as they could in these harsh and barren surroundings. They set up tents on the patches of cleared land and built fires to keep warm. For two days the column remained in this makeshift camp on the side of the snow-covered mountain just a few hundred feet below the summit of the pass. There they rested as best they could and awaited Hannibal's next move.

At dawn Hannibal left camp and made his way to the summit. There he stood as the soldiers slowly began to move up to the pass. From his vantage point on the ridge of the pass Hannibal had a view of Italy that took in all the land from the Po Valley to the plains beyond the foothills of the Alps. He had reached his first objective and he stopped to view it from the summit, basking in a brief moment of personal accomplishment. He had brought his army a thousand miles, crossing over difficult rivers and two large mountain ranges. He had fought at every stage of the journey, and now after five months of sweat and blood he stood upon the highest pass in the Alps, looking down upon the land he had come so far to destroy.

The worst of the journey, however, was far from over, for Hannibal still had to bring the army down from the heights of this mountain pass. As the soldiers made their way over the ridge he called out to them as they passed with words of encouragement. He urged them to take heart and continue on. He pointed out the view of Italy below and explained to all who had the strength or the inclination to listen how they were now close to the end of their ordeal. The Alps were the last obstacle protecting Rome, and Hannibal promised his soldiers that after "a fight or two" the city, the very capital of their hated enemy, would be in their hands.[1] The worst, he promised them, was nearly over and from here on there would be no more mountains to climb. As they began their descent from the pass, little did they know that the worst was in fact far from over. As Hannibal led the descent, his men and animals were worn out from constant marching and fighting. Their supplies were exhausted and their spirit nearly gone. Now, ahead of them lay a dangerous path.

It would be three more days before Hannibal would come down from the pass and onto the plains of Italy. Many more men and animals would still be lost on the ledges leading down from the pass, before this army would once more feel level ground beneath its feet. Death was far from finished with the column. What the Gauls had not completed in the gorge they would try again with nature's help to finish on this pass. As the army moved up and over the pass the Gauls continued to harass Hannibal's army in a series of quick and fierce forays. They appeared from the most unexpected of places to attack the column in small numbers; their attacks were of short duration and they faded quickly back into the cliffs, disappearing among the rocks from which they had come.

The ill winds of fate continued to blow on Hannibal Barca as he and his army made their way down from the Alps and onto the Italian plains. Coming down from the mountain proved to be far more dangerous than the climb to the pass. Because of the general nature of the Alps, the descent of the mountain on the Italian side was far steeper and more treacherous than the ascent had been on the other side. By the time he reached the plains, Hannibal would lose nearly as many men coming down from the pass as he had lost in fighting the Gauls and climbing the mountain.

As the column moved over the pass the scouts ahead had located and marked a track down the mountain, but it was covered with snow. In various places layers of ice had to be cut away to make footing on the path possible. The going was slow and tedious. If a man or an animal stumbled on this section of the narrow and dangerous track, it was usually certain to be fatal. A stumble could mean a fall to the ground. A fall, because of the steep angle of the slope along which the ledge ran, could mean a slide. A slide in most cases could not be arrested because a rolling body gained momentum so quickly on these steep slopes. If the slide could not be arrested immediately—within a few seconds—there was little that could be done to stop a man from falling to his death over the edge of a precipice.

The column began, slowly and painfully, to work its way down along the narrow track across the eastern face of the mountain. The footing became more treacherous the farther the column went and accidents occurred with increasing frequency, men and animals sliding to their deaths into the yawning chasms. There were some who, when they lost their footing, only slid so far as the edge of a precipice. There, unable to be rescued because of the terrain or because a rescue attempt would endanger the lives of others, they had to be left lying in the snow by the edge of the cliff. For some, stranded as they were on the edge, their only choice was either to die slowly from exposure or in desperation take their own lives by allowing themselves to slip over the side.

After several hours of carefully working their way along the ledge, the column had only descended a few hundred feet below the summit of the pass. Then suddenly the column came to a halt on the track. The scouts had come to a place on the ledge where the track had been destroyed by a recent landslide and they could not move forward. Try as they might, the vanguard could not proceed any further along the ledge, for the track ended at a precipice where a section of the mountain had simply been taken away vertically for several hundred yards. At the end of the ledge was a drop of thousands of feet.[2] This section of the track must have always been a difficult place to cross and now it was rendered impossible because of the recent landslide.

As word spread along the column of what had happened ahead, some soldiers began to panic while others became so despondent that they simply gave up, falling upon their packs where they stood in line, unable to endure another crisis. Hannibal was in his usual position at the rear of the column when it came to a halt and he waited several minutes before word finally reached him about what had stopped the army. Slowly and carefully he made his way forward along the ledge to the front of the column in order to survey for himself the problem.

In conference with his engineers and officers, the first idea that surfaced was to create an alternate route several hundred feet above the destroyed section of the ledge. The vanguard of the column followed their orders and began to climb higher up on the mountain slope where there was no track to follow. At first they made some progress because they were able to get good footing in the fresh snow, and advanced slowly up the side of the mountain to a point nearly above the destroyed section of the ledge. But the footing quickly became too treacherous for those who followed.

There was a layer of fresh snow everywhere. It had settled on top of an old layer that had lain on the pass since the previous winter. After the vanguard had climbed along the slope above the missing ledge and the rest of the column began to follow in their tracks, the footing became dangerous and finally impossible. As the fresh layer of snow was trampled by hundreds of boots and hoofs it turned into a slush that quickly froze into a treacherous layer of ice.

As the grade of the slope began to increase sharply above the old track, men began to loose their footing on the ice and slip. Soldiers would fall and then slide down the steep slope to the waiting precipice. There on the barren and snow-covered slopes at nearly ten thousand feet, there was nothing to hold on to. As men began to slide toward the edges of the chasms they clawed desperately around them to find anything that might arrest their slide toward certain death thousands of feet below.

There were men in the column who fell as they marched, and as they struggled to rise under the weight of the loads on their backs, weak from starvation and exhaustion, they could not summon the strength to regain their place in the column. These men simply lay by the side of the track to await death. The pack animals, burdened with what remained of the supplies and weapons, would often drive their hoofs through the soft top layer of snow and become stuck in the older snow below. As these unfortunate animals struggled to free themselves, driven by their panic and whipped by their masters, they fell, often breaking their brittle legs and thus sealing their fate.

After repeated attempts failed to make a new track above the section of the ledge that had been destroyed, Hannibal ordered that a large area on the ridge of the pass and the adjoining slopes be cleared of snow and a camp established. Conferring with his engineers, he determined that the only feasible way down from the mountain was to construct an entirely new track on the ledge to replace the section that had been destroyed. The engineers set about building up and widening the existing track and then proceeded to cut a new path along the side of the mountain. Meanwhile, nearly thirty thousand men waited all along the ridge of the mountain watching the skies and clouds around them and praying to their gods that the weather would hold. When night came, the temperatures plummeted to below freezing and death came into the camp to carry off the weakest in mind and body.

The progress of the engineers on the ledge was eventually blocked when they came to a large boulder in their path. This rock had to be dislodged if they were to continue constructing a new track. So much time and effort had been involved in developing this path that they had no choice but to find a way of removing the rock. Moving the boulder proved to be an impossible task because of its size and weight, so the engineers set about to destroy it. The process they used was an ancient one utilized by farmers for centuries to clear their lands of similar obstructions. The engineers would render the rock friable.

A relay of soldiers was set up that stretched back over the pass and down the other side of the mountain from which they had just come. There on the French side of the Alps, below the snow line, there were heavily forested slopes. They cut down large numbers of trees and gathered quantities of dead wood which they transported back to the top of the pass.[3] By means of elephants, horses and the backs of men, the wood was dragged, passed and carried in a long relay back to the top of the pass. At the site where the boulder blocked the track the engineers built an enormous fire and kept it burning vigorously. Aided by a favorable breeze, which blew on the mountain that day, the fire caused the rock to become hot. Hour after hour the massive fire was fed by wood passed over the ridge by the relay of soldiers.

When the engineers judged that the rock was sufficiently heated, the soldiers passed along the relay their rations of sour wine which were poured on the rock in large quantities. The sour wine was essentially vinegar and its acetic content caused the hot boulder to develop multiple fissures over its surface. The engineers then set to work on the boulder with picks and axes and in short order were able to destroy enough of it to continue creating their path along the ledge. The scouts were able to pass this place and move along the newly constructed ledge to the already existing track on the other side. From there, moving ahead of the column, they reached the valley floor below in a few hours. Within another day the engineers had widened the track all along the ledge enough to allow the drivers and the cavalrymen to bring the supply train and the horses down from the pass to the lower heights.

When the main body of the column reached the lower slopes of the mountain, the soldiers established a large base camp and turned the starving animals out to graze on slopes and pastures that were lush with vegetation. Thousands of feet above, the work on the ridge continued, however, for two more days in order to widen the track sufficiently to compensate for the steepness of grade and so bring the elephants across. By this time the beasts were nearly starved and out of their minds from hunger. They were in such poor condition that it was questionable whether any would survive. Taken to the lower altitudes, however, they were turned out to graze with the other animals and eventually recovered their strength. Miraculously, the ancient sources tell us that all of the elephants survived the crossing of the Alps.

It took nearly four days for the engineers to complete the track and for the entire column to finally come over the pass and descend onto the lower slopes on the Italian side of the mountains. This was by far the most difficult part of the journey, not only because of the nature of the terrain but by the sheer magnitude of the task of moving nearly thirty thousand men and animals over one of the highest and most difficult passes in the Alps, then down along a narrow and treacherous track to the valley below. The task was further complicated because the weather conditions were poor and the army was exhausted from near-starvation and exposure to the elements. There were more casualties sustained in crossing this pass and descending into Italy than in any of the river crossings or battles that the army had fought in the five months since they had first left New Carthage in Spain.

On the lower slopes of the mountains the temperatures were moderate and the land both grassy and well wooded. There was food for the army there because the inhabitants on this side of the Alps enjoyed a better quality of life than the unfortunate wretches who lived on the other. What was left of Hannibal's army—the remnants of a once formidable force of over 50,000 men—was finally able to rest in the foothills of the Italian Alps. For three days they remained in the camp and recovered their strength. Livy commented that recovery for the army was not a simple matter of rest. Men who had become used to weeks of extreme deprivation found recovery to be difficult to adjust to, both physically and psychologically. The early stages of recovery, he commented, are often worse than the sickness itself. The army had become as filthy and unkempt as the animals it led and the barbarians it had fought. The sudden change from hard labor and exhaustion on the higher elevations to leisure on the lower slopes, from starvation to plenty, from dirt and misery to clean living, affected them in a multitude of ways.[4]

As the soldiers assembled at the base camp and the roll was taken, the magnitude of the losses became shockingly evident. When the tally was made among the infantry, only 12,000 African soldiers, 8,000 Spaniards, and a small number of various other mercenaries were left. Among the cavalry, only 6,000 of the original number had survived. Polybius noted that when Hannibal crossed the Rhône River nearly a month earlier, he had 38,000 infantry and more than 8,000 horsemen. Now he had little more than 26,000 men left, and because of what they had been through "they had come to look more like beasts than men."[5]

Hannibal had lost the greatest number of his soldiers and horsemen in the time between the ambush in the gorge and the climb over the pass—all in the space of a little more than a week. Livy comments that 36,000 men were lost and a considerable number of pack animals, from the time Hannibal crossed the Rhône until he descended into Italy.[6] Polybius comments only that Hannibal lost nearly half his force making his way over the passes of the Alps.[7] This must have been, from the numbers killed and lost, statistically one of the greatest noncombat military debacles in history.

Exactly where Hannibal crossed the Alps is a question that has been asked time and again over the centuries by scholars, laymen, soldiers and emperors. Scholars have identified half a dozen likely possibilities, yet following the publication of each theory disputes and arguments have broken out and the debate has been intensified rather than settled. Looking at each of the possible passes that has been suggested over the years, and then comparing them to what the ancient sources have to say and what visits to the sites themselves reveal, the number can be quickly narrowed to two most likely possibilities.

Allowing for the complex terrain of the Alps and knowing that

Hannibal could not have followed a direct route from the Rhône River to the plains of Italy, the only two probable courses through the mountains become evident. However, by comparing each of these routes and the passes to which they lead, it is possible to arrive at a single conclusion regarding exactly which pass Hannibal used to cross the Alps.

We know from the ancient sources that Hannibal covered the distances of the march in stages and within given time periods. First, we know that he marched four days from the place where he crossed the Rhône to the "island," where he settled the dispute between the two brothers. Second, we know that from the "island" he marched ten days and nearly a hundred miles along an unnamed river, and into the foothills of the Alps. Third, we know that the first ambush happened on the tenth or eleventh day after he left the Rhône, as he was passing through a gorge and preparing to climb a pass. After five more days of marching, Hannibal came to another gorge where he was ambushed a second time. Finally, we know that the second ambush occurred in a place that was less than a day's march from the final pass where Hannibal crossed over the Alps and came down into Italy.

In terms of miles we know from Polybius that the distance Hannibal marched from the Rhône River across the entire range of the Alps, from west to east, was about 150 miles. With this information, it remains to examine the two routes proposed by scholars over the centuries and see how each one compares both with the descriptions provided in the ancient sources and with a site survey.

According to the traditional view, which has prevailed among scholars for centuries, Hannibal left the Rhône near Valence and followed the Isère River east for ten days. During those ten days Hannibal covered about 100 miles and arrived with his army near the site of the modern town of Saint-Pierre-d'Albigny, a few miles past Grenoble.

At this point Hannibal would have been faced with a choice. Either he would have to continue along the Isère toward the Alps or he would deviate from the river and follow another route along the Arc River. If he had turned southeast and followed the Arc along its valley, Hannibal would have marched past the site of what is today the town of Modane. By this route he could have crossed over the Alps and into Italy by either the Mt. Cenis Pass, a relatively easy route, or by the Col du Clapier, a more difficult one.

If Hannibal had decided to bypass the Arc River, and continued to follow the Isère east, his army would have passed by what is today the town of Bourg-Saint-Maurice. From there he could have crossed over the Alps and descended into Italy by way of the relatively easy Little St. Bernard Pass.

Scholars who favor the Isère route are divided as to which course Hannibal took. Among the earliest scholars, most favored the Little St. Bernard[8] and the Mt. Cenis passes. More contemporary scholars who support the Isère route, however, have argued in favor of the Col du Clapier. The Isère route and the three passes to which it leads have been popular since it was first proposed in the literature in the sixteenth century.[9] Over the last four hundred years this route and its two variations have been advocated by the majority of scholars interested in the subject.[10]

Even though indications are that the Little St. Bernard was an important route between Gaul and Italy[11] long before the time of Hannibal, it is unlikely that he crossed the mountains by either this pass or the Mt. Cenis. As we shall later see in greater detail, these two passes, like so many others that have been proposed, do not fit the descriptions provided by Polybius and Livy in their accounts of the crossing. Nevertheless, either the Little St. Bernard or the Mt. Cenis may well have been Hannibal's intended route over the Alps since we know that he was probably headed for an easy pass.

The reality of the situation is that neither one of these passes fits the descriptions in the ancient sources and this fact becomes readily apparent during a site visit. Either led astray by treacherous guides or simply lost, Hannibal was forced to deviate from his original route and climb over the mountains by a more difficult and unknown pass. There are also strong indications in the ancient accounts that Hannibal may have simply gotten confused in the Alps after the initial ambush. Faced with critical shortages of food, deteriorating weather conditions, and driven by the increasing desperation of his men, he was then forced to follow unreliable guides who led him to the highest and most difficult pass in the southern French Alps.

The main attraction of the Isère River route, and probably the reason why it has been popular for so long, is that from an observer's viewpoint, looking at maps several centuries later from the relative comfort of a study or library, it is the simplest and easiest route for Hannibal to have followed. The river begins in the glaciers of the highest mountains on the frontier with Italy and then flows through a relatively wide valley with a very shallow grade all the way to the Rhône. The distance from the confluence of the Isère and the Rhône to the confluence of the Isère with the Arc at Saint-Pierre-d'Albigny is a little over a hundred miles of relatively easy marching. The distance from Saint-Pierre-d'Albigny along the valley of the Arc to the frontier passes with Italy is another fifty or so miles. While the terrain becomes considerably more difficult to march over in the valley of the Arc than in the valley of the Isère, it is still a very passable route. The tracks leading to the valleys and then the passes are relatively easy to cover. The total distance from the Rhône River to these passes along either the Isère or the Arc routes is within the parameters specified by Polybius. This makes it an easy and direct route for an army making its way through the Alps to have followed. Then, what clinches the possibility for many scholars is the similarity of the names Isère and Iskaras. They so closely resemble each other that scholars have been tempted to accept this route as logical and convenient.

Upon closer examination, however, especially when one actually goes into the field and traces the routes, they become neither so logical nor so convenient. The distances are not the main problem. If Hannibal had followed the Isère/Arc route, he would have had to have averaged 6 to 7 miles per day to cover the 150 miles from the foothills of the Alps to Italy within the twenty-five-day period Polybius recorded. This is a reasonable distance to have covered in that time given that route, especially since the Isère riverbed is not too difficult to hike along. At times, Hannibal was probably able to actually double that average daily figure in those places where the terrain was easier to march over. In addition, he had an escort provided by Brancus for a large part of the march along the river as a guarantee of safe passage through hostile territory. So one could expect that he would have made very good time along this part of the march.

If Hannibal had elected to follow the Isère River all the way to the Little St. Bernard Pass it might have taken him a little longer since the distance is farther than by the other routes proposed, although not significantly so. From Saint-Pierre-d'Albigny Hannibal could have followed the Isère to Bourg-Saint-Maurice and then over the Little St. Bernard. The total distance from the Rhône to the Little St. Bernard is about 180 miles and would have required Hannibal and the army to cover at least 8 miles per day on average.

A major problem associated with the Isère route is that Polybius specifies that the first ten days were used marching along the river toward the first ambush point. It is difficult to find a place along the Isère River suitable for the ambush described by both Polybius and Livy. If we establish, purely for the sake of argument, that the first ambush occurred in the Gorges de la Bourne, as has been suggested by some scholars, then Hannibal would have had to cover the distance from the gorge to the Little St. Bernard Pass, about 135 miles, in less than two weeks. In that period of time we know that only eight of those days were given over to marching and that the other seven were taken up with fighting and resting. Eight days, based on the author's experience in this area of the Alps, might not be enough time to cover that distance, even with reliable guides and relatively easy march terrain.

The same problem of reconciling distances and time is also evident in tracing the route of Hannibal along the Arc River to either the Clapier or Mt. Cenis passes. While the distances from the Rhône River to either of these two passes is a bit shorter than the distance to the Little St. Bernard, Hannibal would still have had to average about 13–14 miles per day to stay within the time frames given by Polybius. Again, this is possible but highly unlikely, given the nature of the terrain in the valley of the Arc and the vast numbers of people and animals that had to be moved along the route.

The first time Hannibal was ambushed by the mountain tribes he spent the better part of a day fighting them and a second day capturing their town, and then recuperating from the battle. After he captured and sacked the mountain town, Hannibal marched for three days without further delays over easy country and arrived at a wide valley. From there he continued to march another two days along that valley with local guides leading the way to a spot where he was ambushed a second time. The second ambush occurred while his column was entering another gorge. The column fought a day and a night to extricate itself from the second ambush and then took another day to reach the summit of the final pass over the mountains. This represents a total of nineteen days since the Carthaginians left the Rhône River.

From the end of the first ambush to the time when Hannibal finally reached the summit of the pass, eight days were consumed. If Hannibal had averaged eight miles per day he could have covered sixty to seventy miles in this time period. Using the Gorges de la Bourne as the site of the first ambush, because it is the only place the author was able to identify as a possible ambush site along the Isère route, and measuring the distances from there to the Clapier or Mt. Cenis passes, one concludes that it is doubtful Hannibal could have reached either pass within the time frame given by Polybius. The distance from the Bourne gorges to either the Mt. Cenis or the Clapier is in the same general range as the distance from the Little St. Bernard. Thus, even if the Gorges de la Bourne is accepted as the first ambush site, the distance from there to the pass is too far to have been covered within the time reported in the histories. The matter is further complicated by the fact that the distance from the Rhône along the Isère to the Gorges de la Bourne is considerably less than the 100 miles specified by Polybius in the manuscripts.

Looking at the second route that Hannibal might have used, the Drôme/Durance route, the distances and time frames become much easier to reconcile. This route becomes far more feasible, especially since the terrain in many places lends itself more readily to sites for the first and second ambushes.

From the site of the first ambush and the captured town, Hannibal marched three days, and according to both Polybius and Livy he made good progress because the other mountain tribes left him alone and the route was unobstructed. On the fourth day (the seventeenth after leaving the Rhône) he entered a valley and encountered a delegation of Gauls from the mountain tribes of the area who offered to lead him over the final pass and into Italy. These Gauls led the column for two days along the valley before they took it into a gorge where it was ambushed again. The sources are very clear that Hannibal was ambushed the second time at only a day's march from the pass that he used to cross the Alps. This means that considering the four passes identified so far—the Little St. Bernard, the Mt. Cenis, the Clapier and the Traversette—one needs only to construct a hypothetical line of march from the summit of each pass back for a distance of some 8 to 15 miles to find a suitable place for the second ambush.

Looking first at the Little St. Bernard Pass and backtracking a distance of eighteen miles, one comes to the town of Bourg-Saint-Maurice along the Isère River. The road from the town to the pass begins at an altitude of about 1300 meters and rises through a series of switchbacks to 1800 meters. Finally, at the top of the pass the altitude registers 2188 meters. The route is relatively easy to follow. There are no gorges or other places suitable for the ambush along the way. Moreover, it is not feasible to think that Hannibal could have covered nearly 20 miles after the second ambush, given the severe mauling his column had suffered at the hands of the Gauls.

Starting on the summit of the second pass, the Mt. Cenis, at 2081 meters, and backtracking roughly the same distance, one comes to the villages of Lanslebour-Mont Cenis, Termignan, Sollières and finally Bramans. All these villages and towns are situated along the Arc River and are within a day's hike from the pass. The author, however, could not find one suitable ambush site between any of these villages and the pass. The distance from Bramans, the town farthest away, to the summit of the Mt. Cenis is 14 miles.

From the Col du Clapier to these same towns and villages the distance is 12 miles. There are no suitable spots anywhere along the route between Bramans and the Clapier for an ambush. This is not to say that the terrain is not rugged, merely that there are no steep gorges or narrow defiles as described by Polybius and Livy. Nor for that matter are there any particularly hazardous areas to climb or hike along this particular route.

The final pass to consider is the Col de la Traversette, just north of Mt. Viso, beyond the origins of the Guil River. This is the highest and most remote pass in the southern French Alps—and in this author's view the most likely to have been used by Hannibal. There are a number of good reasons for selecting this pass. First, measuring the distance from the summit of the pass back along the route for 15 miles, one comes to a nearly perfect site for the second ambush. This gorge fits all the descriptions provided by Polybius and Livy, and after a site visit the arguments in its favor become all that more persuasive. It now remains to look at the pass itself in greater detail.

After the second ambush Hannibal had no choice but to press ahead and seek a way out of the valley in which he had become trapped, in order to get his army over the mountains and into Italy. He could not go back through the murderous gorge from which he had just come, so the only way out was to follow the valley to its end and climb over whatever lay in his path; In this case, at a height of nine thousand feet, the treacherous Col de la Traversette.

There are other ways out of the valley of the Guil today. For example there are the Col d'Izoard and the Col Agnel as well as a half dozen other smaller and more remote passes. Some of these lead to other valleys in France while others lead directly to Italy. It is unlikely that Hannibal knew about any of them, and furthermore, even if he did, they can be difficult to find and even worse to follow if one does not know the area well. The paths to many of these passes lie close to the site of the second ambush and may well have been under the control of the Gauls at the time and thus not accessible to Hannibal.

The most accessible pass, the Col d'Izoard, lies in a westerly direction relative to the valley, and would have required Hannibal to move away from his objective, Italy. The route over this pass does not lead directly to Italy but in the opposite direction and back into the valley of the Durance. This would have required several more days, perhaps even a week of difficult marching, and another pass to climb, before the column would eventually have crossed into Italy by a circuitous route leading to the Col de Montgenèvre. By this time in the march starvation and fatigue were beginning to exact as many casualties as battle, and it is doubtful that Hannibal would have been inclined to take this route even if he could have fought his way past the Gauls and gotten to it.

The Col Agnel on the other hand would have taken Hannibal directly into Italy over an easy route, but, as mentioned, the entrance to the valley that leads to this pass is, even today, difficult to find and located very close to the scene of the ambush. It is, however, interesting to note that while hiking along that valley one day the author came upon a small plaque attached to a rock which designates the Col Agnel as the pass of Hannibal. There is nothing particularly significant about finding this relatively modern plaque attached to the rock. The author stumbled across a similar plaque attached to another "Pierre d'Annibal" the year before, also by accident. While crossing the Col de la Moulière (2800 meters) the author had become temporarily trapped in a remote valley where the only way out had been blocked by an avalanche. Trying to find another route to leave the valley, he came upon this second "Hannibal's Rock" located between the Col de la Moulière and the entrance to the Col de la Cayolle. Neither of these passes is anywhere near the Italian border and the findings of these plaques should not be considered significant. Someone just nailed them there.

As a result of the second ambush, Hannibal had lost nearly two days to fighting and regrouping. On the morning of the second day he left the column early with an advanced detachment to scout the valley ahead to its end. There he was confronted by an intimidating group of mountains dominated by a giant, Mt. Viso. Located to the left of Mt. Viso, the second highest mountain in the Alps (its summit is in Italy), is the Col de la Traversette. The pass sits cradled in the bosom of this giant and somehow Hannibal found the energy and courage to climb or crawl his way to its highest reaches. There the vanguard of the column must have established a base camp a few thousand feet below the summit of the pass, and over the next two days Hannibal brought the army up to the camp where they rested for two more days.

When did Hannibal cross the Alps? At what time of year? We know from the ancient sources that it took him five months to travel from New Carthage to where he came down from the Alps and into Italy. We know as well that he left Spain and crossed the Pyrenees sometime in the late spring or early summer of 218 B.C., perhaps late May or early June. He crossed the Rhône and followed it to the "island," arriving there sometime in midsummer. He probably stayed with Brancus, settling the fraternal squabbles and re-equipping and resting his army until near the end of August. Hannibal would have begun the ascent toward the Alps in early September, and since we know from Polybius that he spent nearly three weeks marching and fighting his way through the mountains he would have reached the pass by the end of that month or early in October.

Polybius writes that Hannibal was making his way through the Alps "near the period of the setting of the Pleiades, when the snow was beginning to be thick on the heights."[12] The Pleiades are a group of stars in the constellation Taurus, of which six are visible to the naked eye in the northern sky. They were named after the seven nymphs of Diana, who, according to ancient mythology, were transformed into a group of stars to escape the amorous depredations of the giant Orion. Livy confirms what Polybius specified as the season of the year when he writes that "it was now the season of the setting of the constellation of the Pleiades."[13]

While precisely when Hannibal crossed over the pass is subject to differences of opinion, there is general agreement among scholars that the period is sometime in a six-week period beginning in late September. There have been scholars who contend that the term "setting of the Pleiades" is no more than a general term that was used by the ancients to signify the onset of the winter season.[14] As a result of these differences some scholars favor placing Hannibal's crossing in September, while others have designated October,[15] or even a date as late as November.[16] In any event, we know that when Hannibal reached the upper reaches of the mountains snow had begun to fall on the slopes and conditions were deteriorating.

While there are many passes in the Alps by which one can cross into Italy, the one used by Hannibal had certain distinct characteristics as described by the ancient sources. Very few passes in the Alps conform closely to these descriptions. From the ancient sources we also know that a number of passes were known to travelers and soldiers at that period in history. Some of these are recounted by Polybius and others by different ancient historians.

The first pass described was through Liguria and close to the Tyrrhenian Sea.[17] This is probably the coastal pass in the Maritime Alps known today as La Turbie. The pass is located at the site of a monument erected by the Emperor Augustus in the first century B.C. on the heights of the Grand Corniche above what is today Monaco. The second pass mentioned in the ancient literature is referred to only as the pass by which Hannibal crossed the Alps.[18] It is specified as located in the territory of the Taurini in the Cottian Alps, but no further information is given. The third pass was in the country of a Celtic tribe called the Salassi and is generally regarded as being the Little St. Bernard. The last of the passes is located in the territory of the Raeti, another Celtic tribe, and is probably the Brenner Pass.

Another ancient writer, Varro, makes reference to a pass through which the Roman general Pompey passed on his way to the wars in Spain in 60 B.C.[19] Pompey himself, in a letter to the Roman Senate wrote of having opened a road over the Alps different from Hannibal's.[20] This is generally considered by scholars to have been the Montgenèvre.

Further complicating the question of which pass Hannibal used to cross the Alps is the matter of Hannibal's younger brother, Hasdrubal. In an attempt to aid Hannibal in Italy, Hasdrubal assembled a relief force and, following pretty much the same route from Spain as his brother, came through France and crossed over the Alps in 207 B.C. There are references in the ancient sources to the pass used by Hannibal's brother but they specify that when he reached the Alps he crossed by a different pass than did Hannibal.[21]

From the accounts of Polybius and Livy we know that the pass by which Hannibal crossed into Italy had several distinct characteristics.[22] First, we know that the pass, on the French side, had a gorge near it in which Hannibal and his army were ambushed. That gorge is described as particularly narrow, steep and treacherous. Beyond the gorge was a large rock that dominated the valley floor and on which Hannibal regrouped his forces after the ambush. Both the gorge and the rock are a relatively short distance from the pass that Hannibal used to cross the Alps. With this information and some careful site surveys we can begin to narrow the choices.

Of the two routes under consideration, the Isère and the Drôme, the former does not fit the descriptions as readily as the latter. The author could not find any gorge or large rock within a day's hike of either the Mt. Cenis or Clapier passes that fit the descriptions provided by Polybius and Livy. The approach along the Arc River shows no such gorge and large rock positioned anywhere within eight to 20 miles of either of these two passes.

The approach to the Col du Clapier is through a pleasant valley with little arduous climbing. The valley is wide enough to accommodate a sizable army and there are abundant supplies of fresh water everywhere. It is an ideal route to follow in that it is easy to walk, supplied by water along the way, and offers some protection from ambush and the elements. The problem is that is does not have a gorge and large rock anywhere within a day's march of the pass.

From the Col de la Traversette, however, within a day's march are just such a gorge and large rock. This in and of itself is compelling evidence in favor of this pass, but the case for the pass becomes stronger the more one investigates. In no other valley leading to any of the other passes considered for this book are there another defile and rock juxtaposed like these and within the radius of a day's march to the summit of a pass. The gorge is approximately 18 miles from the summit of the pass, and the rock is less than 15. Hannibal's army could have completed this march in a long day, even after suffering heavy losses. The march along the valley leading to the pass is not difficult from the gorge on.

The next body of evidence concerns the pass itself. We know from the manuscripts that the climb to the pass from the French side is not as difficult as the descent is into Italy. It needs to be noted that the Alps in general show a gradual ascent from the French side and then a very precipitous and sudden drop on the Italian side. This is a characteristic of the entire southern Alpine range and becomes readily apparent when the mountains are viewed from the air. The Alps gradually increase in height as one moves from the Rhône Valley east for a distance of nearly a hundred miles, until they attain their full measure (4500 meters) at the Italian frontier.[23] Then they plunge almost vertically straight down to the valleys below and extend gradually by foothills onto the plains of Italy within just a few miles. Most of the passes on the French-Italian frontier have this characteristic, however, so it is of little value in helping to identifying Hannibal's pass.

The pass which Hannibal used, according to the ancient historians, had near or at its summit an area large enough for an army to have encamped and rested for two days. This is probably the most significant factor of all and has frequently been used by scholars as the determining variable in debating which pass was used by Hannibal. A number of scholars have dismissed the Col de la Traversette from considerations at the outset, because they argued it lacked this camp ground at or near its summit. Scholars have traditionally expected this ground to be located right on the top of the pass and in this regard they have erred.

Experience in the mountains shows that this is rarely the case, especially on the higher passes. A plateau several hundred feet below the pass is just as practical for use as a camping ground as one on top of the pass, where weather conditions could make camping for two days next to impossible.

The Col du Clapier has almost always been favored because it has a wide and level plateau over the final mile leading to the pass. One climbs to this plateau by an easy grade and then walks nearly a mile along practically level ground to the pass. At this stage there is virtually no climbing to be done, for it is a nearly level walk to the ridge. The army of Hannibal could easily have encamped along this plateau for several days in relative safety. There is also a lake on this plateau which has never been mentioned by any of the scholars who favor the Clapier as Hannibal's pass. The lake measures approximately 900 by 200 meters, yet there is no mention of it in any of the ancient or contemporary sources. It is significant enough that it should have been mentioned, but it is possible that the lake either was not there two thousand years ago, which, given its relatively small size is possible, or that it was frozen and covered with snow when Hannibal passed and thus was not visible.

The Traversette has been criticized by many scholars because they maintain that it does not have a level stretch of ground near the summit suitable for a campground. Located at the end of a narrow valley and cradled in the breast of Mt. Viso, the Col de la Traversette has been accurately described by scholars as "nothing more than a narrow ledge perched high up in the Alps."[24] This pass was first suggested in the literature as Hannibal's pass in 1805,[25] but was largely forgotten or ignored after that until the early part of this century. When first one and then later a second noted British scholar[26] revived the suggestion of the Traversette in the early 1900s they were greeted with profound skepticism.

Advocates of the classical approach criticized scholars who advocated the Traversette because the pass did not possess a campsite at or near its summit suitable for Hannibal to have rested his entire army for two days.[27] Even its chief proponent, these critics argued, did not dare dispute this "fatal shortcoming" and "remained silent on the subject."[28]

Scholars who dismissed the Traversette might have done so because it is such a remote and difficult pass to reach that there is little likelihood any of them ever visited it. In fact there are indications that it may have been purposely avoided; the pass was for years an unauthorized border crossing between France and Italy and a route frequented by smugglers well into the 1970s. Scholars may have avoided it not only because of the difficulty of the climb but as well because of "the ease with which triggers are pulled in that area."[29] Even today, the pass is considered remote in spite of some development, and is rarely climbed by tourists, even in summer. It is impossible to cross the pass from late October until early July. Several times over the last six years the author has tried unsuccessfully to reach the summit between the middle and end of June but was forced to turn back each time because of the snow and unsettled weather conditions. It has only been in the months of July and August that he was able to reach the summit on several occasions.

The pass is located just to the left of Mt. Viso, at a height of 3000 meters, and is not visible from the valley floor. It is a high pass by Alpine standards and considered difficult to climb. An experienced hiker, under ideal weather conditions, and with caution, can reach the summit in less than three hours of hiking and climbing. Halfway up the mountain, about an hour from the summit, one comes upon a very wide plateau. Its appearance is unexpected, given the nature of the terrain. This plateau is remarkably broad and fed by streams from several sources. Hannibal could well have rested his troops here and then moved them up and over the pass in stages as his engineers completed a needed roadway. For years, critics of this pass have dismissed it because they argued it had no campground for Hannibal's army, yet the suitable campground does exist.

The ancient sources maintain that the pass Hannibal used was one of the highest in the Alps and had snow on it all year.[30] Livy writes that the pass was covered with snow from the previous winter. This means that the pass had to be at an exceptional altitude. Passes below 3000 meters in this area of the Alps rarely have snow on them all year round. It would be surprising to find a pass below 2500 meters with snow on it. The author has spent the last six summers climbing the passes in the Queyras and the Cenis Valley and has yet to see a pass with snow on it at under 3000 meters. Some scholars have argued that climatic conditions might have been different two thousand years ago and that the snow line could have been much lower. The most recent published research in this area indicates that climatic conditions two thousand years ago were essentially the same as they are today.[31]

The fact that Polybius and Livy both agree that the pass was one of the highest in the Alps and would have had snow on it all year allows us to rule out many of the perennial scholars' favorites such as the Little St. Bernard (2188), the Montgenèvre (1850 meters), the Larche (1991 meters) and the Mt. Cenis (2081 meters). These passes are too low to have year-round snow. The author has visited the Montgenèvre, Larche and Mt. Cenis in July and August a number of times over the last several years and has never once seen any snow on any of them.

The fact that the pass would have had snow on it all year long

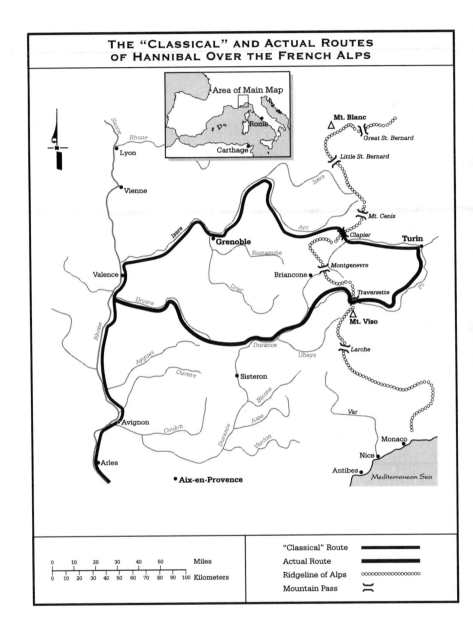

THE "CLASSICAL" AND ACTUAL ROUTES
OF HANNIBAL OVER THE FRENCH ALPS

mitigates in favor of the Traversette. The valley of the Guil ends where three very high mountains, Viso (4000 meters), Granero (3200 meters) and Aiguillette (3300 meters) come together and form a solid white wall. The Traversette, located between Mt. Granero and Mt. Viso, is the only way over this barrier, and because of its height and position relative to the sun the western face of the pass usually always has considerable amounts of snow on it even in the height of summer.

Livy and Polybius both wrote that the pass Hannibal crossed had a view of Italy. Polybius wrote that the Carthaginian's men were despondent and exhausted from marching, fighting and climbing. Many were starving from lack of proper food. So he called his men together and "relied on the actual sight of Italy, which now stretched out before them."[32] Polybius wrote further that Hannibal directed his men to look toward the plains of the Po and in the direction of Rome. In this way he restored their confidence. Livy wrote that "getting on the move at dawn, the army struggled slowly forward on snow-covered ground. Seeing the hopelessness of utter exhaustion in every face that passed him, Hannibal climbed ahead to a vantage point that afforded a view of the Po Valley and Italy beyond. There he pointed out to his despondent men the view and told them that they were climbing over the very walls of Rome.[33]

The ancient sources also tell us that the pass which Hannibal used led to a valley that in turn led directly to the city of Turin. In this regard only two of the six passes considered lead directly to Turin. The Clapier is the nearest and the most direct to the city, while the Traversette leads to the Po Valley, which in turn leads directly to Turin. The other passes, such as the Montgenèvre, the Little St. Bernard and the Larche are all facing the wrong direction in relation to Turin.

When the various other passes of the French Alps are evaluated against these characteristics, most may be ruled out immediately. They are either too low, or they do not lead directly to Turin, or their descents are not difficult enough. In addition, only a few passes in the entire Alpine range offer the view over Italy described by Polybius and Livy.

Among the classical passes, the Little St. Bernard and the Mt. Cenis are not consistent with the descriptions provided by Polybius and Livy. Both are too low, they have no view of Italy, and they are at the wrong radius to Turin. The Col du Clapier, on the other hand, does fit the descriptions of the manuscripts and has as well a long and impressive list of historical supporters.[34] Considering the revisionist passes, the Mt.Genevre and the Col de Larche are ruled out for the same reasons as the Little St. Bernard and the Mt. Cenis. They are not consistent with the descriptions of the sources. The Col de la Traversette, however, matches the descriptions found in the manuscripts and, like the Clapier, warrants serious consideration.

The thinking among scholars who have favored the Clapier crossing is that Hannibal must have been headed for the much easier Mt. Cenis nearby when he fell into an ambush set by the Celtic tribes. Both Polybius and Livy noted that the ascent of the pass was relatively easy but the descent was perilous. The ascent toward the Clapier is easy and the descent into Italy is difficult. Under favorable conditions it takes less than three hours to descend the valley floor. The ease of the ascent and the difficulty of the descent are consistent with the accounts of the ancient sources,

Polybius and Livy both wrote that Hannibal had a wide view of the Po Valley and the plains of Italy from the summit of his pass. The Clapier does not have a direct view of anything from its summit. Several meters away from the ridge, however, there is a promontory from which, under ideal weather conditions, a view of the valley below can be had. This is not the commanding view of the valley of the Po and the plains of Italy that one imagines on reading the accounts of Livy and Polybius, however, it is a view of the valley below, which leads to Turin.

Livy relates how Hannibal stood on the ledge of the pass and, pointing out the plains of Italy below, inspired his tired and despondent men to continue on to Rome.[35] While the view from the Clapier promontory is impressive, it is not inspirational. Some scholars have tended to dismiss the entire account of the view as so much "rhetorical embellishment" by the ancient authors and have ignored it in formulating their own theories of the route.[36] In this author's opinion the view is an important consideration and should not be dismissed so lightly. In fact it is one of the key factors in determining the pass.

The Col du Clapier, at 2500 meters, is one of the highest passes in the Alps, meaning it could have had year-round snow at the time of the crossing, if not every year.[37] There was no snow to be found anywhere on or near this pass when the author conducted his site visit to it in the summer of 1994.

Among all the passes, indeed the Clapier is the most direct to Turin. Livy recounts in his history how Hannibal descended the pass and came to the land of the Taurini.[38] Polybius merely comments that Hannibal came down from the Alps and onto the plains of Italy.[39] The Clapier fulfills most of the criteria mentioned in the ancient sources; nevertheless, a site visit raises concerns that tend to compromise its position.

The main problem with the Col du Clapier is the location of a smaller pass in an adjacent valley. This pass, the Petit Mt. Cenis, is a far easier and safer way to descend into Italy than the Clapier. Even if, as the ancient commentators contend, Hannibal was led into the valley of the Clapier by treacherous guides, or even if he lost his way in the valley, there is nothing in the surrounding terrain that would have prevented him from utilizing this far less difficult route. In fact, by abandoning the climb to the Clapier, even within a kilometer or two of the pass, he could have easily crossed into the next valley by the Col du Petit Mt. Cenis.

This pass is small and relatively low and it connects the valley of the Clapier with the valley of the Mt. Cenis. The pass is parallel to the mountain range and thus does not cross the higher mountains. The attraction of this pass is that the route to Italy from there is easy and direct. There is no precipitous descent. The pass is easy to find relative to the Clapier and takes less than one hour on foot to traverse over relatively level ground. This fact, coupled with the lack of a view of Italy, compromises, in the author's opinion, the viability of the Clapier as Hannibal's pass.

Looking at the Traversette, the climb from the plateau to the summit requires, even in the height of summer, ropes and picks because there is considerable snow that accumulates just below the summit.

While there is no doubt that the path to this pass has changed over the centuries, the basic approach has certainly remained the same since Hannibal crossed two thousand years ago and, like Hannibal, a modern climber must follow the same route. The last 500 meters to the summit involve climbing a snow chute that cannot be avoided. There is simply no other way to the top, even in summer. The author has seen considerable amounts of snow each time he has climbed to the pass over the past five summers. The problems encountered in walking over this snow even in August are remarkably similar to those described by Polybius and Livy. As Hannibal and his men climbed, footing became increasingly difficult because of the snow. Soldiers and especially pack animals became stuck and unable to move, or footing on the ledges became slippery and often fatal.[40] The author has encountered the same conditions each summer he has climbed the pass.

The summit of the pass is ten meters wide and in every respect true to its description as a "narrow ledge perched high in the Alps." The view in every direction is spectacular. Under ideal weather conditions there is a view of the Italian plains in the distance below and of the River Po winding its way through the valley toward Turin. It is an inspiring sight and one that never ceases to thrill, no matter how many times the pass is climbed. One can easily imagine Hannibal standing on any of the large rocks above the pass and urging his men on while pointing out the view.

The descent into Italy is very difficult. It can be done by an experienced hiker in about three hours, but the footing is extremely dangerous and requires attention. The path down has been destroyed in places by Italian or French authorities over the centuries to render it useless in time of war or to discourage smugglers. This only adds another element of difficulty to an already dangerous situation.

A tunnel a few meters under this pass was dug in 1490 by the Duke of Saluzzio as a shortcut under the dangerous ledge. The tunnel was blocked for a number of years but has recently been opened and climbers are able with light and ropes to make their way under the pass and come out onto a ledge overlooking Italy.

In the final analysis, trying to definitively locate Hannibal's pass without archaeological evidence is admittedly a difficult if not impossible task. Until the Alps give up the remains of an elephant, or a Carthaginian officer, or an African or Spanish cavalryman, we will never know for certain exactly where Hannibal crossed. The possibility of discovering the archaeological evidence, however, is not as remote as one might think. During no other period in history have scholars had the access to the Alps and the technological assistance that they have today. While still dangerous, modern developments and technology have made these once formidable barriers accessible to even amateurs for research purposes. Satellites, helicopters and airplanes have allowed aerial surveys to be conducted which yield views of the valleys, ridges and peaks never before available on such an accurate and detailed scale. Developments such as inexpensive and portable metal detectors have allowed professionals and amateurs alike to investigate areas of the Alps that heretofore would have been dismissed from consideration as too difficult or inaccessible for investigation by traditional methods.

The Alps have also become winter and summer vacation spots for hundreds of thousands of tourists each year. As these vacationing hordes descend on the mountains each season, someone, given the right set of circumstances and a little luck, may come upon the physical evidence. Consider the recent story of a vacationing German couple who, while "tramping over a commonly used Alpine pass," found the body of a man who died over five thousand years ago preserved in a glacier.[41] That chance discovery is causing scientists and historians to reconsider many of their cherished beliefs and to begin looking for signs of ancient human activity in the more desolate and higher valleys and passes of the Alps.[42]

Even if the Alps give up evidence that points to a Carthaginian crossing, there is still the matter of Hasdrubal's Carthaginian relief force that came through the Alps over a decade after Hannibal. While the two brothers followed the same general route from Spain, Hasdrubal, perhaps warned by Hannibal not to follow in his exact footsteps, crossed the Alps by another pass in 207 B.C. Thus, any archaeological evidence found in the Alps which pertains to the Punic Wars, unless it contains a specific reference to Hannibal, could further add to the mystery and uncertainty of the pass rather than clarify the matter.

Still, barring new archaeological evidence that would answer the question once and for all, it is this author's view that the Col de la Traversette—one of the most difficult, remote and highest passes in the French Alps—was the one used by Hannibal to enter Italy. He lost thousands of men in the crossing and the survivors were forced to suffer an excruciating ordeal, but as subsequent events were to prove, he was able to get enough fighting strength through. There is also no doubt that Hannibal would have taken an easier route if he had been able, or if he had known how to reach one. Following the second deadly ambush, he may have thought that pitting his men against even a difficult crossing into fertile Italy was preferable to remaining in barren country among the fierce and treacherous Gauls.

On the approach to the Traversette the ambush sites can be identified, as well as the huge rock around which the army gathered after the battle in the second gorge. On the pass itself the campground, the year-round snow and the narrow ledge match the characteristics recorded in the ancient sources. The view of Italy from the summit of the pass is exactly as described and the hazardous descent leads toward Turin. It is difficult to find another pass through the Alps that meets these essential criteria.

Modern visitors to the area who are interested in recreating Hannibal's experience in the Alps may well want to attempt the trip, perhaps starting at the gorge where the second ambush took place, a day's march away from the pass. The crossing along Mt. Viso, however, is not recommended for any but experienced climbers, and then only in summer. For other readers interested in Hannibal's actual experience, perhaps the following description from Silius Italicus in Book III of his *Punica* will suffice:

> Here everything is wrapped in eternal frost, white with snow and held in an icy grip. The mountains are stiff with cold so that even though they tower to the sky, the warmth of the sun cannot soften them . . . shutting out with their shade even the light of heaven. The joys of

spring never come to this region, nor the charms of summer. Winter dwells alone on these dreaded crests, and guards them as her perpetual abode. Here, in this Alpine home, the winds and tempests make their dominion and men grow dizzy amid the lofty crags.[43]

NOTES

[1] Livy, Bk. XXI, Sec. 35.

[2] Livy, Bk. XXI, Sec. 36.

[3] For comparative purposes the Traversette has a heavily forested area on the French side while the Clapier has no forests nearby.

[4] Livy, Bk. XXI, Sec. 39.

[5] Polybius, Bk. III, Sec. 60.

[6] Livy, Bk. XXI, Sec. 38.

[7] Polybius, Bk. III, Sec. 60.

[8] Warmington, *Carthage.*

[9] W.W. Hyde, *Roman Alpine Routes*, p. 206.

[10] Among the proponents of this passage over the Alps have been the famous historian Edward Gibbon, 1763; C. Denina, 1792; J.A. de Luc, 1818; Letrone, 1819; Ladoucette, 1820; Wickham and Cramer, 1820; J.L. Larauza, 1826; H.L. Long, 1831; R.Ellis, 1853; W.J. Law, 1866; Colonel Hennebert, 1878; Colonel Perrin, 1887; Dr. Ollivier, 1889; Theodore Dodge, 1891; J. Fuchs, 1897; W.H. Bullock Hall, 1898; W. Osiander, 1900; P. Azan, 1902; D.W. Freshfield, 1914; G. DeManteyer, 1944; D. Proctor, 1971; J.F. Lazenby, 1978.

[11] Hyde, p. 207.

[12] Polybius, Bk. III, Sec. 54–55.

[13] Livy, Bk. XXI, Sec. 35.

[14] Mommsen, *History of Rome*, p. 133 (footnote).

[15] Hyde, p. 198.

[16] Ernle Bradford, *Hannibal*, p. 67.

[17] Strabo, opus cited. Varro, another ancient writer, refers to this pass as "*una quae est iuxta mare per Ligures.*"

[18] Varro writes: "*altera qua Hannibal transiit.*"

[19] Varo writes: "*tertia qua Pompeius ad Hispaniense bellum profectus est.*"

[20] Sallust, Bk. III. This is probably the Montgenèvre.

[21] Varro refers to a fourth pass, "*quarta qua Hasdrubal de Gallia in Italiam venit.*"

[22] Polybius, Bk. III, Sec. 53–56, and Livy, Bk. XXI, Sec. 36.

[23] See the slide shot from aircraft at 10,000 meters or on a relief map of Alps.

[24] Dennis Procter, *Hannibal's March in History*, p. 203.

[25] Denina, *Tableau historique.*

[26] Cecil Torr, *Hannibal Crosses the Alps*, and Gavin deBeer, *Hannibal, Hannibal's March, Alps and Elephants.* The pass was also proposed some years earlier by Cecil Torr.

[27] Proctor, p. 203. This is Proctor's big mistake. "Not surprisingly, the Traversette, perched high in the mountain, yields no such area (camping ground). Even deBeer, its chief defender, agrees it is only a narrow ridge." The Traversette very definitely has a campground at least the size of the Clapier (Proctor's choice), if not larger.

[28] H. Ferrand, *Alpine Journal*, p. 426, H.S. Wilkinson, *Journal of Hellenic Studies*, pp. 269–271, W.W. Hyde, *Roman Alpine Routes*, p. 208, and D. Proctor, *Hannibal's March*, p. 203.

[29] deBeer, *Hannibal's March.*

[30] Polybius, Bk. III, Sec. 53–56, and Livy, Bk. XXI, Sec. 36.

[31] *Washington Post*, August 13, 1997. A report on temperature over time indicates that conditions two thousand years ago were essentially the same as today. The research was based on indicators such as tree rings, isotope analyses in coral reefs and ice cores. The research was based on data collected and analyzed by the National Center for Atmospheric Research in Boulder, Colorado, and the Intergovernmental Panel on Climate Change.

[32] Polybius, Bk. III, Sec. 54.

[33] Livy, Bk. XXI, Sec. 35.

[34] Among the supporters of this route and the Mt. Cenis throughout history have been Julius Caesar, Pompey, Constantine, Napoleon, Maccaneo and Giorio (16th century), Larauza (1826), Mace (1852), Maissiat (1874), Perrin (1887), Hall (1898), Azon (1902), Colin (1904), Spencer-Wilkinson (1911), Torr (1925), Hyde (1935), Lavis Trafford (1956), Hoyte (1960), Proctor (1971), Lazenby (1978), Rivet (1988), and Coninck (1992). The Clapier and the Mt. Cenis are frequently grouped together because of their very close proximity as is explained in greater detail in the text.

[35] Livy, Bk. XXI, Sec. 35, and Polybius, Bk. III, Sec. 54.

[36] Hyde, p. 210.

[37] According to most sources, Hannibal crossed the Alps sometime between the end of September and the middle of October. For a September crossing,

see Walbank, Sumner, or deSanctis. For an October crossing, see deBeer, Devos or Proctor. For a November crossing, see Mommsen.

[38] Livy, Bk. XXI, Sec. 38.
[39] Livy, Bk. XXI, Sec. 38, and Polybius, Bk. III., Sec. 56.
[40] Polybius, Bk. III, Sec. 54.
[41] *Washington Post,* October 15, 1992, p. A-2.
[42] *New York Times,* December 19, 1995, p. C-9.
[43] Silius Italicus, *Punica,* Bk. III, Sec. 479–93.

CHAPTER VII

❧ · ❧

THE WAR IN ITALY

The soldiers who came down from the Alps with Hannibal in the fall of 218 B.C. were a ragged and exhausted lot who looked "more like animals than men."[1] Of the nearly fifty thousand who had followed Hannibal into Gaul that summer, less than half were left. Most had been killed or lost either in the fighting along the route or in the crossing of the mountains. There is no doubt that some had deserted. From the accounts of Polybius and Livy[2] we know that there were only about 20,000 infantry and 6,000 cavalry who descended onto the plains of Italy to form the core of the small army with which Hannibal would challenge the mightiest power in the ancient world. Almost all of the pack animals had been lost, killed or eaten along the way, but, miraculously, all of the elephants and many of the horses had survived.

For the next two weeks Hannibal rested his men at the foot of the mountains so they could recover from the exhaustion brought on from months of marching and fighting, and the last few weeks of climbing. The elephants, along with the horses and pack animals that survived the last difficult weeks, were close to death when they were led down from the mountains, but after several days grazing in the lush fields, and resting in the temperate conditions of the lower elevations, they recovered much of their strength.

The area of Italy in which Hannibal and his army first camped when they came down from the mountains was probably somewhere along the Po Valley west of modern-day Turin. Both Polybius and Livy make reference in their works to the fact that when Hannibal came out of the Alps he descended onto the plains of the Po and moved into the area of a large tribe of Gauls called the Taurini. This tribe had been waging war against the Insubres, another of the Gallic tribes that inhabited the area and one that allied itself closely with Hannibal.[3]

At first Hannibal sent emissaries to the principal city of the Taurini, probably at Turin, to persuade them to receive him as a friend and ally against Rome. When the Taurini rebuffed these overtures, Hannibal moved his army closer to their city; and after the Taurini refused a final offer of cooperation, he laid siege to it. Following three days of vicious fighting, his mercenaries breached the walls. Inside the city they put all the surviving defenders to the sword and made slaves of their women and children. The slaughter of the Taurini had an immediate effect on the neighboring tribes. Many of the Gauls were so intimidated by how quickly and brutally Hannibal had taken the city that they immediately sent emissaries to pay homage to him and to declare their willingness to join him as allies.

In taking the town Hannibal displayed a keen understanding of the value of psychological warfare. His assault on the Taurini was probably intended more to push the other tribes of the Po Valley into joining him than to punish the unfortunate inhabitants of that doomed city for refusing cooperation. He probably welcomed the opportunity to demonstrate to the local natives that the once bedraggled army that had struggled down from the Alps was a force to be reckoned with, and not to be feared less than Rome. As a result of this first victory, Hannibal expected to substantially increase the size of his army in both infantry and in cavalry.

Following his victory over the Taurini, Hannibal could not afford to allow his men more than a few days to rest. A Roman army under the consul Scipio had already crossed into northern Italy and was moving west, searching for them. Hannibal needed to augment his depleted forces with fresh recruits from the Gallic tribes for what was sure to be a major battle with the Romans.

While a large number of these tribes throughout northwestern Italy had pledged to join him as allies, the sudden arrival of Scipio with a sizable force of legionaries at the Po River near Placentia caused many of them to temper their initial enthusiasm. Most of the tribes preferred to remain neutral, in fact if not in word, for a while longer while they awaited the outcome of the first few confrontations between the Romans and the Carthaginians. While the Gauls made grandiose promises to Hannibal about their bravery in battle and what they would do to the Romans, the numbers of men-at-arms they provided him, as well as the quantity of supplies, were not as generous as he had expected.

As Scipio moved west and north of the Po River looking for Hannibal, he too pressed into service many of the Gauls who lived along the route. While they ostensibly joined the Roman army as allies, probably out of compulsion, the area of northern Italy that lay behind the advancing Roman army became rife with discontent and on the verge of insurrection. All that was needed was some sign to give the Gauls confidence that Hannibal could defeat the Romans.

He was ready to provide that sign. For psychological as well as strategic reasons, Hannibal believed that if he could defeat Scipio the Gauls would rise up across northern Italy and flock to join his standard. The result of such a massive defection of allies would severely weaken the Romans, both physically and in terms of propaganda. With the Gauls marching behind his standard, Hannibal would have access to vast quantities of supplies, and other cities and towns throughout Italy would begin to waiver in their allegiance toward Rome.

When Hannibal first received word that Scipio was approaching the Po Valley, he was impressed with the decisiveness of his Roman adversary. Only a few weeks earlier Scipio had been at Marseilles, and already he had completed a difficult sea voyage back to Rome, raised an army and was now marching west. The Roman army that Scipio was leading into northern Italy, however, was not of the same quality as the one he had commanded at Marseilles. The army at Marseilles, much larger and more experienced than his current one, had been placed under the command of his brother, Gnaeus, and sent on to Spain. Scipio had returned to Italy where he raised a new, though inexperienced, army of legionaries. As this army moved north into the Po Valley, Scipio merged it with the garrisons that had already been posted at Cremona and Placentia.

Scipio thus had an army of novice soldiers and defeated veterans—a poor mix both militarily and psychologically. Many of the veterans among the garrison troops were suffering from low morale. They had been defeated by the Boii and the Insubres in a revolt a few months earlier. Others, the more inexperienced, had only recently been drafted into the Roman army and they were fearful at the prospect of meeting Hannibal and his mercenaries on the battlefield. Scipio had not had the opportunity or time to build their confidence and mold them into the type of cohesive fighting force he would need to confront the Carthaginians.

When Scipio had left Marseilles he was sure that Hannibal and his mercenaries would perish in the mountains from starvation or die at the hands of the warlike Celtic tribesmen who lived along the route. Still, he could not risk the chance that Hannibal might survive the crossing, so he marched his new recruits mercilessly across Italy, first north and then west, joining with the remnants of the legions at Placentia and Cremona along the way. Another Roman consul, Tiberius Sempronius Longus, had been sent to Sicily earlier that year with a large army to prepare for an invasion of Carthage. When Scipio had returned to Rome and reported to the Senate that Hannibal was attempting to cross the Alps, Sempronius was recalled to the Italian mainland with his army and ordered to move north. Since it would take Sempronius some time to be able to move his army from Sicily to northern Italy, Scipio was left to delay Hannibal as best he could.

The Roman army at the time of the Second Punic War was composed of legions. These legions were its primary unit, and rather than being organized along territorial lines, each was composed of men drawn from throughout Italy. Most of these infantrymen were simple farmers who had some property, even if only a modest plot of land, yet they had come together in a time of crisis to fulfill their duty to Rome as citizens. At the time of the Punic Wars a legion usually consisted of from 4,500 to 6,000 men. The mainstays of the legion were its heavily armed infantry, who were divided into maniples of between 300 and 400 men. Each maniple was formed into three lines for combat.

The typical Roman order of battle was for the first line to charge the enemy and attempt to break its ranks. If this did not succeed, the second line would try while the first retreated through the ranks. The first line consisted of younger men, the second line those who were somewhat older and more experienced, and the third line the true veterans of the legion. These lines were staggered so that during battle the first line could retreat or advance as needed through the second without disrupting it. This battle formation allowed one line to advance as another was tiring and retreating. The third line formed the reserve and was held back until the most crucial point in the battle, at which time it was committed to combat. This formation gave the legion considerable flexibility and would prove in the years to come, with some modifications, to be an effective technique that would allow the Roman army to eventually become the most powerful and well-organized fighting force in the ancient world.

In addition to the legions the Roman army also had contingents made up of Italian "allies." These were neighbors of Rome, who had been pressed into service by treaty and usually formed the cavalry detachments and reserves that accompanied each legion. The cavalry was held in reserve or would skirmish on the flanks of the enemy. These tactics had been the standard fare of the Roman army for years, and while simple they often proved effective against an enemy of lesser skill and commanders of lesser resourcefulness. Against Hannibal, as the Romans were soon to discover, they would prove ineffective.

As the distance between the two armies narrowed and a confrontation became inevitable, both commanders began to move more cautiously. Scipio was the first to move into position for the battle as he crossed the Po and established himself on the banks of a tributary, the Ticinus (Ticino). This river is just a few kilometers south of modern-day Milan near the city of Pavia. There Scipio assembled his army and addressed them in a manner typical of the time. A formal speech or exhortation by a commander to his troops before battle was a Roman tradition. The commander's speech was intended to be a morale booster and the army of Scipio needed a heavy dose. Most of the soldiers in the assembled legions were simple illiterate farmers, and probably did not understand fully why they had been called from their fields, drafted into the army and marched halfway across Italy to fight this North African.

The name of Hannibal had been respected and feared at Rome since the destruction of the city of Saguntum in Spain months before. His reputation as a master of battlefield tactics as well as his fierceness in combat were well known in Roman military and political circles. Scipio explained to his army that this was a righteous war against a perfidious enemy who had come to devastate their lands. He explained how Hannibal had broken the truce of the First Punic War and treacherously attacked Roman allies at Saguntum. Now with an army of mercenaries he had crossed the Alps and was coming to destroy Italy.

To alleviate the fears of his inexperienced soldiers on the eve of battle Scipio recounted how Roman men-at-arms in Sicily had defeated Hannibal's father, Hamilcar, during the First Punic War. Then he told the army how Hannibal and his mercenaries had fled from Roman soldiers just a few weeks before, when they landed at Marseilles. Scipio urged his men to take heart since in a day or two they would not be facing men-at-arms on the battlefield, but "ghosts and the mere shadows of men." This army of mercenaries, Scipio recounted, was nothing more than a ragtag column of misfits who had been starved, beaten and exhausted by their trek over the Alps. They were little more than "half-dead men, cold, dirty and neglect-ed," "riding lame animals" and "fighting with broken weapons." Scipio boasted that after the Roman victory the legionaries would hardly be justified in taking pride in what they had won on the field of battle because the cold, the snow and the ice of the Alps had already done most of their work for them.

As for Hannibal, Scipio portrayed him as no more than "a young upstart and criminal, drunk with ambition." The peroration of the speech was one that leaders have used for centuries to rouse the spirits of their men and motivate them to fight. The Roman consul exhort-ed his countrymen to fight for the honor of their wives and the lives of their children against an enemy who had come to their land to take everything from them.

In the privacy of his thoughts that night, Scipio must have experienced considerable anxiety and self-doubt. He knew that the outcome of this battle might well determine the course of the war and the future of the Roman Republic. Hannibal would be a formidable adversary. He and his army had subdued the Celtic tribes of Spain and southern Gaul and had crossed the Alps at the onset of the worst season of the year. The mercenaries were veteran soldiers moving under the direction of a skilled and resourceful commander who could not be taken lightly. Late that night, a lone wolf made its way into the Roman camp. Throughout the hours of darkness it moved about the camp, killing any soldiers who crossed its path. Before dawn it made its escape as quietly and treacherously as it had come.

In the camp of the Carthaginians a few miles away, Hannibal prepared his men for their first confrontation with a Roman army. He formed his men into a great circle around a number of Gauls who had been captured in the Alps. The Gauls were offered the opportunity to fight each other in individual gladiatorial combats for their freedom. Each victor would be given his freedom and a horse while each loser would be freed from his bondage by death. The contests began, and as the fighting proceeded the assembled army was impressed to see the Gauls fighting with such spirit to win their freedom.

After the combats Hannibal explained to the army how what they had just witnessed was not staged to entertain them but in order for them to comprehend the gravity of their own situation. Fate and circumstances, he alleged, had bound the Carthaginian army in heavier and stronger chains than those which had imprisoned the Gauls who had just fought. The mercenaries were isolated in Italy and there was no escape from what lay ahead, nor was there another way home. Behind them were the Alps, which because of the winter season they could not re-cross, and in front of them was a Roman army which they could not avoid. To their side was a wide sea for which they had no ships. The mercenaries had no choice but to fight and win a decisive victory. Their very survival depended on the courage and skill they would display in battle, for the price of defeat would be a cruel death and an unmarked grave in Italy. However, the rewards of victory would be spoils and glory for each man beyond anything their imaginations could comprehend. For each soldier who fought bravely Hannibal promised there would be wealth beyond measure. Rome—in fact all of Italy—could be theirs for the taking. There would be gold, silver and slaves enough to make every man among them a king. Hannibal promised those who fought hardest tax-free land of their choice in Italy, Africa or Spain.[4]

As for the Roman army that would stand before them on the field of battle, what had the brave and experienced mercenaries to fear? This Roman army was composed of new recruits and a few veterans who had already been beaten by the Gauls only a few months before. The Roman commander and his soldiers were still strangers to each other and would be no match on the field of battle against the experienced and fearless men who had followed Hannibal through Spain and Gaul and over the Alps.

Hannibal recounted with pride the diverse regions and nations from which his soldiers had been drawn. He recognized the veteran infantry and skilled horsemen from North Africa and the brave, loyal allies from Spain. He praised his own countrymen from Carthage for their courage and resolve in enduring so much hardship to recover the honor of their city stolen from them by the Romans in the last war. Last of all, he welcomed his new allies, the Gauls from northern Italy, who had joined him to free their land from Roman oppression.

Hannibal praised his army for coming to Italy to battle a pernicious and rapacious race intent on enslaving the world. This army, he contended, was about to strike a blow for the freedom of men everywhere in the ancient world. On a personal note, Hannibal recounted to his veterans how he had grown to manhood among them in their camps. He told with pride and nostalgia how as a young officer he had learned the arts of war under their watchful eyes and how they had voted him their commander upon the murder of his brother-in-law, Hasdrubal.

Hannibal concluded his speech by reminding his men that in this war there was no retreat. Either they moved forward to victory or they died where they stood. After they had marched a thousand miles, forded rivers, and climbed mountains—fighting nature and the Gauls every mile of the way—they were preparing for their first battle against the Romans and perhaps their greatest moment. To prove that his words were his sacred bond Hannibal prayed to Jupiter before the assembled army. Then upon the sacred altar of the god he crushed the skull of a lamb with his right hand while his army shouted its bellicose approval.

The first battle between the Romans and the Carthaginians, in spite of the extensive pre-fight rhetoric of the commanders, turned out to be little more than a cavalry skirmish on the banks of the river Ticinus. However, it reinforced the nervous apprehension with which the Romans viewed the invaders and helped set the psychological tone for the much larger battles that were to come.

The Ticinus is a tributary of the Po River located a few kilometers south of Milan near the town of Pavia. Scipio had constructed a bridge over this river and he brought his cavalry over it and to the opposite bank. There he engaged the advanced elements of the Carthaginian cavalry. In short order the African horsemen of Numidia showed their skill in dominating the open ground by the river and outmaneuvering the Romans. Hannibal's African cavalry inflicted a quick and decisive defeat over the inexperienced Roman horsemen. During the skirmish Scipio was wounded and quickly surrounded by Carthaginians, who, like a pack of wolves, began closing in for the kill. According to Livy's account,[5] the wounded Roman commander was rescued from certain death by his seventeen-year-old son, also named Scipio. The boy, who would one day earn the appellation "Africanus," allegedly rode full gallop into the midst of the Carthaginians and diverted them long enough for his father to be rescued.

The Roman defeat at the river Ticinus forced the elder Scipio to retreat to the safety of the walled city of Placentia. There he established his camp on a secure stretch of land on the east bank of the Trebbia River, another tributary which flows into the Po, and awaited the arrival of Sempronius Longus with his larger army that was moving up from the south.

As news of the victory at the Ticinus spread among the Gauls, they sent ambassadors to Hannibal to pledge their support for his war against Rome. The Gauls promised to join him and bring with them large quantities of supplies for his army. When Hannibal and his forces arrived near Placentia, they arrayed themselves in front of the Roman camp. There, each day, elements of the African cavalry taunted the Romans, challenging them to come out and do battle. Scipio, still badly wounded, ordered his soldiers to remain in camp and sought to buy the time needed for Sempronius' army to arrive. Many Gauls who were serving with the Roman army as auxiliaries, however, were impressed by the daring and bravado of Hannibal; each day, as the Carthaginian cavalry came within sight of the Roman camp and challenged the legions to do battle, they grew more enamored of him. Finally, these Gauls decided to go over to the Carthaginian side. Waiting until the early-morning hours, they deserted the Roman camp in large numbers and crossed over to join Hannibal. Before they left, some of the Gauls decapitated Roman soldiers who were sleeping near them and took the severed heads to Hannibal as symbols of their new allegiance.

After the Gauls had deserted the Roman camp, Scipio left Placentia and crossed to the western bank of the Trebia to establish a more secure campsite in the hills. There he had the army construct a wide ditch in front of the camp and erect a palisade behind it. The new camp became well fortified and, because of the hilly terrain and the rocks, Scipio was able to neutralize the advantage that Hannibal held over the Romans in cavalry and elephants.

When Sempronius arrived at Placentia he was eager to fight Hannibal as soon as possible. Scipio urged caution, warning the new commander that it would be more prudent for the legions to break off contact with Hannibal as it was now December and weather conditions around Placentia had begun to deteriorate. It had, in fact, become very cold and was starting to snow. Scipio believed that if there were little fighting and thus no chance for looting, the Gauls who had joined Hannibal would quickly tire of the inactivity and return to their towns and villages for the winter. Then Hannibal would be without allies or a source of supplies; his army would be reduced to foraging for food throughout the barren countryside while the Romans would be in secure winter quarters. The Roman soldiers could use the winter to recover from their defeat at the Ticinus and improve their confidence and skills through additional training. Then, when the time was right, perhaps in late spring, the legions could leave the security of their camp and hunt down the Carthaginians.

Sempronius, however, would not hear of delay. Because Scipio was still recovering from his wounds, he took command of both armies, and after designating a small garrison to guard the camp he ordered the remainder of the troops into the field against Hannibal. The army that Sempronius led in battle in December 218 B.C. consisted of about 16,000 Roman legionaries, 20,000 Gallic and Italian "allies of Rome" and about 4,000 cavalry. With the addition of his own Gallic allies, Hannibal was able to put into the field about 30,000 men. While the Romans enjoyed a superiority over Hannibal in terms of numbers, they nonetheless lacked a great deal in terms of competent leadership and experience.

When Sempronius joined Scipio in his new camp the Romans held a clear defensive advantage. Hannibal could not risk a frontal assault against the camp because of its fortifications and the Romans' numerical advantage. The Romans could hold out against Hannibal indefinitely. He had to find a way to draw them from their secure position in the hills and onto the open plains east of the Trebbia. There the Romans would be vulnerable to the Carthaginian cavalry and elephants. At the same time, Hannibal had to be careful how he engaged the Roman infantry on open ground since their advantage in numbers could cause many casualties among his veteran soldiers.

In reconnoitering the area between the river and the open plains near his camp Hannibal found a place where he could conceal a substantial number of his soldiers and cavalry. The place was along a small tributary of the Trebbia thick with scrub and brush. In the early light of the overcast winter skies, especially with rain or snow falling, Hannibal believed he could hide some of his men in the scrub, where they would lie unnoticed by the Romans. The legionaries would be focused on the enemy forces in front of them as they moved into battle and unaware that elements of Hannibal's army were hidden behind them. At a crucial point in the battle these troops would emerge from hiding and attack the Romans from behind.

The most difficult part of the plan was to find a way to lure the Romans out of their camp, across the Trebbia River, and onto this open ground. Hannibal knew that Scipio was too prudent a commander to venture into dangerous territory. Sempronius, however, was a new and unpredictable variable. The new Roman commander was an impulsive and ambitious man; for his own political reasons, he wanted to force a decisive battle with Hannibal as soon as possible. While Sempronius knew that Scipio's plan to avoid fighting Hannibal and to wait out the winter in quarters was strategically sound, he was under intense personal pressure to strike a decisive blow and thus secure his political future at Rome.

Hannibal would exploit the impulsive character of Sempronius to his own advantage. He sent a detachment of Numidian cavalry to the Roman camp at dawn, where they taunted and goaded Sempronius into action. Their enticement was carefully orchestrated to anger the Romans and draw them out of their camp before they had time to eat their breakfast or prepare their horses and arms for battle. While the Numidian cavalry were taunting the Romans, the Carthaginian mercenaries consumed their morning meal and prepared themselves for the forthcoming battle in the comfort of their camp. They readied their weapons and even took the precaution of coating their bodies with oil as insulation against the cold of the day.

When Sempronius saw the Numidian cavalry posturing outside the Roman camp and heard their taunts and jeers he could not contain himself. Instead of thinking, Sempronius reacted, just as Hannibal had hoped he would. He ordered his troops into the field, and as the Roman cavalry came pouring out of their camp they were in disarray and without a clear plan. The Numidians on the other hand had a prepared plan of action: they feigned a frightened retreat, drawing the Romans farther and farther away from the security of their fortifications. Sempronius, caught up in the emotion of the moment, and tasting victory, impulsively ordered the entire Roman army to follow the cavalry out onto the field for battle.

That morning in December 218 B.C. was bitterly cold and it had begun to snow lightly just before dawn. The Roman soldiers and their animals had left camp without breakfast. At first, as they charged after the Numidian cavalry, they were fueled by their adrenaline and the illusion that the enemy was fleeing from them. As the Numidian cavalry retreated, the Romans developed a false sense of confidence that drew them more and more distant from the safety of their camp. Flushed with the anticipation of an easy triumph, they believed they were driving Hannibal and the Numidian cavalry before them. Sempronius was certain that the day was his while Scipio, confined to his tent by his wounds, worried at the outcome.

Nearly the entire Roman army, cavalry and foot soldiers alike, chased the retreating Numidians to the banks of the Trebbia and then plunged into the river itself. Once in it, they found the water colder and running deeper than usual because of the snow and rain from the previous days. As they struggled to the far bank of the river and began to assemble for battle, the Romans began suffering from the effects of the wet cold as well as from their lack of food.

The Carthaginians were assembled at the far end of the plain, waiting for the Romans to be drawn up in battle order. They had eaten a good breakfast and undertaken all their preparations for combat in the comfort of their camp. Hannibal now prepared for the Roman assault by moving his infantry into a wide rank of some 20,000 men. He divided his cavalry, 10,000 horsemen, and placed them on both flanks of the army. Then he further reinforced the infantry by placing the elephants on both sides of them. The mercenary army patiently awaited the Romans.

After the Romans crossed the Trebbia, their officers managed to establish some order and began to draw them up in their usual battle fashion. The legionaries advanced over the open ground in three lines and their pace became slower and more labored the farther they moved. Men and animals were cold, wet, hungry and tired. A half-mile before they had even engaged the enemy, many began to falter in the lines. As the distance between the two armies closed, the Numidian cavalry turned and charged back on the Roman flanks. There they inflicted heavy casualties, and continued to hinder the Roman infantry after they had engaged the Carthaginian infantry in

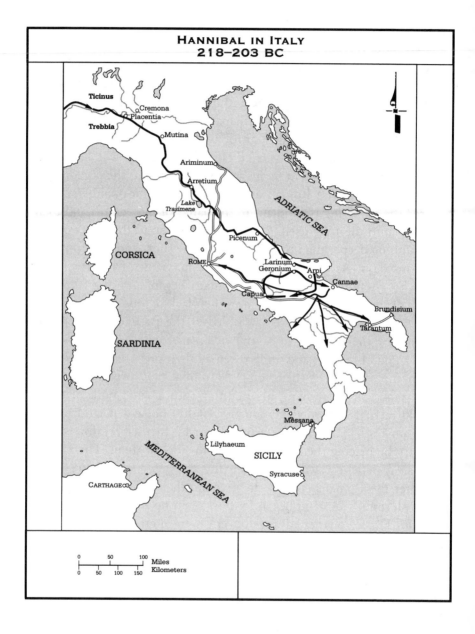

HANNIBAL IN ITALY
218–203 BC

Ticinus

Cremona
Placentia

Trebbia

Mutina

Ariminum

Arretium

Lake
Trasimene

ADRIATIC SEA

Picenum

CORSICA

ROME

Larinum
Geronium

Arpi

Cannae

Capua

Brundisium

Tarentum

SARDINIA

Messana

MEDITERRANEAN SEA

Lilyhaeum

SICILY

Syracuse

CARTHAGE

| 0 | 50 | 100 | Miles |
| 0 | 50 | 100 | 150 | Kilometers |

front of them. The two armies clashed head-on and became a static wall of flailing swords and spears.

At a crucial point, once the Romans were fully engaged and neither line could move the other, the troops Hannibal had hidden behind the Roman lines emerged from their cover. Led by Hannibal's younger brother Mago, they charged the Romans from the rear. The sudden appearance of these Carthaginians threw the Roman army and its commanders into confusion, then panic. The psychological effect on the Romans was more than Hannibal had anticipated. The flanks of the Roman infantry, hard-pressed by the Carthaginian elephants, began to cave in and were eventually forced back to the river. The Roman center, now under attack from all sides, was being badly mauled. By mid-day the light snow had turned into a cold, driving rain as the Roman position became increasingly more hopeless.

Driven by desperation, a large contingent of Roman infantry at the center of the battle line managed to push their way through the Carthaginians in front of them. With nowhere to go except east, they made their way to the safety of their old camp at Placentia. The defection of this large force, estimated at 10,000 men, gave numerical superiority on the battlefield to Hannibal. Not only did he now have the tactical and psychological advantage over the Romans but he had the greater strength that allowed him to crush what little resistance was left. Those elements of the Roman army that were not able to retreat to the river were isolated and killed by the elephants and the Numidian cavalry. Mercenaries pursued the fleeing survivors and drove them headlong into the river. By this time, the day had become so cold and the rain so heavy that the Carthaginians finally broke off their pursuit and turned back to their camp.

They were exhausted but elated. Their first major victory against a Roman consular army had been decisive. There could be no question about the outcome of the battle on the Trebbia that day. Outnumbered by the Romans, Hannibal had used the weather, the terrain, psychology and superior tactics to devastate a numerically superior enemy. The losses among his mercenaries were small for such a major engagement; the majority of the casualties had been taken by his Celtic allies in a scenario that would be repeated over and over during the Second Punic War. Hannibal would place his unreliable "allies" along the center of the battle line as so much fodder. There they would absorb the brunt of the Roman attack and sustain the highest casualties while Hannibal would use his skilled and disciplined mercenaries on the flanks or behind the main battle lines, as needed, to turn the tide of battle in his favor.

Hannibal had fought and won his first major battle in Italy with only a relatively small number of Celtic allies at his side. While the tribes of the Po Valley had been quick to declare their allegiance to Hannibal, they proved hesitant to back their words with actions. They had sent emissaries to Hannibal before the battle at the Trebbia with promises of material support, but few tribes actually sent the numbers of men and quantities of supplies that had been promised. The Gauls, for the most part, waited on the sidelines during the first round of the conflict, hedging their bets, and waiting to see who would gain the upper hand: Sempronius or the invader.

The next night following their defeat, Scipio and Sempronius led the survivors and the garrison out of their camp in the hills and proceeded to the safety of a larger fortified Roman camp a few miles away at the town of Cremona. They were able to escape without interference from the Carthaginian mercenaries, who were camped just a few miles away. Hannibal may have allowed the Romans to escape that night because his own men were so exhausted from the fighting that he could not risk another encounter. In secure quarters at Cremona, Scipio settled in for the winter with the remnants of the army, while Sempronius left for Rome to explain the defeat to the Senate.

During the winter of 218–217 B.C. Hannibal still did not receive the quantities of men and supplies he had been promised from the Gauls of the Po Valley. As the winter became harsher, and his need for supplies and reinforcements more acute, his anger toward the Gauls increased. Finally he sent out raiding parties to plunder their towns and villages in order to gather the badly needed supplies and to force the Gauls into committing themselves to one side or the other. Attacking town after town in northern Italy that winter, and the mercenaries subjected the unfortunate inhabitants to every imaginable form of cruelty and brutality. As a result, some of the Celtic tribes joined Hannibal as allies; others turned to Rome for protection. Scipio, meanwhile, sat at Cremona unable or unwilling to move. The harsh weather of that winter only added to the misery of both the Celts and the Carthaginians. It was intolerably cold that year, and as the winter wore on all but one of the elephants died.

At Rome, Sempronius had returned to a city and Senate near panic. The Romans demanded to know how two Roman consuls and their armies could be defeated by the Carthaginian and his mercenaries. Sempronius at first attempted to minimize the extent of his defeat on the banks of the Trebbia. He tried to blame the defeat on the snow, the rain and the cold. Initially the Romans accepted this version of the events, but as the details became known and the magnitude of the defeat surfaced, the mood at Rome changed. Sempronius lost favor and eventually disappears from the historical accounts. The Romans, however, pulled together as a people and the Senate took measures to raise new armies to combat Hannibal.

The Senate had a total of ten legions to commit to the next phase of the war. Two of those legions were already fighting in Spain under the command of Scipio's younger brother. There was a legion in Sardinia and one in Sicily. Two legions were held in reserve for the possible defense of Rome, and four were left to be sent to northern Italy to fight against Hannibal. New consuls were designated for the forthcoming year: Gaius Flaminius and Geminus Gnaeus Servillius. They were given orders by the Senate to raise additional troops and to elicit help from the Greek cities of southern Italy and Sicily.

The Roman strategy for fighting Hannibal was reformulated. The new plan was to use the Apennine Mountains, which run through central Italy, as a natural defensive barrier against the enemy. The two new consuls with their armies were first sent to the mountains in northern Italy by different routes. Flaminius, who had taken command from Sempronius, established himself at Arretium (just southeast of modern-day Florence, at the town of Arezzo). Here, the consul and his army established themselves to guard the central passes of the Apennine range and block the main approach to Rome. Servillius went east, around the mountain range, to the Adriatic coast of Italy and stationed his army at Ariminum (near modern-day Rimini). There he would be in position to block any attempt by Hannibal to come around the mountains and down the eastern coast.

In the spring of 217 B.C., Hannibal was ready to take his army to invade central Italy. He now had a larger and better equipped force than the one he had come over the Alps with months before. Many of the Gauls had joined him and marched with his soldiers, although he still regarded them as unreliable and treacherous allies. So deceitful did Hannibal find the Gauls that while on the march he often wore wigs and other disguises to change his appearance.[6] Although he may have had various reasons to appear among his troops incognito, it is important to remember that Hannibal had first taken command of the army in Spain after his brother-in-law, Hasdrubal, was suddenly murdered by a Celt.

From his scouts Hannibal learned that the Romans held the main roads from the Apennine Mountains into central Italy. In searching for an alternative route he learned that there was a little-used and treacherous road through the swamps and marshes northwest of Arretium and just south of the Arno River. The route would bring his army into central Italy and behind Flaminius. As his army began the march over the western part of the Apennines, Hannibal placed the Gauls between his African and Spanish troops and his Numidian cavalry. In this way he had his "allies" carefully controlled. His cavalry insured that the Gauls kept up the pace, for they were prone to complaining, malingering and deserting when the going got rough.

When the army entered the marshes south of the Arno (somewhere west of today's Florence), the footing for the first contingents of soldiers was not bad. While the water was ankle deep, the ground underneath was fairly firm. For the Gauls who followed behind these soldiers, however, the footing became far more difficult. The already marshy soil had been further softened by the thousands of soldiers and animals who first passed through and now, for the Gauls, the ground became all but impossible to traverse. While they complained and bemoaned their lot, the fearful-looking Numidian cavalrymen kept them moving.

The army spent four days and three nights moving through the marshes, with only brief times out for rest. The men struggled through the dismal swamps suffering from fatigue at first and then from disease and fever. Most of the pack animals died in the mud and the soldiers were able to catch a few hours' sleep each day by resting on their corpses. Many of the horses became lame as their hoofs rotted from walking continually in water. Hannibal rode on the last surviving elephant, Syrus. As a result of the fever that coursed through the army he developed an infection and became blind in his right eye.

When the army finally came out of the marshes they emerged into a region of Italy north of Rome known as Etruria, a land rich in natural resources and with a prosperous people. Seeing the prosperity of the land, the Gauls quickly recovered from their fatigue and lethargy. They could scarcely contain themselves at the prospect of looting and plundering the peaceful towns and villages. As part of his strategy for this next stage of the campaign, Hannibal decided to allow his troops to plunder the countryside and satisfy their impulse to murder, rape and pillage.

The plundering also played, psychologically at least, into Hannibal's strategy for dealing with the Roman army. He was sure that Flaminius, like Sempronius, was an impulsive commander. The consul would be unable to restrain himself as he watched the mercenaries and the Gauls plunder the Italian countryside so close to Rome. Hannibal reasoned that if he could draw Flaminius away from the security of his encampment at Arretium and onto a more unfavorable battleground, he could defeat another Roman army.

Indeed, when reports reached Flaminius that Hannibal and his mercenaries were raiding the countryside he exploded into a blind rage.[7] Some of the officers around him cautioned against pursuing Hannibal and they warned Flaminius about the Carthaginian cavalry. Flaminius would not listen to their advice. He was more concerned with his public image at Rome and in resolving the issue with Hannibal quickly. In fairness to this newly elected consul, for him to leave Hannibal unchallenged and with the initiative in the new war promised unsettling consequences in terms of Rome's maintaining its allies—not to mention its army's morale. For his part, Hannibal purposely began to burn towns and villages close to the Roman camp. When Flaminius saw the pillars of black smoke rising into the sky he led his army out of bivouac, intent on finding Hannibal and forcing him to fight.

Hannibal meanwhile turned his column south and began to march toward Rome, incinerating and devastating the countryside on either side of his advancing army. This was psychological warfare at its most effective and Flaminius took the bait. Just north of the city of Cortona, Flaminius located Hannibal's army. Hannibal measured his pace and led Flaminius farther and farther south, into the area of Lake Trasimene in central Italy.

As Hannibal marched past the lake a few miles ahead of Flaminius, he discovered the perfect place for an ambush. It was a narrow and level plain enclosed by steep cliffs on one side and the lake at the other. Access to the place was through a narrow passage that ran along the foot of the hills. Hannibal led his troops onto the plain and placed contingents of his African and Spanish troops at one end. The Celts and the Carthaginian cavalry were positioned at the other end while infantry were positioned near where the Roman column would have to pass as it entered the plain. The narrow track of land between the hills and the lake offered little room for the Roman army to maneuver, but it provided excellent cover for Hannibal's forces. All of the positioning of the troops was carried out under cover of darkness so that at dawn the mercenaries were in position and silently awaiting the arrival of the Roman column.

On the morning of the battle, in June 217 B.C., a thick mist hung over Lake Trasimene and extended over much of the plain between the hills and the lake. Flaminius led his troops onto the plain just after dawn. Even though the mist was thick, and clung so low to the ground that the scouts could see little more than a few feet in front of them, the stubborn Roman commander ordered his troops forward. Once the entire column was well onto the plain, the trap was sprung. Hannibal's army attacked the Roman column from three sides simultaneously. Most of the Romans were cut down while they were still in marching order. The attack came so swiftly and at such close quarters that few of the legionaries were even able to wield their weapons. They were marched to the slaughter that morning by the brave intentions combined with the tactical incompetence of their commander.

Flaminius, confused and demoralized when the trap was sprung, was isolated with a few of his guards and killed by the Celts. His armor was stripped from his body and carried off as a battle prize. The Romans in the rear of the column were trapped between the lake and the Numidian and Celtic cavalry, which charged down on them from the hills. Many of the Romans ran to the lake and in a desperate attempt to escape swam out into the depths. There many drowned, pulled under by the weight of their armor, while others, in water up to their necks and frightened, turned to face the mercenaries pursuing them. Their arms raised above the water in surrender and uttering the most pitiful cries for mercy, the Romans begged to be spared. The African and Celtic cavalry drove their horses into the water and cut down the legionaries where they stood, like so many reeds in the marches.

A contingent of 6,000 Romans managed to break out of the ambush and escape to a nearby village. After the battle Hannibal sent his Spanish troops to surround the village and the Romans laid down their arms, surrendering without further resistance. When the mist cleared at noon that day, the battle was already over. Nearly 15,000 Romans lay dead on the field, most having been slaughtered where they stood in line of march or in the act of surrender. When the Roman prisoners were assembled before Hannibal, they numbered nearly another 15,000 men. Hannibal bound the Romans in chains but freed those who had fought beside them as allies, urging these men to return to their homes with the message that Hannibal had come to wage war on Rome, not on the Italian people. When the tally of Carthaginian troops and allies was made, Hannibal discovered he had lost fewer than 1,500 men, most of them Celts.

After taking time to honor and bury his own dead, Hannibal assembled his officers and planned the next stage of the campaign. Livy reports that so furious was the fighting that morning at Lake Trasimene that neither the mercenaries nor the Romans ever realized the area had been shaken by an earthquake that did considerable damage to many of the towns and villages nearby.[8]

When news of the defeat at Lake Trasimene reached Rome, terror spread throughout the city. Crowds surged through the streets and massed before the Capitoline Hill seeking words of explanation and reassurance from the city fathers. Women ran in frenzied groups from one gate of the city to the other seeking news of their men who had been with Flaminius. Then, just before sunset, the city magistrate Marcus Pomponius addressed the crowd from the steps of the Senate and made the first official pronouncement. "We have been beaten in a great battle"[9] was all he would say to the crowd before he turned and went back inside.

Over the next several days, crowds of women kept vigil by the city gates and watched the roads to the north for signs of any who had survived the battle. As stragglers slowly began to drift into the city the women pressed them for news of their loved ones. Then, when the Romans thought things could get no worse, they received news that a cavalry detachment of some 4,000 Romans, which had been sent by the consul Servilius to support Flaminius at Trasimene, had been ambushed by Hannibal and slaughtered to the last man.

The Senate stayed in session from sunrise to sunset each day to debate Rome's next course of action. In desperation the senators resorted to a measure reserved only for the most dire of circumstances. With one consul dead, and the other, Servilius, isolated in the north, the Senate took the extraordinary measure of appointing a dictator to rule the city for six months. All senatorial and consular powers were suspended during the period of the dictatorship while one man ruled Rome. Quintus Fabius Maximus was appointed by the Senate as dictator and entrusted with the defense of the city and the conduct of the war against Hannibal.

The Senate was forced to recognize that the war against Hannibal in the countryside had been lost, and for the immediate future Hannibal could go where he wanted in Italy. As they prepared for the defense of Rome, their only thought was to fortify the city and save themselves from the Carthaginian mercenaries. Hannibal, however, defied all conventions when he turned his army away from Rome and marched to the city of Spoletium (Spoleto), a few miles away from Trasimene. From there he continued toward the Adriatic coast. While his victory at Lake Trasimene had opened the road to Rome and brought him within a hundred miles of the capital, Hannibal did not march on the city. Many historians believe that the city would have fallen at that point and the war would have ended in a decisive Carthaginian victory.

Taking Rome, however, was not Hannibal's strategic objective. His original strategy had been to disrupt the Roman confederation and isolate Rome from its allies. He had already defeated the Roman legions in three battles, and so he elected to remain with his original plan and allow sufficient time for it to work. By turning south he hoped that the Roman allies there would welcome him and that his army might become the catalyst for an insurrection against Rome which would sweep across Italy. Another reason Hannibal may have avoided a direct assault on Rome is that he did not have the siege machinery, such as massive battering rams, high towers and powerful catapults, that would be needed to breach the thick city walls. The siege of Rome might have taken weeks or months to carry out and Hannibal could not afford to remain in one place for that long. There would probably have been logistical problems because the country-side around Rome might not have contained the resources he needed to supply his army during a long siege.

As Hannibal headed toward southeastern Italy, the success of all his plans was predicated on a belief that the cities there would defect from the Roman alliance. As he moved south through central Italy, however, the gates of the major cities allied with Rome remained bolted as their inhabitants on the ramparts cautiously watched his army pass on the horizon. When Hannibal arrived in southern Italy, only a few of the cities there renounced their allegiance to Rome and joined him. As he moved from one province to another, his men plundered the countryside and ravaged everything in their path. His army of mercenaries and Gauls now became a band of criminals devoted to plundering and looting; they raped, murdered and robbed their way throughout the Italian countryside. From Apulia on the east coast of Italy to Campania on the west coast they accumulated vast stores of treasure and thousands of slaves. The cities of central and southern Italy were reluctant to join his cause, however, in spite of his military victories. Hannibal was trapped within Italy, and forced constantly to be on the move.

Quintus Fabius Maximus, the dictator of Rome, was a different kind of general from those who had taken the field against Hannibal early in the war. He was a careful and calculating man who formulated his strategy with considerable thought. Now he assessed the situation and was content for the immediate future to shadow Hannibal at a safe distance and avoid full-scale battles. Fabius believed the way to defeat Hannibal was to allow time and attrition to work in Rome's favor. Rome had the manpower and the resources to wait him out.

Since Hannibal had not marched on Rome after the battle of Trasimene, Fabius was able to take his army into the field and follow Hannibal into southeastern Italy. Fabius was convinced that Hannibal could not be defeated in open combat, at least not on battlefields where he was able to chosoe the ground and conditions for fighting. The way to defeat Hannibal, Fabius believed, was to put vast numbers of Roman troops into the countryside, divided among a number of consular armies. These armies could then move against those Italian allies who had left the confederation and make examples of them; this would serve as a deterrent to other cities thinking of defecting. If Hannibal did not divide his forces and offer protection to his allies, then many of them would be vulnerable to Roman attack, since he could not be everywhere at once. Support for Hannibal would diminish in Italy as it became obvious that he could not protect his allies and that the price of defection from Rome was steep.

Fabius also planned to keep Hannibal moving in the countryside and deny him a steady base of support. Without adequate supplies and reinforcements it would be only a matter of time before the mercenary army would weaken and its numbers diminish. As Rome controlled the seas around Italy, Hannibal could not be reinforced and supplied from Carthage. While Hannibal was tied down in Italy, Roman troops were putting pressure on the Carthaginians in Spain. Fabius expected that eventually the Romans would subdue Spain and then launch an attack against Carthage, one that would force Hannibal to finally abandon his Italian campaign and return home to defend his city.

The cost of this strategy would be high in terms of Roman resources and manpower. It meant the Roman people would need to be patient and willing to tolerate Hannibal's presence in Italy, perhaps for years. Hannibal had become like a virus in their body politic. He would have to be tolerated until time caused him to subside and die. Fighting Hannibal in this way meant enormous financial strain on the Roman economy as well as the willingness of the people and the Senate to commit large numbers of men to the army.

From the southeastern province of Apulia Hannibal moved into Campania and onto the plain between the River Volturnus (Volturno) and Mount Massicus. Fabius and his army shadowed the Carthaginians, avoiding any large scale confrontations. They often remained in the mountains where they could erect a formidable defensive position if Hannibal attacked. In time, Hannibal would have to leave the plain and return to Apulia for the winter; meanwhile, Fabius blocked all the passes over the mountains that separated these two provinces.

When Hannibal found himself cut off from the passes he devised a clever ruse to outsmart the Romans. He moved the Carthaginian army close to a particular pass and the Romans positioned themselves immediately to block it. Hannibal waited until nightfall and then drove nearly 2,000 oxen straight toward the Roman camp. His men had attached torches to the horns of the animals, and when the Romans saw thousands of these lights moving rapidly toward them they believed Hannibal was launching a surprise attack. As the Romans prepared to do battle with the oxen, Hannibal and his army marched over another pass and into Apulia.[10]

By 216 B.C. the Senate and people of Rome had begun to tire of Fabius' strategy. Many senators were unsettled at seeing the Roman army passively hiding in the mountains while Hannibal burned and looted the countryside. Positive results from the strategy had not been forthcoming and the humiliating episode with the oxen did not help. Fabius was recalled to Rome when his period of dictatorship expired and two new consuls were elected. Neither of the new consuls, Lucius Aemilius Paullus or C. Terentius Varro, had had any experience fighting Hannibal. Their elections constituted a political decision on the part of the Roman Senate to abandon the strategy of Fabius and force a decisive battle with the Carthaginian.

In preparation for the new campaign the Romans taxed their resources, both human and material, to the limit. The Senate raised a combined force of nearly 80,000[11] soldiers and placed it under the joint command of the two new consuls. This massive army was ordered to find Hannibal and destroy him. While it was unusual for the Romans to amass a single force of this size and commit it to a decisive battle, what they did was an indication of just how desperate they had become to rid themselves of Hannibal. They had reached a point psychologically where they could no longer tolerate his presence in Italy. The Roman strategy was to overwhelm Hannibal and his mercenaries with massive numbers in a direct infantry attack. As the consuls Varro and Paullus set out from Rome at the head of their legions, Fabius is alleged to have warned of impending doom with the words: "If Varro drives straight into the battle, as he has pledged to do, then there will be another loss more terrible than Trasimene."[12]

Hannibal had established himself for the winter near the Adriatic coast, just north of Apulia, at the town of Gerunium (in the province of Molise). The area was rich in wheat and other supplies that Hannibal needed. In the late spring he moved his army farther south into Apulia and established his camp at Cannae, a ruined fortress that had been used as a storage facility by the Romans. All around his camp at Cannae were fields of ripening crops, especially early summer wheat, which provided his men with food. There Hannibal patiently awaited the arrival of the Roman army and planned his next move.

By late July of 216 B.C., the Roman army arrived within sight of the Carthaginian camp at Cannae. The consuls ordered their camp to be established in the plain within sight of Hannibal, where they believed their massive assault would be most effective. The consuls shared a dual command of the legions in an unusual and ineffective way. They alternated command of the army on odd- and even-numbered days. Under this system no consistent strategy developed between the two leaders. Serious signs of division arose between Paullus and Varro and these became particularly acute at Cannae over the question of tactics.

Paullus considered the ground on which the Roman army had encamped too bare, and thus dangerous. He feared it would give Hannibal an advantage in battle when he utilized his cavalry. Paullus argued to move the camp farther west into the safety of the hills. Varro, however, who would take command the following day, wanted the camp to remain where it was in preparation for a massive frontal assault on the mercenaries and a quick resolution of the conflict. He openly criticized Paullus for coming too heavily under the influence of his friend and mentor at Rome, the cautious Fabius. Varro prevailed and the camp remained on the plain. For the next several days preparations were being made in both camps for the forthcoming battle.

At dawn on August 2, Varro was in command and he ordered the Roman army to cross to the east bank of the River Aufidus (Ofanto). There he positioned his cavalry along the river on his right, placing the legions in the middle and his allied cavalry on the left. The deployment of troops initially followed the standard Roman pattern. Then Varro deviated from convention and ordered that the maniples be brought much closer together than usual. This move greatly reduced the ability of the maniples to maneuver, for the Roman battle line had now deliberately become very narrow and very deep. Varro intended to achieve an overwhelming concentration of force in the center of his army and use it to burst through and trample the Carthaginian infantry. The push through the center would be such a massive thrust that the mercenaries would simply be overwhelmed by sheer numbers. The mass of 80,000 Roman soldiers would destroy anything in front of it, and all the superior tactics of Hannibal and the fighting skills of the mercenaries would have little or no bearing on the outcome.

On the opposite side of the plain near Cannae, Hannibal began to deploy his troops along the river as well. He was able to put approximately 40,000 infantry and 10,000 cavalry into the field for battle. Facing the Roman cavalry on his left wing he positioned his Spanish and Celtic horsemen. On the opposite wing he placed his Numidian cavalry. The infantry were arranged between the two wings of cavalry in a long convex line composed primarily of Gauls and Spaniards. Behind this infantry line and slightly to either side of it Hannibal positioned his heavily armed African veterans.

As the Romans advanced over the plain that morning they had the sun in their eyes and a light wind blowing dust toward them. When the two lines clashed, the mercenaries were able to resist the force of the Roman onslaught for a short time. Then, as the Roman attack increased in intensity and the full force of the line was brought to bear, the mercenary line began to give way under its weight and pressure. Still the mercenaries would not collapse completely and permit a breakthrough. Then, either by design or circumstance, they slowly began to bend their line inward at the center and formed a pocket that engulfed the vanguard of the Roman line. The more deeply the leading edge of the Roman mass pushed into this pocket, the more densely packed it became. The African infantry held back, moving to either side to allow the Roman army, which now resembled a wedge, to penetrate deeper and deeper. What the Romans thought was success was really another trap being prepared by Hannibal.

While the two infantry lines clashed, cavalry battles were in progress on both wings of the armies. The Celtic and Spanish horsemen on Hannibal's left had completely destroyed or dispersed the cavalry on the Roman right. They then circled behind the mass of Roman infantry and joined the Numidian attack against the cavalry on the opposite wing. In short order both wings of the Roman cavalry were destroyed, and the Spanish, Celtic and Numidian cavalry were now free to attack the rear of the Roman infantry line anywhere at will. Most of the Roman infantry by this time had become wedged into a tight pocket and were surrounded by the Carthaginians on three sides. They were so constrained by the sheer mass of their line that most of the Roman soldiers were unable to use their weapons. They could only crowd together in a large mass pushing straight ahead. With their cavalry free to enclose the rear, the Carthaginians had now surrounded the entire Roman army of some 80,000 men and had begun a massacre of unimaginable proportions.

As the Carthaginians began to press the encircled Roman forces more aggressively, order among the legions began to disintegrate and their casualties mounted quickly. It is impossible to determine with accuracy the Roman losses, but Polybius writes that only 390 cavalry and 3,000 infantry were able to escape.[13] Among the captured there were only 10,000. Livy recounts that 19,000 Romans escaped and 4,500 were taken prisoner. He states that over 50,000 men were killed.[14]

Cannae is often considered the closest thing to a "perfect" victory in the annals of warfare. However, like many other events in Hannibal's life it has attracted speculation aimed at separating truth from legend. Could 50,000 well-armed and trained Roman soldiers in fact have been killed by a like number of Hannibal's mercenary troops? It seems that patriotic Romans themselves did not disavow that casualty figure and perhaps even took a perverse pride in how it expressed the magnitude of both Roman sacrifice and Hannibal's lethal genius.

Some modern scholars have agreed that a slaughter of that size could have taken place, given the dust blowing into the legionaries' eyes, their unmaneuverable mass and the fact that they had become encircled. Others maintain that there were numerous Roman break-outs unrecorded by history because the conscripts simply disappeared back to their provinces and villages. If a determined centurion led 60 men through the thinly stretched Carthaginian line, the enemy would have been unable to pursue lest the encirclement be further breached, allowing even more Romans to escape. In this scenario, any Romans breaking out would have been bid good riddance while the Carthaginians surrounding the main force found their task made easier. The point of the encirclement was to contract until it reached the center of the packed Roman mass. Although the best of the Romans were no doubt inclined to stand firm at the onset of the debacle, as the day progressed it may have been the bravest of the legionaries who led or joined the breakouts. The Roman mass left within the circle might have been largely comprised of the weakest, who were clinging to the largest number of compatriots, the wounded and those who were immobilized by panic.

Starting at a certain point, arbitrarily for example 17,000, any actual figure for the multitude of dead lying on that small field after the battle would have fully justified Cannae's reputation as a colossal disaster for Rome. When the remnants of the army were counted, reflecting those who had gotten away and not reported back for service, a loss as high as 50,000 could have been evident. In any event, the Roman losses on that day were the worst in their history of warfare. Varro, the architect of the disaster, managed to escape the carnage and return to Rome while Paullus, with about 30 military tribunes and 80 senators, died on the field of battle. Among the mercenaries, Hannibal lost 1,500 Spaniards and 4,000 Gauls.[15]

As Fabius had predicted, the disaster at Cannae was even worse than the debacle at Lake Trasimene. In one of the rarest of historical instances, an army vastly superior in numbers to its adversary had been encircled and destroyed. Hannibal won at Cannae because he had outthought his enemy again and carefully orchestrated the various elements in his army to accomplish his plan. His main infantry line bent before the Romans without breaking, whereas his African infantry on the left and right slowly and methodically enveloped the Roman mass. The Carthaginian cavalry destroyed the Roman cavalry on the flanks and then entered the main fray to turn the tide of battle in Hannibal's favor. It had been a well-coordinated effort, successful because of the discipline and experience of the mercenary units and the careful planning and battlefield coordination of their commander.

With the Roman army destroyed at Cannae, nothing stood between Hannibal and Rome but an open road. His elated officers urged him to take the initiative and march on the city immediately. Maharbal, the Carthaginian cavalry commander, told Hannibal he could be dining in the Roman capital within five days if only he would press his advantage. Yet Hannibal, as at Lake Trasimene, refused to deviate from his original strategy. It was at this time that Maharbal made his angry remark, "You know how to win a battle, Hannibal, but not how to use one."[16] Hannibal's refusal to march on

Rome after Cannae saved the Republic.

When news of the defeat at Cannae reached Rome, the citizens became so fearful of their demise that panic swept the city. Many of the rich quickly made plans to leave Italy for more secure foreign shores, while others, rich and poor alike, flocked to the temples and begged the priests to consult the sacred books for divine guidance. So frightened did the Romans become at the prospect of Hannibal taking their city that they lost all reason and resorted to human sacrifice. This was an uncharacteristic thing for them to do, for they were not a people normally given to this type of behavior.[17] In the central marketplace of Rome the people assembled to watch the sacrifice of a man and women from Gaul, followed by the sacrifice of a couple from Greece. Thinking that they had appeased their gods, the Romans recovered their sanity and turned to the defense of their city.

In preparation for what they thought was sure to be an immediate attack on the capital, the Senate ordered that all males sixteen and older report for military duty and that two new legions be formed from slaves. Criminals and debtors were released from the prisons in large numbers and pressed into military service. In an effort to raise the morale of the people, women were forbidden to mourn in public and required to remain at home until conditions were stabilized. The Senate acknowledged that Fabius had been right all along in his strategy to avoid engaging Hannibal in set-piece battles. Thus, from that moment until the end of the war in Italy, in 203 B.C., the Romans never fought another major battle with Hannibal.

The year 216 B.C. marked the apex of Hannibal's campaign in Italy and the height of his military career. He had defeated the Romans repeatedly over the last two years and there was no force that could effectively challenge him for control of Italy. He could range wherever he liked and nothing could resist him. As a result of the Carthaginian victory at Cannae, almost all of southern Italy abandoned Rome and defected to him. Many of the towns and cities in the provinces of Apulia, Campania, Lucania and Bruttium went over to Hannibal while Greek cities in Sicily, such as Syracuse, abandoned their alliance with Rome and declared for Hannibal. Philip, the Greek king of Macedonia, eager to drive the Romans from Illyria (modern-day Albania, Bosnia and Croatia), concluded a pact of mutual assistance with the Carthaginians. Hannibal was within the proverbial inch of achieving everything he had planned.

Even though the Romans were exhausted, demoralized and desperate, and Italy was in chaos, the main Roman allies—Latium, Umbria and Etruria—remained loyal. They supported Rome and provided the vast amounts of supplies and manpower needed for the survival of the Republic.

From this point on, the fortunes of war began to slowly change and Hannibal entered the period of his long and inevitable demise. The Romans would return to the attrition tactics of Fabius. They avoided any large battles with the Carthaginian army in Italy and concentrated on keeping their existing allies loyal and winning back those who had defected. The Romans used their navy effectively to prevent provisions and reinforcements from reaching Hannibal from outside Italy, while they vigorously prosecuted the war against Carthage in Spain and Sicily. All this required enormous sums of money and huge resources of manpower which the Roman people, both individually and in consortia, willingly provided. Over time, the Roman Republic, unlike Hannibal's mercenary army, was able to grow stronger.

NOTES
1. Polybius, Bk. III, Sec. 60.
2. Polybius, Bk. III, Sec. 60; Livy, Bk. XXI, Sec. 38.
3. Polybius, Bk. III, Sec. 60; Livy, Bk. XXI, Sec. 39.
4. Livy, Bk. XXI, Sec. 45.
5 Livy, Bk. XXI, Sec. 46.
6 Polybius, Bk. III, Sec. 78.
7 Polybius, Bk. III, Secs 78 and 82.
8 Livy, Bk. XXII, Sec. 5.
9 Livy, Bk. XXII, Sec. 7.
10 Polybius, Bk. III, Sec. 93; Livy, Bk. XXII, Sec. 17.
11 Polybius, Bk. III, Sec. 109.
12 Livy, Bk. XXI, Sec. 39.

[13] Polybius, Bk. III, Sec. 117.
[14] Livy, Bk. XXII, Sec. 49.
[15] Polybius, Bk. III, Sec. 117.
[16] Livy, Bk. XXII, Sec. 51.
[17] Livy, Bk. XXII, Sec 57.

EPILOGUE

As word spread throughout Italy that Hannibal had destroyed the consular army at Cannae, a number of cities and towns in the southern part of the country defected from the Roman confederation. While all of the cities that left the alliance did not necessarily declare for Hannibal and join him, their defection meant that their resources were no longer available to Rome and that they had been effectively neutralized for this last long stage of the war.[1] Many of these cities and towns saw this as an opportunity to take advantage of the Roman crisis and establish their own independent course by playing off one side against the other. As events would subsequently show, however, this proved to be a dangerous game and many of these cities and towns were destroyed as a result.

Hannibal was now anxious to gain control of a port city in southwestern Italy so that he could establish a supply and communication line with Carthage. He made repeated attempts to take the city of Naples but the inhabitants managed to withstand his assaults. Several other cities in the area managed to keep Hannibal and his army at bay as well, eventually forcing him to abandon the idea and retreat back into the countryside. From this point on, the nature of the war changed dramatically. There would not be any more large-scale battles between the Romans and the Carthaginians. From Cannae in 216 B.C. until the end of the war in 202 B.C. the conflict became a war of attrition. Hannibal moved from place to place with the Roman army always following at a safe distance.

The Romans prepared to meet the crises in Italy head-on. They kept a high level of morale during these difficult years, which inspired

Polybius to devote an entire book (VI) to a detailed examination of their qualities as a people and their institutions. The Romans learned from their years fighting Hannibal. He taught them that there was more to warfare than just great clashes between massive armies and there was more to fighting than just pushing and shoving. There were important elements to be manipulated before and during a battle, like surprise, weather conditions, terrain and psychology. The Romans at the beginning of the war had not been professional soldiers. They elected two governing consuls who also commanded the armies. When the Second Punic War began they had little understanding of the principles of large-scale command; either they divided the legions between the consuls or they alternated command on different days. By the end of the war they were beginning to develop a professional, experienced officer corps that eventually was on a par with the best Hannibal could put into the field.

Fabius Maximus was returned as consul in 214 B.C. with M. Claudius Marcellus as his colleague. The Romans undertook to recover several of the towns in Campania and Samnium which had gone over to Hannibal; and the Roman recovery after Cannae was nothing less than remarkable. In the three years from 216 B.C. until 213, Hannibal achieved very little in Italy. In 212 he managed to capture Tarentum (Taranto), after which the cities of Metapontum, Thurii and Heraclea defected to him. From the winter of 212–211 B.C. onwards Hannibal retreated to the extreme south, where he remained with the exception of brief excursions to the center of Italy, until the end of the war.

In 210 B.C. Hannibal attempted the march on Rome that he should have tried after Trasimene or Cannae. As he marched along the road toward the city, reports reached him about how heavily fortified it was. It was apparent the enemy would not emerge from behind their walls so when he was within five miles of Rome he abandoned the effort and turned his army back to the south. One, entirely believable, account has it that Hannibal himself approached the city's gate with a small escort and hurled a javelin at it in frustration.

In 209 B.C. Fabius, holding his fifth consulship, recaptured Tarentum. The previous year the Romans had taken back the city of

Capua north of Naples. Roman commanders were becoming wiser and more cautious in the field against Hannibal. They purposely avoided situations that were tactically favorable to him or where they might be subject to ambushes. Still there were times when they fell into some of his cleverly laid traps, such as when a Roman force sent from Tarentum to Locri was ambushed near Petelia and the consuls killed. Hannibal recovered a signet ring from one of the dead consuls, Marcellus, and used the seals to forge documents. Using these documents Hannibal attempted to retake the city of Salapia by trickery, but failed when the forgeries were discovered by the Roman garrison commanders.

In 207 B.C. Hannibal's brother Hasdrubal left Spain with a relief army and crossed the Alps in an attempt to reinforce his brother in Italy. Hasdrubal's messengers were captured by the Romans as they tried to reach Hannibal in southern Italy. Their captured documents revealed the plans of the two brothers to unite their forces in the province of Umbria in central Italy. The Romans dispatched an army under the consul M. Livius Salinator north to intercept Hasdrubal when he came down from the Alps. When Hasdrubal discovered the Roman army waiting for him, he avoided a confrontation and tried to escape along the Via Flaminia, the main Roman highway, to his meeting place with Hannibal. The Roman army pursued him and caught him at the Metaurus River. There the Carthaginian forces were massacred and Hasdrubal was killed. The Romans cut off his head and delivered it to Hannibal's camp as a "gift."

After the death of his brother, Hannibal retired to Bruttium and avoided any further aggressive actions against the Romans. In 206 B.C. there was virtually no military activity in Italy. In 205 Hannibal's other brother, Mago, landed by sea at Genua in another attempt to bring him reinforcements. Two Roman armies were sent north to meet the threat. Mago, however, successfully concluded a treaty with the Ligurian tribes of northern Italy and conducted numerous operations against the Romans in the area until 203 B.C., when he was defeated by a consular army and seriously wounded. Mago was recalled to Carthage and died of his wounds on the sea voyage home.

While the Romans had undertaken to follow a cautious, even passive, plan against Hannibal, they decided to prosecute the war vigorously against Carthage in Spain. Despite Hannibal's continued presence in Italy, Roman forces and supplies were sent to Spain, where, under the leadership of the Scipio family, they conducted a series of successful campaigns. While the two elder Scipios eventually were killed in the fighting, the younger Scipio won a succession of battles in Spain between the years 211 and 205 B.C. that turned the tide of the war and brought Spain completely under Roman domination. The Scipios had not only prevented the Carthaginians from sending reinforcements from Spain to Hannibal in Italy, but they succeeded in extending Roman control over much of the Iberian peninsula. After the war, Spain would remain a Roman possession for the next several hundred years.

In 205 B.C. Scipio the Younger was assigned the task of preparing for an invasion of Carthage from Roman bases in Sicily. In 204 Scipio invaded North Africa and landed near Utica. As a result of several military defeats at the hands of the Romans over the winter of 204–203 B.C., the Carthaginians sent word to Hannibal to return home and defend the city. While waiting for Hannibal to return the Carthaginian senate opened peace negotiations with Scipio. A provisional agreement was reached to end the war, but then Carthage broke the terms of the treaty by attacking a Roman convoy off the coast of what is today Tunis. By the time Hannibal returned to Carthage the fighting had resumed. He opened negotiations with Scipio at once and offered generous terms for a peace accord: the Carthaginian proposal was based on a Roman occupation of Sicily, Sardinia and Spain. Scipio, under pressure from political elements at home, was determined to weaken Carthage to the point where it would no longer be a threat to Rome in the future. Hannibal's terms were therefore rejected and the armies began to move into position.

The Roman armies faced Hannibal once more on a field of battle, but this time it was in Africa and only a few miles from the walls of Carthage. The Roman army was in the hands of an experienced commander who had fought against Hannibal and survived three times. What's more, Scipio had studied Hannibal and his tactics, and learned from the Roman defeats in Italy. Both armies were about equal in size—40,000 men—and they met on a wide plain. Hannibal had assembled a large force of elephants but the Numidian cavalry that had always been the decisive factor for him against the Romans in Italy was now fighting on the other side. The Numidian king Masinissa, seeing the handwriting on the wall, had allied himself with Rome a few months earlier. He was now fighting with the Romans in the expectation that he would be rewarded handsomely when Carthage was destroyed. The African king no doubt anticipated that at the war's end he would reclaim the lands that had been lost to the Carthaginian Queen by his ancestors centuries before.

The battle opened with a frontal attack by the Carthaginian elephants against the Roman lines. This time the Romans were ready for them. They had anticipated this type of attack and so had practiced and perfected their tactics of defense. When, in prior years and in prior wars, Roman legions had run before the elephants or tried to stop them by their massed numbers, this time the maniples shifted into files on command. The charging beasts raced uselessly down the lanes formed by the legionaries and through the army, inflicting little damage. Scipio then moved his troops rapidly back into formation and, using the same tactics that Hannibal had employed at Cannae, attempted to envelop the Carthaginian army. Hannibal, however, would not be drawn into the type of trap he had used so many times over the years on the Romans. The Carthaginian army had a third line composed of its most experienced troops which was kept well back from the first two lines fighting in the battle. From this position, the line of veterans functioned not only as a reserve force for the troops in front of them, but they were able to prevent any flanking movement by the Romans by shifting their position to meet developing threats on the flanks. For several hours neither line could gain an advantage in the fighting.

Finally the Numidian cavalry, allied with Scipio, drove off Hannibal's cavalry on the flanks. They then made a wide circle and came in against the rear of Hannibal's force well behind the third line. The Battle of Zama was slowly coming to resemble Cannae, only this time it was Hannibal who was trapped within. Most of the Carthaginian army was annihilated that day, but Hannibal survived and quickly sued for peace. Scipio offered the same general terms as had been offered in 203 B.C. but he doubled the indemnity. Masinissa was rewarded by Rome for his services as an ally when he received all the African land around Carthage that had been held by him and his forefathers before the war.

Under the terms of the peace treaty Carthage was forced to surrender all her war elephants and dismantle her navy. Further, the Carthaginians were required to remain within a carefully delineated sphere in the Mediterranean and pay Rome an enormous war indemnity in fifty annual installments.[2] The Roman Senate ratified the treaty and Scipio was given the task of administering the terms. The presence of Hannibal in Italy for sixteen years had had a profound effect on the Roman Senate, and fear of another invasion became foremost in their deliberations on how to treat Carthage in the future.

Under the treaty Rome and Carthage remained formally at peace for the next fifty years (201–150 B.C.). Roman power over Carthage was considerable in that period but the city was not destroyed, and as long as the indemnities were paid on time the Carthaginians were allowed to go about their business. Successive rulers of Carthage placated and conciliated Rome in all circumstances and the annual payments were made ahead of schedule. The city prospered and in the year 200 B.C. Hannibal was elected chief magistrate with the support of the mass of voters against the oligarchs.[3]

After he assumed office Hannibal implemented various democratic and financial reforms. His enemies, however, sent word to the Roman Senate that he was plotting to resume hostilities and was in secret communication with Antiochus III, an enemy of Rome in Asia Minor. A Roman senatorial "fact finding" mission was sent to Carthage to open an inquiry into Hannibal's actions. Hannibal left for Syria before they arrived. Antiochus was the ruler of a vast empire in what is now modern-day Syria and he had an interest in expanding his empire west, into Greece. His activities in the east concerned the Romans, who were interested in expanding in that general direction themselves. The two were on a collision course and Hannibal saw an opportunity to continue his struggle against Rome. He offered his services to Antiochus, who regarded him, as did much of the ancient world, as an expert in fighting the Romans. Hannibal convinced Antiochus that it would merely be a matter of time before the Romans would cross into Asia and that the eastern ruler would have to come to terms with them sooner or later. Antiochus placed Hannibal in command of his navy.

By October 190 B.C. a large Roman army had crossed into Asia Minor, and the war with Antiochus III ended quickly in a Roman triumph at the Battle of Magnesia that year. Among the terms of the peace treaty were that Hannibal be handed over to the Romans. Immediately, Hannibal fled Asia Minor, first to the island of Crete with a vast sum of gold, later to the neighboring state of Bithynia, in what is today northern Turkey.

On the island of Crete Hannibal settled into a villa but he soon aroused the interest of the local authorities when they realized who he was and heard rumors that the enemy of the Romans had brought with him great sums of gold. Hannibal made a great public showing of depositing a sizable number of large, narrow-necked jars in the Temple of Diana for safekeeping by the Cretans. He had secretly filled most of each jar with lead and then covered the last several inches near the top with gold coins. The jars were then sealed for all to see and the Cretan authorities volunteered to guard the temple and its contents for him.

The authorities quickly lost interest in Hannibal, who spent his days in the comfort and tranquility of his garden villa. In that garden were a number of unremarkable bronze statues of varying sizes. They were placed in a haphazard fashion and blended in with the generally unkempt state of the garden; many were simply lying on their sides. What the Cretans did not know is that Hannibal had filled these statues with the bulk of his fortune in gold coins. Months later, when Hannibal left Crete, the local authorities made no effort to stop him as he loaded his household goods and his statues onto the ship that took him and his family to Bithynia.

The ruler of Bithynia, Prusias I, had remained neutral during the war between Rome and Antiochus, but war between Rome and Bithynia became inevitable. Hannibal could not remain on the sidelines, and offered his services to the king. Hostilities began in 187 B.C. and lasted until 183, when Prusias lost the war. The Romans demanded the surrender of Hannibal. This time he was tired of running; at age sixty-four, he committed suicide in Bithynia in 183 B.C.[4] At the age of sixty-four Hannibal took poison. Taking poison, before his death he uttered the words "Let us now put an end to the anxiety of the Romans who could not wait for the death of this hated old man." With his death the Romans breathed freely for the first time in fifty years. Hannibal was dead; Rome went on to conquer the known world.

Hannibal possessed the abilities of a military genius. He displayed throughout the war years an understanding of battlefield tactics and psychology as well as an ability to apply them to varying situations. At Cannae he accomplished probably the most amazing feat of arms in ancient history. Hannibal held a capacity for personal leadership second only perhaps to Alexander the Great. He took a diverse group of mercenaries—Africans, Spaniards, Gauls and Greeks—and molded them into a cohesive and efficient fighting unit, imbuing them with such a sense of loyalty that they stayed with him throughout the war years without a single mutiny. While Roman historians have often portrayed him as a monster—cruel and perfidious—there is no indication that he did anything more than remain within the parameters of the accepted usages of ancient warfare.

The Second Punic War came down to the question of whether Hannibal's military genius and the skill of his mercenary army could be overcome by greater reserves of manpower and resources. The Roman Senate and people showed a durability and a resolve that enabled them to continue during the dark years following Hannibal's descent from the Alps. Eventually, Rome's greater strength prevailed.

By the time of the Third Punic War, the Roman Republic had already begun to transform into what would become the greatest empire in ancient history. The conflicts with Carthage, grueling and traumatic as they had been, elevated Rome from the dominant city on the Italian peninsula to the dominant power in the Western world. The final war lasted three years and resulted not only in the deaths of people but of a civilization. Carthage was erased from the map. At first the Romans were determined never to allow a new city to emerge on the site, but a hundred years later Julius Caesar, who had an eye for strategically valuable locations, ordered that the site be colonized with Roman veterans and the cycle of life began once more.

NOTES
[1] Polybius, Bk. III, Sec. 118; Livy, Bk. XXI, Sec. 61.
[2] Polybius, Bk. XV, Sec. 18; Livy, Bk. XXX, Sec. 37; Appius, Punica, Bk. 54, Sec. 234–38.
[3] Livy, Bk. XXXIII, Sec. 45
[4] *Cambridge Ancient History*, Vol. VIII, p. 531.

SELECT BIBLIOGRAPHY

The following manuscripts were examined at the Bibliothéque Mazarine, Institut de France, Paris:

Casaubon, Isaac. *Polybii*, 1609 and 1617.
Cluver, Phillip. *Italia Antiqua*, 1624.
Gronovius, Jacques. *Titi-Livii Patvini Historiarum*, 1670.
Holstein, Lucas. *Italia Antiqua Annotationes*, 1666.
Obropaeus, Vincent. *Polybii Historiarum*, 1530.
Perotti, Nicolas. *Polybii Historiarum*, 1530.
Sigonio, Carlo. *T. Livii Historiarum*, 1555.

Other Sources:

Abbott, Jacob. *History of Hannibal.* New York: Harper and Co, 1849.
Azan, Paul. *Annibal dans les Alps.* Paris: Oran D. Heintz, 1902.
Baedaker's Southern France. Leipziç: Baedaker Publishers, 1907.
Bagnall, Nigel. *Punic Wars.* London: Hutchinson, 1990.
Baker, George. *Hannibal.* New York: Barnes and Noble, 1967.
Bath, Tony. *Hannibal's Campaigns.* Cambridge, UK: Stephens, 1981.
Bonus, Arthur. *Where Hannibal Passed.* London: Methuen, 1925.
Bosworth-Smith, R. *Carthage and the Carthaginians.* New York: 1879.
Bradford, Ernle. *Hannibal.* New York: Dorset, 1981.
Cambridge Ancient History, Vol. VIII. Cambridge University Press, 1991.
Carcopino, Jerome. *Profils de Conquérants.* Paris: Flammarion, 1961.
Cary and Scullard, *History of Rome.* New York: St. Martin's Press, 1983.
Les Celtes and les Alpes. Chambéry: Le Musée, 1986.
Centini, Massimo. *Sulle Orme di Annibale.* Turin: Piemonte, 1987.

Charles-Picard, Gilbert. *Hannibal.* Paris: Hachette, 1967.

Colin, Jean. *Annibal en Gaule.* Paris: Chapelot, 1904.

Coninck, Francis de. *Hannibal à Travers les Alpes.* Montélimar: Ediculture, 1992.

Connolly, Peter. *Hannibal and the Enemies of Rome.* London: Mac-Donald, 1978.

Cope, Anthony. *The History of Two Most Noble Captains.* London: Hovy, 1590.

Cottrell, Leonard. *Enemy of Rome.* London: Evans, 1960.

deBeer, Gavin. *Alps and Elephants.* New York: Dutton, 1956.

———. *Hannibal.* New York: Viking, 1969.

———. *Hannibal's March.* New York: Viking, 1967.

Denina. *Tableau historique, statistique, et moral de la haute Italie.* Paris: 1805.

Devos, Gabriel. *D'Espagne en Italie avec Annibal.* Vaison-la-Romaine, France: Voconces, 1966.

Dodge, Theodore. *Great Captains.* New York: Kennikat, 1968.

———. *Hannibal.* London: Houghton, 1891.

Ellis, Robert. *Treatise on Hannibal's Passage of the Alps.* Cambridge, UK: Deighton, 1853.

Flaubert, Gustave. *Salammbô.* London: Penguin, 1977.

Fox, Joseph. *Hannibal, Enemy of Rome.* Chicago: Adams, 1990.

Freshfield, Doughlas. *Alpine Pass of Hannibal.* London: 1886.

———. *Hannibal Once More.* London: Arnold, 1914.

Glanville, Terrell. *Hannibal's Pass Over the Alps. Classical Journal* 17 (38), May 1921–22.

Granzotto, Gianni. *Annibale.* Milan: Mondadori, 1980.

Guillaume, Augustin. *Annibal Franchit les Alpes.* Montfleury: Editions des Cahiers des Alpes, 1967.

Haight, Elizabeth. *Carthage and Hannibal.* Boston: Heath, 1915.

Hall, R. *Romans on the Riviera.* Chicago: Ares, 1898.

Houghton, Eric. *White Wall.* New York: McGraw Hill, 1961.

Hoyte, John. *Trunk Road for Hannibal.* London: Bles, 1960.

Hyde, W.W. *Roman Alpine Routes.* New York: American Philosophical Society, 1935.

Jacobs, William. *Hannibal: An African Hero.* New York: McGraw Hill, 1973.

Jiménez, Ramon: *Caesar Against the Celts.* New York: Sarpedon, 1996.

Johnston, Johanna. *Story of Hannibal.* New York: Garden City, 1960.

Juvenal. *Decimi Iunii Iuvenalis Saturae.* London: Macmillan, 1963. (E.G. Hardy).

Lamb, Harold. *Hannibal.* New York: Doubleday, 1958.

Lancel, Serge. *Carthage: A History.* Oxford, UK: Blackwell, 1992

Larouza. *Histoire critique du passage des Alpes par Annibal.* Paris: 1826.

Law, William J. *Alps of Hannibal.* London: Macmillan, 1866.

Lazenby, J.F. *Hannibal's War.* Warminster: Aris and Phillips, 1978.

Linke, Otto. *Die Controverse über Hannibals Alpenubergang.* Breslau, Germany: Neumann, 1873.

Livy. *Ab urbe condita,* XXI–XXII. Leipzig: Teubner, 1971 (T.A.Dorsey).

——. *Hannibal est a nos portes.* Extraits d'Histoire Romaine de Tite-Live.

Paris: Gallimard, 1977. (Gerard Walter).

Mace. *Description du Dauphiné.* Paris, 1852.

Maissiat. *Annibal en Gaule.* Paris, 1874.

Melvin, M. *Expedition Alpine Elephant.* Cambridge, UK: University Press, 1980.

Mommsen. *History of Rome,* Vol. II. New York: Scribner, 1887.

Montanari, Tommaso. *Annibale.* Rovigo, Italy: Stabil, 1900.

Morris, William. *Hannibal.* New York: Putnam, 1897.

Nepos, Cornelius. *Vie d'Annibal.* Paris: Presses Universitaires de France, 1968.

Osiander, Wilhelm. *Der Hannibalweg.* Berlin: Weidmannsche, 1900.

Pernoud, Jean. *Annibal.* Paris: Juilliard, 1962.

Perrin, Jean. *Etude sur Annibal.* Paris, 1887.

Peyramaure, Michel. *Les Colosses de Carthage.* Paris: Laffont, 1969.

Polybius. *History of Rome.* Cambridge: Loeb, 1923. (Patton).

Powers, Alfred. *Hannibal's Elephants.* New York: Green, 1944.

Prieur, J. *L'Itinéraire transalpine d'Hannibal.* Chambéry: Musée, 1986.

Proctor, Dennis. *Hannibal's March in History.* Oxford: Clarendon, 1971.

Rivet, A.L.F. *Gallia Narbonensis.* London: Mackays, 1988.

Rowland, Robert J. *Rome's Earliest Imperialism.* Extrait de Latomus, 1983.

Seibert, Jakob. *Hannibal.* Darmstadt, Germany: Wissenschaftliche, 1993.

Silius Italicus. *Second Punic War.* London: Roycroft, 1672. (Tho. Ross.).

Taleb, Mirza. *Hannibal, Man of Destiny.* Boston: Branden Press, 1974.

Thirion, Jacques. *Alpes romanes.* Yonne, France: Zadiaque, 1980.

Torr, Cecil. *Hannibal Crosses the Alps.* Cambridge, UK: University Press, 1924.

Toynbee, Arnold J. *Hannibal's Legacy.* London: Oxford, 1965.

Vaccarone, R. *Ball del club Alpino Italiano,* No. 41, 1880.

Vanoyeke, Violaine. *Hannibal.* Paris: France Empire, 1995.

Walbank, Frank. *Historical Commentary on Polybius.* Oxford: Vol. I, 1957, Vol. II, 1967, Vol. III, 1979.

Webb, Robert. *Hannibal: Invader from Carthage.* New York: Watts, 1968.

Whitaker, John. *Course of Hannibal Over the Alps Ascertained.* London: Stockdale, 1794.

Wickham, Henry. *Dissertation on the Passage of Hannibal Over the Alps.* London: Whittaker, 1828.

Wilkinson, Spenser. *Hannibal's March Through the Alps.* Oxford: Clarendon, 1911.

Zanelli, Dario. *Annibale.* Novara, Italy: Istituto Geografico de Agostini, 1978.

INDEX